THE LOST SUBMARINES OF PEARL HARBOR

Ed Rachal Foundation Nautical Archaeology Series

The Lost Submarines of Pearl Harbor

The Rediscovery and Archaeology of Japan's Top-Secret Midget Submarines of World War II

James P. Delgado, Terry Kerby,
Hans K. Van Tilburg, Steven Price, Ole Varmer,
Maximilian D. Cremer, Russell Matthews

Texas A&M University Press | College Station

First edition

This paper meets the requirements of ANSI/NISO Z39.48-1992 (Permanence of Paper).
Binding materials have been chosen for durability.
Manufactured in China by Everbest Printing Co. through FCI Print Group ♾

Disclaimer: The views expressed by the authors of this book are not necessarily the views of NOAA, the Department of Commerce, or the United States Government.

Library of Congress Cataloging-in-Publication Data
Names: Delgado, James P., author. | Van Tilburg, Hans, author.
Title: The lost submarines of Pearl Harbor / James P. Delgado, Terry Kerby, Hans K. Van Tilburg, Steven Price, Ole Varmer, Maximilian D. Cremer, Russell Matthews.
Other titles: Ed Rachal Foundation nautical archaeology series.
Description: First edition. | College Station: Texas A&M University Press, [2016] | Series: Ed Rachal Foundation nautical archaeology series | Includes bibliographical references and index.
Identifiers: LCCN 2016012118 (print) | LCCN 2016014294 (ebook) | ISBN 9781623494667 (printed case: alk. paper) | ISBN 9781623494674 (ebook)
Subjects: LCSH: Midget submarines—Japan. | World War, 1939–1945—Naval operations—Submarine | World War, 1939–1945—Naval operations, Japanese. | Pearl Harbor (Hawaii), Attack on, 1941. | Pearl Harbor (Hawaii)—History, Naval—20th century.
Classification: LCC V859.J3 D45 2016 (print) | LCC V859.J3 (ebook) | DDC 940.54/26693—dc23
LC record available at http://lccn.loc.gov/2016012118

Contents

Foreword

ALTHOUGH UNDERSTANDING HISTORY IS SO VITAL TO UNDERSTANDing our future, it is often difficult to draw attention to its meaning and lessons. But there are certain events and subjects that can and have drawn people to them. For a wide range of Americans, and others, there is a no more compelling event than the December 7, 1941, attack on Pearl Harbor. The mysteries surrounding how it happened, what happened, and the secret weapons that were involved continue to stimulate great interest in every generation since and will likely continue to stimulate the curiosity of future generations. One of the last remaining and persistent mysteries of the Pearl Harbor attack is that of the Japanese midget submarines. It is a fascinating story of innovation, courage, secrets, and failed expectations. And it is a story of not only the morning hours of December 7 but the years before, to develop these weapons, and the years after, where they were deployed in the great Pacific War, and how they fared as weapons of war.

This book contains many lessons worthy of contemplation: What were the key participants in the saga thinking? Who was making decisions? How was the Japanese Navy organized and operated, and in the end, how did desperation set in and affect people and events? Equally valuable to think about when reading this book is how researchers have carefully unraveled the story over many years, exploring to discover the lost submarines and assemble the physical evidence to complete the story. For those who seek to explore and discover, there are insights in how advanced technology, partners, and forensic archaeology work in unison.

I myself was involved in a few of the submersible expeditions to the *Ward* midget submarine outside of Pearl Harbor and thought I knew a lot about Japan's top-secret midget submarines. Reading this book showed me how little I actually knew of the full story. The authors have brought together a heretofore unavailable body of information that is woven together in a blend of academic scholarship, good storytelling, and pointed insights that finally renders a full understanding of midget submarine aspects of the Pearl Harbor attack and their role in the greater war in the Pacific.

All mysteries are only unanswered questions in the absence of facts. This book resolves the mystery of these secret weapons and their use and, if read carefully, offers lessons that can be of value today. Just as Japan was not the only nation developing midget submarines in secret (many others also were), development of "secret weapons" continues apace today. These efforts are always wrestling with many of the same institutional, personal, technological, and political considerations that brought "Japan's secret midget submarines" to Pearl Harbor on December 7, 1941.

Daniel J. Basta

Acknowledgments

A LARGE NUMBER OF FRIENDS AND COLLEAGUES SUPPORTED the research necessary for this book, providing opportunities and information freely from the beginning of our research in the 1980s. Terry Kerby and Steve Price, whose detailed research in the archives and on the seafloor revealed two Pearl Harbor midget submarines off O'ahu, are at the forefront along with Burl Burlingame. Burl's pioneering book, *Advance Force Pearl Harbor*, was the first and remains the definitive book on the role of Japanese submarines in the Pearl Harbor attack. Burl also went the extra mile and provided his digital image files in an incredibly generous measure of support.

We also wish to thank Daniel J. Lenihan, former chief of the National Park Service's Submerged Resources Center (NPS SRC); Larry V. Murphy, friend, colleague, and fellow submarine archaeologist and chief of the NPS SRC; and David L. Conlin, PhD, the current chief of the center. It was Dan Lenihan and Larry Murphy who began the now decades-long study of the Pearl Harbor submerged battlefield along with Larry Nordby and Jerry Livingston, Gary Cummins, and Jim Adams from the NPS. They invited full participation and fully shared all they found, as well as offering profound insights not only at Pearl Harbor but also at other Pacific War sites, including their archaeological documentation of a Pearl Harbor–type midget submarine at Kiska, Alaska. Daniel J. Martinez and Robert Chenoweth, both then from the USS *Arizona* Memorial, as well as B. J. Dorman, then with the Pacific Fleet Submarine Memorial, also opened doors and provided invaluable material in the 1980s and 1990s. Additional material and files were provided by curator Nancy Johnson Richards and Charles R. Hinman, the director of education and outreach, in 2015.

Documenting the saga of HA-19, the midget submarine captured after the Pearl Harbor attack, began with an assignment from Edwin C. Bearss, then the chief historian of the National Park Service, in 1987. Work on the craft's history was assisted greatly by the late James Charleton of the NPS History Division, Kevin Foster, and J. Candace Clifford of the NPS Maritime Heritage Program, known at that time as the National Maritime Initiative. Henry Vadnais, then the chief curator of the Naval Historical Center (now the Navy History and Heritage Command), as well as Chuck Haberlein of the Curatorial Branch, John Reilly of the Ships' History Branch, and Mike Walker and Katherine Lloyd of the Operational Archives of the NHHC, made ready access to the US Navy's records and materials. More recently, Alexis Catsambis also assisted with research, for which we are grateful. Pearl Harbor historian David Aiken was also helpful, providing key information from his research on American and Japanese casualties on December 7, 1941.

The gracious support of Bruce Smith, superintendent of the Admiral Nimitz Museum in Fredericksburg, Texas, where HA-19 ultimately was placed on display, is also very much appreciated. Bruce provided interior access to the submarine and shared the museum's research.

We are also grateful to Don Birkholz for providing copies of his surveys of HA-19 and of a later Type C (*hei-gata*) midget submarine in Guam. Ensign S. D. Kramer, USN, provided interior access to the Guam submarine. We are also grateful for the assistance of Richard Davis, then the territorial archaeologist for Guam. Additional materials on midget submarines were provided by Bob Patten of the National Geographic Society and Steve Burns, then with National Geographic Explorer, who sent research leads and video footage. The Submarine Force Library and Museum in Groton, Connecticut, provided materials on the salvage and recovery of HA-8, now on display there next to USS *Nautilus* (SSN-571). Former director Bill Galvani was very helpful, as was acting director Steve Finnegan. During research there, EMC Randy Wade provided interior access to HA-8. Documentation of the Nishimura submarine was made possible by former director William (Bill) Wilkenson of the Mariners' Museum in Newport News, Virginia. Archaeological documentation of the craft was done by James Delgado in collaboration for former curator David Baumer, who worked diligently and with tremendous devotion to the project.

A number of friends in Australia facilitated access to the remains of HA-14 and HA-21 in Sydney. The Australian National Maritime Museum's exceptional temporary exhibit, "Hitting Home," provided the opportunity during a museum conference in 1992. Curator Mariea Fisher opened her copious research files, while Jenni Carter provided photographs. Kevin Fewster, PhD, then the museum's director; senior curator Lindsey Shaw; and curator Mark Staniforth provided other support. David Jenkins, author of *Battle Surface!*, the definitive book on Japanese submarine operations against Australia, was a great help and provided many leads and graciously supplied a number of illustrations and also read the manuscript, offering a number of helpful edits. Lewis J. Lind, director of the Garden Island Naval Dockyard Museum in Sydney, opened the surviving conning tower section of HA-21 and provided access to many artifacts and materials. Peggy Warner, coauthor of *Coffin Boats*, graciously provided the means to contact her major sources in Japan. Wendy Burkwood with the National Archives of Australia was another tremendous help and provided digital files of the exhaustive RAN records on HA-14 and HA-21 in 2015. In Japan, Mitsuharu Uehara was very helpful, and Bill Lise graciously undertook research and tracked down sources in the Japanese Defense Agency's War Library in 1997. Randy Sasaki translated key sections of the Japanese Midget Submarine Association's landmark 1984 work, *Ah Tokushu Senkotei*.

R. W. "Bob" O'Hara, commissioned to conduct research, did great work in the Public Records Office, Kew, in 1996 and provided the admiralty records for the midget submarine attack on Diego Suarez in 1942. Research and materials pertaining to midget submarines in Papua New Guinea were provided by Peter Stone of Oceans Enterprises of Yarram, Victoria, Australia, as he completed his book, *Rabaul's Forgotten Fleet*; Stone first wrote in 1993 and shared what he knew about HA-53, the Rabaul submarine. We are also grateful to Don Silcock, Robert (Bob) Halstead, Fritz Herscheid, Dietmar Amon, and Beo Brockhausen for additional information on both the Rabaul and the New Ireland (Kavieng) Type B and C midget submarine wrecks of HA-53 and HA-52.

Stan Cohen and Brian Garfield, as well as Dan Lenihan and Larry Murphy, provided research and information on the midget submarine base and surviving craft at Kiska. Ewan

Stevenson graciously shared his research and images from his ongoing work with the midget submarines in Guadalcanal's waters, as featured on his tremendous website, Archaehistoria.org, on the page concerning the archaeology of World War II in the Solomon Islands. Ewan is examining a number of sites there, and his reports are available online at http://www.archaehistoria.org/index.php/solomon-islands-archaeology. Mike Mair, longtime friend, with Joy Waldron, another longtime friend and author of the recently published *Kaiten*, shared research and introduced us to Michael Harris, who provided a copy of and permission to use his late father Sid's image of the *kaiten*-hit USS *Mississinewa* burning and capsizing at Ulithi prior to sinking. We also acknowledge the detailed research into war diaries and after action reports by Robert "Bob" Schwemmer and acknowledge his amazing ability to find deeply buried sources in the online sections of the National Archives. We also thank Pam Ribbey of Agoura, California, who shared her research and pointed us in the direction of Captain Roger Pineau's fascinating letter of June 1956 in the NHHC archives.

There are a variety of great Internet-based resources, but in particular, we want to single out and thank Jonathan Parshall and his associates, especially Bob Hackett and Sander Kingsepp, who manage the submarine page of http://www.combinedfleet.com, which is truly an exceptional online resource. The pages on submarine operations (http://www.combinedfleet.com/sensuikan.htm) are an amazingly well-detailed resource, and we benefited greatly from the pages on midget submarine operations (http://www.combinedfleet.com/midgets.htm). We are also grateful for Bob Hackett's review of the manuscript.

We also wish to thank the following institutions and organizations for the use of their facilities, materials, and images: Burl Burlingame and Don Silcock, US Naval History and Heritage Command, Washington, DC; the United States Naval Institute, Annapolis, Maryland; the Hawai'i Undersea Research Laboratory of the University of Hawai'i; the USS *Arizona* Memorial (now Valor in the Pacific National Monument), Pearl Harbor, Hawai'i; the Australian National Maritime Museum, Sydney; the Australian National Archives, North Melbourne; the Australian War Memorial, Canberra; the Garden Island Naval Dockyard Museum, Sydney; the Mariners' Museum, Newport News, Virginia; the Admiral Nimitz Museum (now the National Museum of the Pacific War), Fredericksburg, Texas; the US Naval Base in Agana, Guam; the Pacific Fleet Submarine Memorial Museum, Pearl Harbor, Hawai'i; the Public Records Office, Kew, United Kingdom; the Submarine Force Library and Museum, Groton, Connecticut; the Imperial War Museum, London; the Submerged Resources Center, National Park Service, Lakewood, Colorado; and the staffs of the Vancouver Maritime Museum, Vancouver, British Columbia, Canada, and the West Vancouver Memorial Library, Vancouver, Washington.

Editing of this book was undertaken by Rachel Paul of Scribe Inc. Layout was by Tim Durning of Scribe Inc. for Texas A&M University Press. The process of external and internal peer review is an essential part of scholarly publishing, and we acknowledge and thank the A&M reviewers, Dr. Kevin J. Crisman and Mark K. Ragan. Kevin in particular was a tremendous help, with a number of very good suggestions and edits that went above and beyond the call of professional courtesy and substantially helped us focus some key points. We also acknowledge the ongoing support of editor Thom Lemmons and, as always, appreciate working with him and the incredible team at Texas A&M University Press.

While grateful to all who helped in the assembly of material for this book, and for the comments of reviewers, any and all errors and omissions are the responsibility of the authors.

THE LOST SUBMARINES OF PEARL HARBOR

Introduction

The Japanese attack on Pearl Harbor on December 7, 1941, was a combined aerial and naval assault that covered a large area of sea, sky, and ground. Like a number of naval battles in World War II, the events and combat at "Pearl Harbor" took place within a vast battlefield landscape that encompasses hundreds of square miles when all aspects of the attack are considered. As Potter et al. (2000) have noted, battlefield archaeology reflects that

> the actions of military units on a battlefield are based on the tactics of the prevailing military wisdom of the day; they are not random. Therefore, one should not expect the debris of battle to be distributed randomly over a battlefield. The tactics employed on a battlefield do leave their traces in the archaeological record. Subsequently, if natural forces or human activities do not significantly disturb, mix, or mask all or parts of the battlefield, it should be possible to identify and define artifact patterns created by the tactical positions and movements of individual military units. (Potter et al. 2000:13)

The first archaeological study of Pearl Harbor, which began as a study of the iconic battleship USS *Arizona* in 1983, expanded in 1988 "to be full submerged cultural resources study of World War II remains in Pearl Harbor" (Lenihan 1990:3). This included not only the sunken battleships *Arizona* and *Utah* but also the sites of other battleship casualties salvaged postbattle, aircraft crash sites, and a search in the "1,000 + foot deep defensive perimeter outside the harbor mouth for a Japanese mini-sub reportedly sunk by the destroyer USS *Ward* more than an hour before the aerial attack began" (Lenihan 1990:3). While the concept of battlefield archaeology was emerging in the field of historical archaeology (Scott et al. 1989; Snow 1981), it had yet to find its analog in nautical or maritime archaeology in 1988, and the concept of the maritime cultural landscape was just emerging (Westerdahl 1992).[1] What was significant in the USS *Arizona* Memorial/Pearl Harbor project was research driven by the realization that "the remains of the USS ARIZONA, the USS UTAH, the Japanese planes and submarines that initiated the attack and even the bullet holes in the buildings of Hickam and Wheeler fields, comprise a material statement that archeologically and symbolically preserves the reality of World War II in a manner that could never be replicated by books, films or pictures" (Lenihan 1990:8).

The expansion of the USS *Arizona* project to encompass the entire submerged Pearl Harbor battlefield was one of the first to address a naval battle as a larger site than a localized individual

USS *Shaw* explodes during the Pearl Harbor attack, one of many iconic images of a combined aerial and undersea assault. (Library of Congress, LC-USZ62-16555)

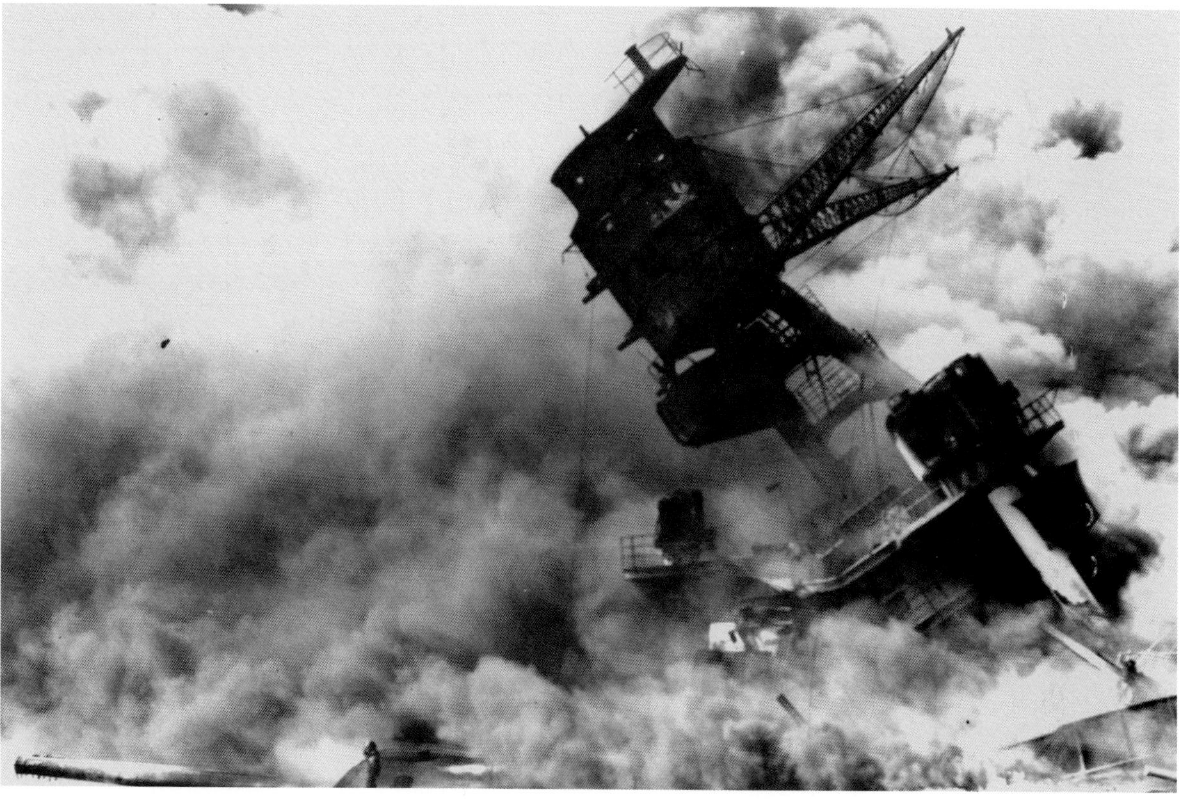

USS *Arizona* burns on December 7, 1941. The cataclysmic loss of the battleship dominated the memory of that day. (Naval History and Heritage Command, NH 97379)

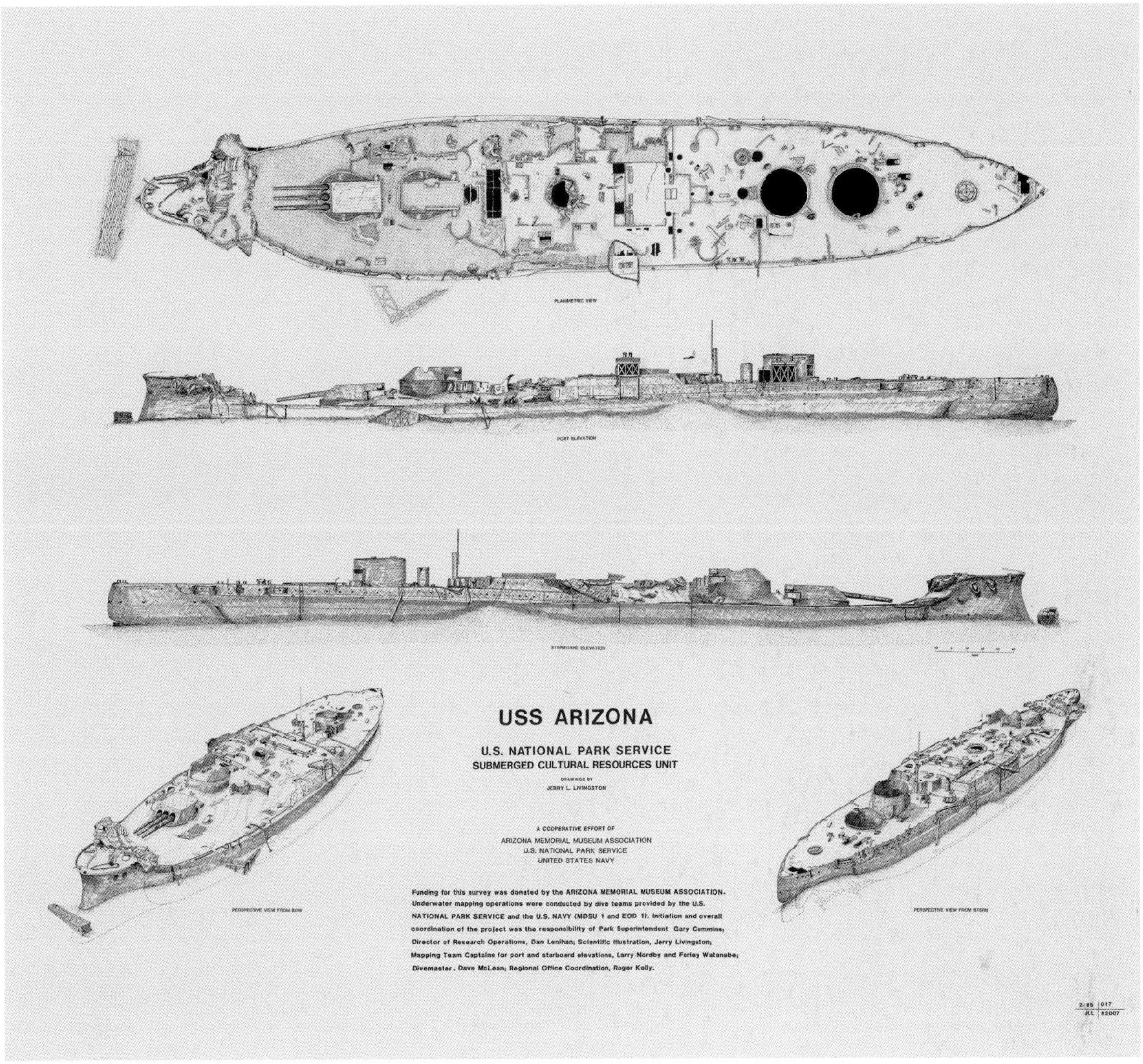

The sunken USS *Arizona*, the beginning point of the battlefield archaeological study at Pearl Harbor. (National Park Service, Submerged Resources Center; drawing by Jerry L. Livingston)

loss or victory. It came at the same time Martin (1975; also see Martin and Parker 1988, 1999) was similarly making larger level assertions about the Spanish Armada's unsuccessful campaign against England through a series of wreck sites and Gould (1983) was offering a theoretical comparison between the larger archaeological signature of the armada and downed aircraft from the World War II Battle of Britain as the "archaeology of war" (Gould 1983:105–42).

What has transpired since the 1980s has been an increasing interest in the archaeological study of naval battlefields, focusing on engagements such as the Revolutionary War naval battlefield at Valcour Bay on the New York side of Lake Champlain (Cohn et al. 2003); the Civil War encounter between the Confederate submarine *H. L. Hunley* and USS *Housatonic* off Charleston, South Carolina (Conlin and Russell 2006); and US Civil War naval engagements in the Ogeechee River of Georgia (Lydecker 2005), an ongoing larger landscape of the naval siege and battles for Charleston undertaken by the South Carolina Institute of Anthropology and Archaeology (SCIAA). Other studies focus on the naval battles off the Egadi Islands between

Pearl Harbor, once the setting of native Hawaiian fishponds and harvests, transformed in the early twentieth century into a bastion of American naval power. This image, oriented to the northwest, was taken sometime around 1940. It shows battleships moored alongside Ford Island (center and left), with the Navy Yard to the left and the Supply Base and Submarine Base at center-right and right. (Naval History and Heritage Command NH 54301)

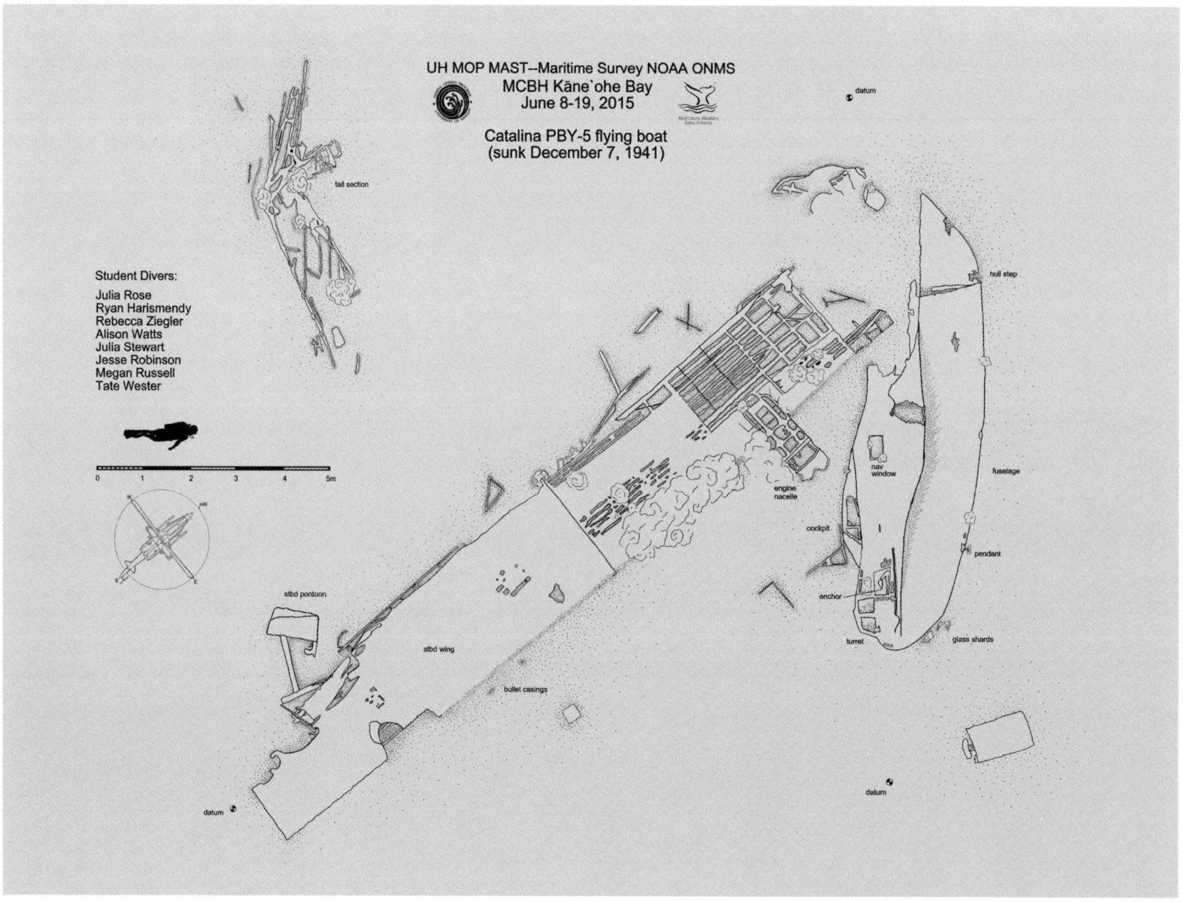

One element of the archaeological site that is the battlefield of December 7, 1941, the wreck of a PBY at Kaneohe, as mapped by the National Oceanic and Atmospheric Administration (NOAA) and University of Hawai'i. (NOAA's Office of National Marine Sanctuaries, Maritime Heritage Program / University of Hawai'i Marine Option Program)

Roman and Carthaginian forces off what is now Trapani, Sicily, in 246 BC (Tusa and Royal 2012); the naval battlefields of the Mongol invasions of Japan and Vietnam in 1281 and 1284 (Delgado 2006; Kimura 2014; Sasaki 2015); and the offshore remains of the D-day invasion off the beaches of Normandy, as well as German U-boat losses (McCartney 2015), to name a few.

Significantly, work to better characterize and offer a broader context of Pearl Harbor, both as a physical entity (i.e., a naval base with extensive maritime infrastructure) and as part of a larger maritime cultural landscape in Hawai'i and the Pacific Ocean, has continued through the past three decades. It is within this larger context that the battlefield was and is seen to extend beyond the harbor and beyond the island of O'ahu. The battle encompasses multiple sites across the islands of O'ahu and the island of Ni'ihau. It is a three-dimensional area encompassing not only the surface of the land and water but also the skies above the island and the depths that surround it. It extends to the distant position of the Japanese fleet, including the carriers that launched the aerial strike forces, as well as to the waters off the harbor entrance and the waters around what was then Kaneohe Naval Air Station. Here, on the open ocean, the first shots were fired as one of five midget submarines sent to stealthily enter the harbor was intercepted and sunk. These submarines, as well as the larger I-class submarines that carried them across the Pacific and others deployed in a screen to sink American ships fleeing the harbor, were elements in the battlefield. In assessing the archaeology of that larger battlefield, what the archaeological record ultimately revealed is not one but two sunken midget submarines.

The midget submarines have archaeological importance as elements in the larger battlefield landscape of Pearl Harbor. They are also significant in that they are important technological developments that have remained undocumented and misunderstood for several decades. This is

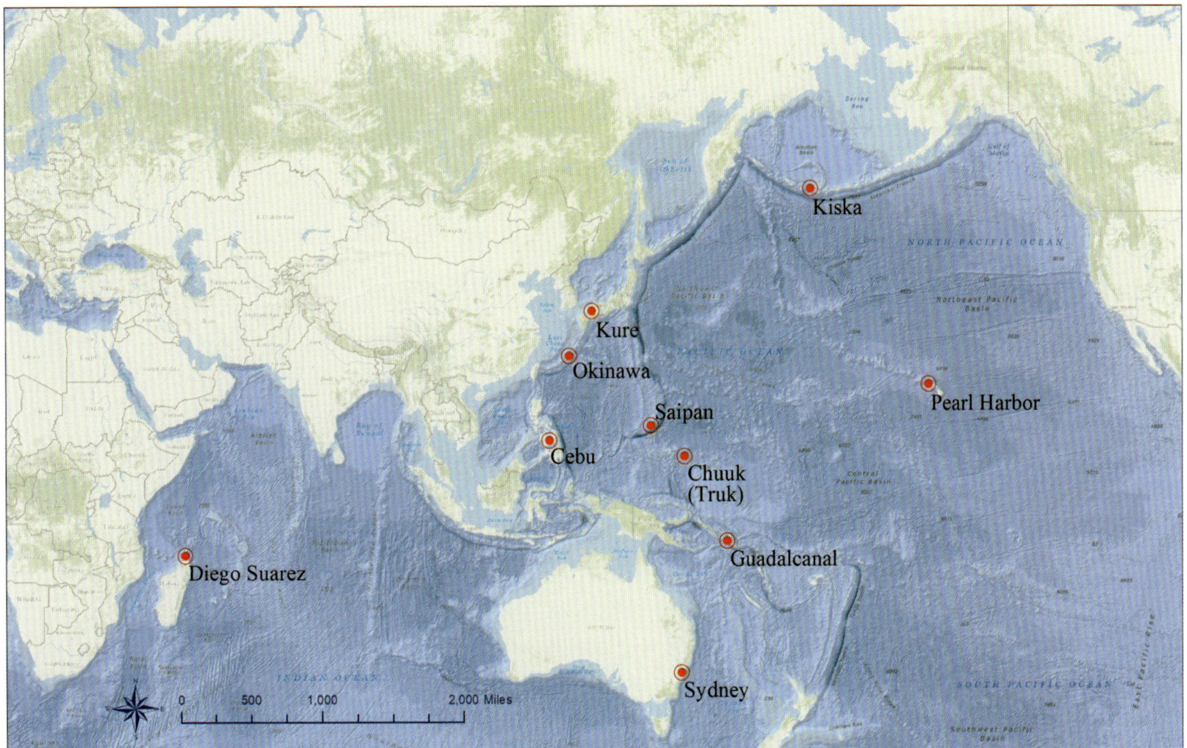

Midget submarine operational areas, 1940–45. (NOAA/Tony Reyer)

due to the postwar destruction of the surviving midgets left afloat, as well as the burning of most records of their design, construction, and operation. Before and during World War II, Japan built a fleet of several hundred midget submarines and human-piloted torpedoes. Cloaked in secrecy and operated in stealth, these top-secret craft were first revealed to the world at Pearl Harbor and then in attacks at Sydney, Australia, and the British fleet anchorage at Diego Suarez on Madagascar in the Indian Ocean. They subsequently were deployed in many other campaigns in the Pacific War, particularly in their last design phase as suicide weapons. Of several hundred of these craft, only a few have survived, their histories and characteristics for the most part lost or forgotten. Confusion and contradictory descriptions of Japan's midget submarines were common during the war years, and to this day, the lack of information about the Japanese midget submarines, as well as the wealth of misinformation about them, has only been corrected in the last decades by detailed forensic archaeological, architectural, and historical research.

Archaeology is more than the excavation of lost cities and forgotten cultures. It is a detailed, methodical approach to the documentation of artifacts, even larger ones like ships and submarines. These craft, like all built things, are the physical expression of people and their times. Archaeology is relevant when studying not only the distant past but also recent times, even when those times are within the memory of living persons.

Archaeology as practiced in the depths off O'ahu and elsewhere is also more than an academic exercise. The results presented in the pages that follow represent decades of work not only by the individuals involved but also by agencies and organizations. The collaboration inherent in the authorship of this book represents an ongoing commitment to work together to locate, document, study, and understand the battlefield and the larger maritime cultural landscape. It also represents a commitment to share the results with the public as well as other scholars and to work together to manage and protect, to the best of our ability, that which survives and rests entombed in the mud, sand, and sea.

The ongoing partnership among the US Navy, the National Park Service, the University of Hawai'i, and the National Oceanic and Atmospheric Administration has existed since the 1980s. That partnership has matured, not only as technology, techniques, and philosophies have evolved, but as time has shown that together as a team we can make a difference for what is necessary to expand our ability to earn the public's trust and ensure that the legacies of the past help project the lessons learned. Wars are caused by many things, and among them is a lack of understanding. Human beings tend to create barriers between us, things that set us apart, and we often overlook our common humanity as well as our increased risk on a fragile planet with limited resources. Indeed, we often war over access to those resources instead of seeking common solutions. When ideologies enter that mix, manipulated by those who seek power at any cost, then humanity faces the types of crises that saw the deaths of millions in the twentieth century. So far, this century and new millennium are also no stranger to crises or war. We are not so naïve as to think that war will cease to be part of human affairs, but it is telling, as students of history, to observe how passions and seemingly impassable divides can fade with time. In the case of the collaboration inherent in this project, once bitter foes now collaborate to study and protect the midget submarine sunk in the opening hours of the Pearl Harbor attack.

In September 1942, newspapers reported on the impending national tour of one of the midget submarines launched against Pearl Harbor and subsequently captured after a failed attempt to enter the battle. The nature of that craft, the ill-fated submarine of Kazuo Sakamaki, "POW No. 1," seemingly spoke to its captors about the nature of both the submarine and of the Japanese themselves. In 1942, the Chicago *Daily Tribune* noted, "Its construction and equipment indicated [it was] truly a suicide detail," quoting one visitor who "after squeezing into the contrivance [remarked], 'They just shoved those Japs inside with the idea they weren't coming out again'" (Chicago *Daily Tribune*, September 17, 1942:7). Belittling the technological achievements of a wartime adversary and labelling experimental submarines as one-way suicide machines is perhaps not unexpected wartime propaganda, given the times. Three quarters of a century later, we know more, and the answer is not that simple—nor was the opinion of 1942 necessarily correct.

By studying that submarine, as well as the others, and by merging the archaeological with the historical records, we see more now. We see propaganda spinning different perspectives on both sides—referring to the Imperial Japanese Navy as both suicidal fanatics and "Hero Gods." We see grieving families and friends in Japan and remorse from commanding officers who nonetheless stay the course and send more young men to die. We see more through objective forensics analysis. We see changes made to improve the chances of success and perhaps crew survival in the adaptations made to the subs sent to Sydney and Madagascar. We see more as Japanese sources and memoirs have become available and have been consulted. With a vaster, richer array of information, and with

Kazuo Sakamaki after seeing his midget submarine for the first time, five decades after the Pearl Harbor attack, at Fredericksburg, Texas, in the spring of 1991. (Burl Burlingame)

the distance of time, we gain a different perspective. We see a weapon relegated to uses it was not designed for, the enthusiasm of youth, indoctrination into an ideology that nurtured obedience and sacrifice, patriotic fervor, and the setting aside of fear and doubt. We see more of the human story other than that captured in headlines. When Kazuo Sakamaki visited his one-time command five decades after his capture, it was said that he smiled, touched the hull softly, and then wept.[2] It was a reminder that he was, like so many others, a young man caught up in something much bigger than himself those many years ago. Is that not a recurrent theme in human events? When we study the past, including battlefields or submarines, archaeologists always confront the reality that we study people as opposed to things. We study ourselves.

CHAPTER ONE

The Development of the Japanese Midget Submarine Program

The development of the submarine as a weapon for naval warfare was a centuries-old dream for some and a nightmare for others.[1] The desire to develop a working submarine began with experiments in undersea warfare in the early eighteenth century when small wood, brass, and copper craft emerged. The Industrial Revolution of the late eighteenth century and the subsequent development of massive foundries to cast and forges to render iron in the nineteenth century brought new submersible craft into existence. In February 1862, one of these craft, developed by Confederate sympathizers during the War between the States, became famous: the human-powered submersible *H. L. Hunley* successfully sank the US warship *Housatonic* with an electrically detonated spar "torpedo."

Although *Hunley* and its crew were unable to escape from their encounter, the "success" of the sinking spurred other inventors. They developed a variety of craft, some for underwater work and others for war, throughout the end of the nineteenth century. One of these inventors, John P. Holland, would ultimately win a design competition for the US Navy, and at the beginning of the twentieth century, Holland's craft inaugurated submarine service for the United States and then other naval powers, including Great Britain and Japan (Delgado 2011).[2]

The marriage of combustion engines for running on the surface, battery power for submerged operations, and self-propelled torpedoes would prove irresistible. In essence, the submarine found its fullest expression as a stealthy mobile torpedo-launching platform. The true advantages of the submarine's inherent stealth would only be realized in warfare.

Japan purchased five American-built Holland boats in 1904 and built two of its own boats using Holland's plans in 1904–5. These craft, commissioned in 1905, were the beginnings of what would within four decades grow into a large Japanese submarine fleet, all part of Japan's rapid development of a modern navy in response to its forced "opening" by Western powers (Boyd and Yoshida 1995:1; Delgado 2011:118). The success of submarines, particularly those of Germany during the First World War, led many nations to expand their submarine fleets after 1918, seeking at the same time greater range,

H. L. Hunley, the first successful combat submarine, as depicted in Charleston during the Civil War. (Naval History and Heritage Command NH 999)

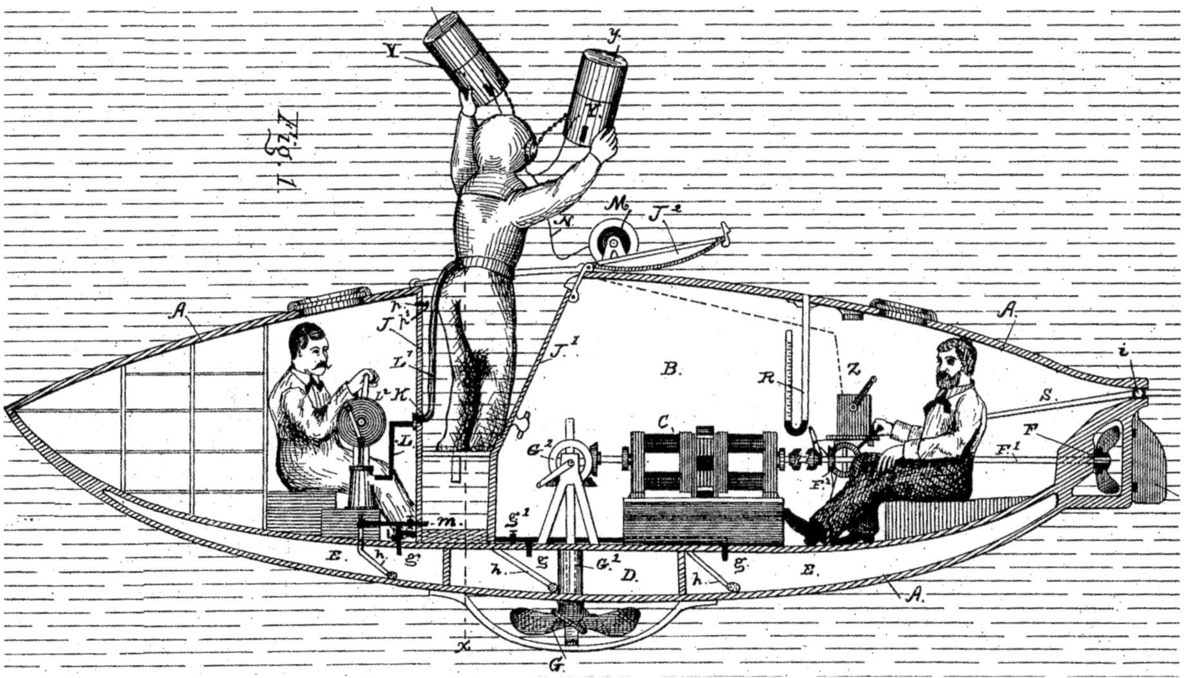

Late nineteenth-century designs included small submarines, which would deploy divers who would attach explosive devices to the target. They presaged later twentieth century designs for some classes of midget submarines. This is Josiah H. L. Tuck's 1884 patent for "Peacemaker," the craft he built and demonstrated but failed to sell to the US Navy. While the US did not pursue the development of small submarines prior to World War II, other navies, notably Japan, had a greater interest in small, "midget" submarines and developed them. (US Patent Office)

USS *Holland* ushered in a new age of submarine warfare at the start of the twentieth century. (Library of Congress, LC-USZ62-50131)

size, and speed for their boats (Evans and Peattie 1997:177–78). Japan's prewar submarine fleet stood at thirteen vessels, including six of the original seven Holland-type craft, an experimental modified Holland boat, five British Vickers C1/C2 boats, and a Japanese-built modified Vickers (Carpenter and Polmar 1986:71). After 1919, the Japanese submarine program commenced in earnest with the construction of Japanese-designed fleet submarines and other large and medium-sized submarines. Starting with what was, in the beginning, an unproven technology, this is simply one of the most successful chronologies of adaptation and innovation in the world.

Japanese submarine doctrine stressed the auxiliary role of the submarine as a supporting arm of the *Rengo Kentai* (Combined Fleet). In keeping with Japan's plans for a decisive naval victory in one great battle—and in the spirit of the Japanese naval tradition of war with Russia, in which small torpedo boats played a symbolically significant role in a surprise opening battle at Port Arthur[3] on February 8–9, 1904—Japanese planners initiated discussions in 1932 focused on creating a fleet of small torpedo-armed craft. That discussion soon turned to *tokushu senkotei* (midget submarines).

Japan's Midget Submarine Program

While the Japanese post–World War I submarine construction program in measure duplicated those of the other naval powers, Japan alone planned for a submarine force that seriously included midget submarines as part of its combat force. This move was inspired by Japanese dissatisfaction with the terms of the Washington, DC, and London naval treaties of 1922 and 1930.

Japan's first submarine squadron in their Holland boats, c. 1905. (US Naval Institute)

Japanese sailors attack a Chinese warship with a torpedo boat during the Sino-Japanese War in this contemporary *ukiyo-e* (woodblock print) by Kobayashi Kiyochika, titled "The Defeat of the Chinese Fleet Near Phungtao, 1894." It is in the use of these surface craft and their torpedoes during battle in Japan's wars with China and Russia that the concept that evolved into the midget submarine program began. (James P. Delgado)

With Japan's number of capital ships limited to a fraction of the US and British fleets, Japanese naval planners investigated a number of programs to compensate for their lack of firepower in an all-out naval gun battle between battleships. Japanese victory in the war with Russia in 1904–5 had been achieved by outgunning the Russian fleet at Tsushima on May 27–28, 1905. That victory reinforced the leadership of the Imperial Japanese Navy's belief in the concept of a "decisive battle" that would win a war (Evans and Peattie 1997:129).

The concept of building a fleet capable of delivering a fatal blow to an enemy in a decisive battle was incorporated into Japanese strategic doctrine in 1907 with the adoption of the "Principles for the Defense of Imperial Japan." The principles focused on Russia as the likely opponent, until February 1928 when they were modified to reflect Japan's new rival for Pacific supremacy—the United States. In that revised plan, Japanese submarines would wage an initial war of attrition against the advancing American fleet, which Japan was convinced would cross the Pacific to engage them (Boyd and Yoshida 1995:5; Carpenter and Polmar 1986:1; Itani et al. 1993:116). Once in Japanese waters, the surviving American ships would be reduced again by surface and underwater torpedo attacks. Finally, Japanese capital ships would engage the last Americans in an artillery duel.

In this battle plan, midget submarines launched by the dozens from surface ships could swarm in to deliver stealthy, crippling blows to the advancing enemy's warships. It was a bold tactical use of submarines, craft hitherto used, albeit successfully, by Germany as commerce raiders in World War I. Captain Kaneji Kishimoto of the Imperial Japanese Navy, the chief of the torpedo section (First Department, Second Section) of the Bureau of Ships, advocated a midget submarine program after his section received a proposal, "Gyorai nikko an" (proposal for human torpedo attacks), in late 1931 from Captain Noriyoshi Yokoo, a veteran of the Russo-Japanese War. In 1904, Yokoo had been part of the initial torpedo boat attack on the Russian fleet at Port Arthur. Yokoo's proposal reportedly called for "releasing a torpedo piloted by one man from

THE FIRST JAPANESE SUBMARINES AND THE LOSS OF NO. 6

Japan was one of the first nations to adopt the submarine into its naval forces. After closely watching the US Navy's trials of its first twentieth-century submarine, USS *Holland* (commissioned in 1900), including the Japanese naval attaché's taking a test dive in the craft, Japan ordered five of the "Holland" boats from the Electric Boat Company in 1904. Shipped partially disassembled to Japan, the boats were completed in 1905, too late to participate in the war with Russia. John Holland, inventor of the eponymous craft, praised the Japanese for adopting a newer design and building two new boats that improved on his earlier craft. Calling the Japanese "incomparably superior war men," Holland noted that by working "independently and indefatigably," the Japanese were "building boats designed and fitted to accompany fleet of any kind of weather for any distance and any speed . . . Japan's boats work; they don't do stunts" (Morris 1966:126).

Japan gained its first submarine martyrs when its newly completed Holland-type submarine No. 6 dived too deep and sank, partially flooded when a valve was stuck open. Trapped on the seabed, the crew of No. 6 slowly asphyxiated in a freezing steel coffin. The commanding officer, Lieutenant Sakuma Tsumoto, wrote a letter to his colleagues explaining what went wrong: "It is with pride that I inform you that the crew to a man discharged their duties as sailors should with the utmost coolness until their dying moments. We now sacrifice our lives for the sake of our country, but my fear is that the disaster will affect the future development of submarines." He begged his superiors "to study the submarine until it is a perfect machine, absolutely reliable. Then we can die without regret" (*Our Navy*, September 10, 1910:16). When the Imperial Japanese Navy located and raised No. 6, it was too late, but the discovery of the letter on Satsuma's body became an international sensation (*New York Times*, May 19, 1910:4; Yamamoto 2005). His name, as well as that of submarine No. 6, inspired the midget submariners of the *kō-hyōteki* corps.

Japanese submariners on a Holland boat, 1905, one of the sister subs of the ill-fated No. 6. The image was first published in the Japanese naval magazine *The Air and Sea*, vol. 6, no. 3, in June 1933. (US Naval Institute)

Captain Kaneji Kishimoto of the Imperial Japanese Navy, an early advocate of a Japanese midget submarine program. (Burl Burlingame)

a mother torpedo" (Itani et al. 1993:116; Kurihara 1974:10–11; Sano 1975:21–23). While torpedoes had actually played only a minor role in the naval war with Russia, the concept of a small, elite force resonated with proponents of warfare conducted in accord with ancient Japanese principles—"the quick, close-in thrust of small groups of warriors against the heart of the enemy" (Evans and Peattie 1997:130).

Inspired by Yokoo's idea, in early 1932, Kishimoto encouraged his superiors to authorize the development of midget submarines. "In a decisive battle between U.S. and Japanese fleets," Kishimoto noted, "we could send out nearly a hundred torpedoes" from a fleet of forty-eight midgets, launched twelve at a time from a mother ship. "It would thus be possible to reduce the enemy strength by fifty percent" (Warner and Seno 1986:10). These "torpedoes" would need to be fast, running at speeds of at least 30 knots, carry two tubes each for launching torpedoes against their targets, and have a range of some 60 km (30 nm; Itani et al. 1933:116). Kishimoto's plan was approved by Prince Hiroyasu Fushimi, chief of the Naval General Staff, on the understanding that despite the suicidal intent of Yokoo's proposal, the midgets would not be developed as suicide weapons. Kishimoto believed that "the operation needed death-defying courage but should never mean suicide" (Itani et al. 1993:117; Warner and Seno 1986:10). In line with the Imperial Japanese Navy's strategy of "using inferior strength against the superior strength of our potential enemy, the U.S. Navy," the midgets would augment the submarine fleet in numerous groups of small but deadly "Davids" pitted against the American "Goliath" (Fukudome 1986:32–33).

Conducted under a program of stringent security, even within the Imperial Japanese Navy, the midget submarine program commenced modestly in October 1932 when the navy accepted a small civilian-built craft for testing. Known as Nishimura Mamesen No. 1, the 8.83 meter (29 foot) craft was the product of Ishimatsu Nishimura, the operator of the Nishimura Fishing Company of Shimonoseki City in the Yamaguchi prefecture. Designed in 1927 and built in 1929, ostensibly to search for pink coral in the "mandated islands" of the Pacific,[4] Nishimura Mamesen No. 1 was a cigar-shaped vessel reportedly displacing 12 tons and capable of diving to 400 meters (Nihon Kaiyo Sangyo Kenkyusho 1976).

The small vessel was powered by two 16 hp electric motors. Unmanned tests of Nishimura's midget were held at Iyo-Nada, a strait on the

The Nishimura prototype submarines. (Burl Burlingame)

Seto Inland Sea,[5] in August 1933. Sleek and without a conning tower, Nishimura Mamesen No. 1 achieved a submerged speed of 24.85 knots. Manned trials, with the craft piloted by Lieutenant Commander Ryōnosuke Kato and Sublieutenant Arata Harada, followed between October 1933 and December 1934. Mamesen No. 1 was successfully operated to a depth of 100 meters and ran at 22 knots for 50 minutes (Itani et al. 193:117). The existence of the craft and the tests were a closely guarded secret, but a photograph and a brief description, smuggled out of Japan, was published in English-language newspapers in 1934.[6]

The naval correspondent of the London *Daily Telegraph*, Hector C. Bywater, reported the following in the May 22, 1934, edition:

> Despite official reticence, the existence of a midget Japanese submarine appears to be fully established. I learn that trials lasting three months have just been concluded at Ito . . . and the remarkable little craft is reputed to have given every satisfaction. . . . The boat can dive to a depth of 164 feet, and remain below the surface for three hours at a time. . . . The type is intended for harbour defence and surprise attacks. Owing to its small dimensions, it can be hoisted on board a large warship, and then launched again to attack enemy shipping in waters where the presence of submarines might never be suspected. In consequence of the success of the first experimental boat, further midget submarines will probably be built for the Japanese Navy. (London *Daily Telegraph*, May 22, 1934)[7]

Following the success of the first craft, Nishimura laid down a second boat in 1935. Nishimura Mamesen No. 2 was fitted with a conning tower and a diesel engine that allowed the sub's batteries to recharge while on the surface. According to Japanese sources, the navy tested the Nishimura craft "for researching under-water sound wave propagation, to find out long range ship-borne anti-submarine device of transportation ship, and for fortress anti-submarine device at Korean Strait (Chosen Kaikyo)" (Nihon Kaiyo Sangyo Kenkyusho 1976). This was the essential original purpose of the midget submarines: they were to be shore-based coastal defense weapons. While the trials found that the conning tower, propeller guards, and other external fittings reduced the submerged speed from 24 to 23 knots, the speed remained exceptional.[8]

In the fall of 1938, the Imperial Japanese Navy decided to build two highly modified "Nishimura boats." These craft, known as Nishimura No. 3746 and Nishimura No. 3747, set the basic form of the midget submarines that would follow. They were laid down at the Kure Navy Yard in July 1939 (Nihon Kaiyo Sangyo Kenkyusho 1976). Four officers from Kishimoto's section of the Bureau of Ships supervised the work. They were Commander Toshihide Asama, a torpedo expert; Commander Takeshi Nawa, a battery expert; Commander Kiyoshi Yamada, who was assigned to the motors; and Commander Ariki Katayama, who worked on the hull (Itani et al. 1993:117; Orita and Harrington 1976:26).

Nishimura No. 3746 was completed in April 1940, and Nishimura No. 3747 was finished 2 months later (Itani et al. 1993:119). These craft were also used in tests beginning in April, when Lieutenant Commander Yoshimutsu Sekio and Sublieutenant Toshio Hori submerged Number 3746 to a maximum depth of a hundred meters (Itani et al. 1993:119). The boat, with a larger conning tower and bow appurtenances to approximate torpedo mounts, ran for 50 minutes at 21.5 knots. At a lesser speed of 6 knots, Number 3746 operated for 16 hours (Nihon Kaiyo Sangyo Kenkyusho 1976).

Experiments in launching the two midgets from the seaplane tender *Chiyoda* on the Sea of Iyo, in the Inland Sea and in the Bungo Strait, took place in August 1940. After ten unmanned launches in different conditions and at various speeds, *Chiyoda* successfully launched a manned

THE NISHIMURA PROTOTYPES

The Nishimura boats were the world's first true midget submarines. Clumsy on the surface, where they were difficult to control and could achieve a scant 6 knot speed, the Nishimura boats were designed as submarines, not as submersibles.[9] With their hulls dedicated to underwater performance, the four anticipated the later, postwar hull forms of the United States' prototypes for nuclear submarines.

Japanese sources describe the first two Nishimura submarines as 20 ton, 36-foot-long vessels with a maximum hull diameter of 6 feet. The vessels were reportedly powered by two 16 hp motors (one held in reserve) and were battery powered. Shizuo Fukui, the former chief constructor of the Imperial Japanese Navy, and as such the preeminent Japanese source on the vessels of the Imperial Japanese Navy that survived World War II, illustrated one of the Nishimura prototypes in his multivolume tome on the Imperial Fleet (Fukui 1980). Fukui was not entirely forthcoming in his description when he termed the craft a *sensui sagyo-sen*, or "diverging boat," built for "gathering corals in the mandated islands . . . by order of a civilian named Nishimura." Fukui noted that the craft was "not used for practical gathering due to some insufficient qualities." The boat was employed, according to Fukui, to search for the sunken I-63 in 1939, and others were built for submarine salvage purposes following this. Fukui rated the Nishimura boats' speed at 4.4 knots and their maximum depth at 200 meters (Fukui 1980:184). Former Japanese submariners familiar with the craft in Japan later rated the speed at 22 to 24.85 knots and the maximum depth at twice that, or 400 meters (Nihon Kaiyo Sangyo Kenkyusho 1976).

The first two prototypes of the *kō-hyōteki* were nothing like the earlier Nishimura craft but instead closely resembled the later versions made famous at Pearl Harbor. All the early boats were kept at Kure by the Imperial Japanese Navy and survived the war. Under the terms of disarmament, three of the boats were scrapped by order of the victorious Americans in 1945. One, identified by the Japanese as prototype No. 3746 (but in fact Nishimura Mamesen No. 2 of 1935), was sent to the United States as a prize of war in 1946 in response to a request from the Mariners' Museum in Newport News, Virginia, for a gift of "certain objects of historical interest" and the decision of the navy to send "one Japanese midget submarine," according to the museum's accession files for the craft. It arrived on May 23, 1946, and was on display for many years as an outdoor exhibit. In 1976, veterans of the submarine program and Nishimura's nephew embarked on a campaign to have the craft returned to Shimonoseki, and the Japanese embassy supported the request, but the museum demurred, noting the craft was used in educational programs. Several years ago, following a redevelopment of the museum, the craft was moved to outdoor storage, where it remains to this day.[10]

The only known surviving Nishimura prototype for the Japanese midget submarine program is in the collections of the Mariners' Museum in Newport News, Virginia, where it has rested since the end of the World War II. (The Mariners' Museum/James P. Delgado)

sub (Itani et al. 1993:119). Japanese naval censor Hajime Fukaya, writing after the war, stated that these experiments were a "complete success," particularly in proving "the feasibility of their utilization in long range operations" (Fukaya 1952:863–64). One spectator, Admiral Soemu Toyoda, chief of the Bureau of Naval Construction, was thrilled: "Even as we watched the successful experiment, we asked ourselves how wonderful it would be if all three mother ships were to advance to the front of the enemy, discharge their target As [the code name for the

HIJMS *Chiyoda*, the "mother ship" of the Japanese midget submarine program. (Imperial War Museum, MH.5948)

midget submarines] and carry out an all-out attack on the enemy. Visualizing such a scene, I felt every drop of blood in my body dancing in my veins" (as cited in Warner and Seno 1986:11).

Notwithstanding the "complete success" Fukaya reported and Admiral Toyoda's excitement, Lieutenant Sekido's later assessment was honest and spoke to the problems future midget submariners faced: "This was a high-speed boat armed with high quality torpedoes manned by a smaller crew, which produced advantages, but I am afraid it also meant problems because of the contradictory requirements of superior capabilities and a small lightweight hull" (as quoted in Itani et al. 1993:129). Sekido complained that the craft required considerable support from the mother ship and that "some of the equipment called for high levels of skill and were easily deranged" and noted the need for a rigid program in which the midget submariners would benefit from "excellent tuning and repair facilities" (as quoted in Itani et al. 1993:129).

In addition, the boat was always rolling and pitching at periscope depth, making acquisition of a target by periscope difficult; the conning tower was frequently exposed, "which in fact cannot be called submerging," noted Sekido; and "attack on the ocean . . . was very, very difficult" (as quoted in Itani et al. 1993:120). Some of these problems were addressed for the first generation of craft that would follow the two test hulls, but many problems were not addressed, as Japanese naval planners were aware that war was coming soon and time was running out to make more significant changes.

In October 1940, ten boats (numbered HA-3 to HA-12)[11] were ordered, followed in December by an order for boats HA-13 through HA-36.

With these hulls ordered, on November 15, 1940, the Imperial Japanese Navy formally accepted midget submarines as a weapon of war and embarked on a secret larger scale program of midget submarine construction (Itani et al. 1993:120). The stage was now set for the mass production of innovative small submarines that would demonstrate extraordinary technological advances. Like the Japanese Zero fighter and the later I-400 series large submarines, the midget craft were major Japanese contributions in the development of the airplane and the submarine. A number of unaddressed Achilles' heels came with the midget submarines as the exigency of impending war pushed aside concerns of Sekido and likely others.

The Karasukojima Naval Armory's torpedo factory at the Kure Naval Arsenal at Hiroshima laid down the first ten of the newly designed midget submarines in October 1940 in a special closed shop on the isolated island of Kurahashijima (Evans and Peattie 1997:273; Orita and Harrington 1976:26). While officially termed Type A boats, the midgets were often referred to by code names. At times called *kanamono*, or "metal fittings," during the design phase, they were later designated *hyōteki*, or "targets" (Fukui 1991:100). They were usually referred to as *kō-hyōteki*, following the Japanese practice of indicating smallness with the appellation of *kō* (Evans and Peattie 1997:273).[12] Thus the target was diminished, masking the deadly potential of the small craft. Submariner Zenji Orita, speaking for his peers, later said that "right up to the government broadcast telling of midget submarine operations at Pearl Harbor, most Japanese Navy men thought these bulbous, cigar-shaped hulls were special targets for use by submarines during firing practice" (Orita and Harrington 1976:26).

Another twenty-four *kō-hyōteki* were ordered before the end of 1941. While owing many of their salient features to the Nishimura prototypes, the *kō-hyōteki* were different in appearance. Built in sections that bolted together, they were larger to accommodate the tubes for two 18 inch torpedoes. The *kō-hyōteki* were also fitted with a taller, more streamlined conning tower than the Nishimura boats (Fukui 1991:100). Each was painted with the character for HA, which is *Romaji* for the third character of kana in *katakana*, the Japanese syllabary. I and RO are the first and second characters and were used to designate first- and second-class subs, and HA was used to designate small, third-class submarines like the midgets. As noted, HA-3 through HA-36 were laid down before the end of 1940, although only thirteen, HA-3 through HA-15, were ready for use when the Pacific War commenced. HA-7 was retained for training, leaving twelve midgets for combat.

Captain Kaku Harada, Imperial Japanese Navy, "father" of the Japanese midget submarine program. Born at Fukushima-ken in 1890, Harada graduated from the Naval Academy in 1913. He entered the Imperial Japanese Navy's submarine service in 1917 and in 1922 assumed his first command. Promoted to captain in 1937, Harada was in command of *Chiyoda* in 1940 when the *kō-hyōteki* program commenced. His rise in command saw him promoted to rear admiral in 1942. After commanding and then surrendering Japanese forces at Cebu, then Vice Admiral Harada died of disease in captivity in September 1945. (Burl Burlingame)

Selecting the Crews

The first *kō-hyōteki* were ready in August 1941, but the program began earlier, in January, when Lieutenant Naoji Iwasa and Sublieutenant Saburo Akieda began testing the new craft with the first two test boats. Iwasa was the chief test pilot for the new craft (Warner and Seno 1986:14). The crews for the first group of twelve midget submarines were selected in April 1941. In all, twenty-four young men who were believed to epitomize determination, a fighting spirit, bodily strength, and physical energy, in addition to being unmarried and from large families, were picked and ordered to the seaplane, now midget tender *Chiyoda*. There they were met by Captain Kaku Harada, commanding *Chiyoda* and the midget submarine program. According to new recruit Kazuo Sakamaki, Harada told the assembled group, "Fellows, you are going to receive a very special type of training from now on [because] you are going in a secret weapon—the midget submarine" (Sakamaki 1949:29).

The Imperial Japanese Navy had selected the midget crews from its already rigidly trained, selective ranks. The navy was one of the world's most respected, if not feared, naval forces. It stood at 287,476 men and 23,883 officers in 1941 (Evans and Peattie 1997:402). Each, particularly the officers, was indoctrinated with the navy's five principle virtues of loyalty, propriety, valor, righteousness, and simplicity.

More than 90 percent of the young men who applied to join the Imperial Navy were rejected. Cadets had to be perfect physical specimens. Yutaka Yokota, a naval petty officer in 1944, was rejected by the Japanese Imperial Naval Academy at Etajima because three of his teeth were missing after a boxing match. When Kazuo Sakamaki, destined to be one of the first class of midget submariners,

CHITOSE, CHIYODA, AND NISSHIN

Built under the provisions of the Second Fleet Replenishment Law, the Imperial Japanese Navy built three 11,203 ton, flush-decked seaplane tenders. *Chitose*, *Chiyoda*, and *Mizuho* carried twelve seaplanes on the deck, while another twelve were stowed below deck in a hangar. The bridge was located forward, with the superstructure also supporting the guns, the aerial mast, and a single stack into which all four boiler uptakes were trunked. Immediately aft of midships, an elevated platform, with four corner supports, mounted three 25 mm guns, the flight operations bridge, and a searchlight. The planes were taken up from the hangar through an opening in the deck beneath the platform with cranes mounted on the platform supports. Rails on the deck allowed the planes to be shifted to the two catapults forward of the platform, near the funnel, and the two platforms aft of the platform.

Chitose was laid down on November 26, 1934, was launched on November 29, 1936, and was completed July 25, 1938. *Chiyoda* was laid down on December 14, 1936, launched on November 19, 1937, and completed December 15, 1938. While *Chiyoda* was the first of the seaplane tenders to be used for midget submarine work, in late 1940, the decision was made to convert *Chitose* to carry twelve Type A midgets in her hangar. Mounted on rails, the submarines were stowed, two abreast and in groups of two, in two rows. Two rails ran aft to the launching ramp, which ran through a hole cut in the stern. The stern was secured by hinged steel doors. All twelve midgets were capable of being launched at a rate of two every 3 minutes in good conditions.

Chiyoda was converted along the same lines as *Chitose* in July 1941. The decision to use the midgets at Pearl Harbor and then again at Sydney and Diego Suarez relegated the former seaplane tenders to a secondary role, and after the Battle of Midway, it was decided to convert *Chitose* and *Chiyoda* to aircraft carriers. *Chiyoda* was first, converted at Yokosuka beginning in December 1942, and was followed by *Chitose* at Sasebo in January 1943. Both were lost as aircraft carriers in the Battle of the Philippine Sea. *Chitose*

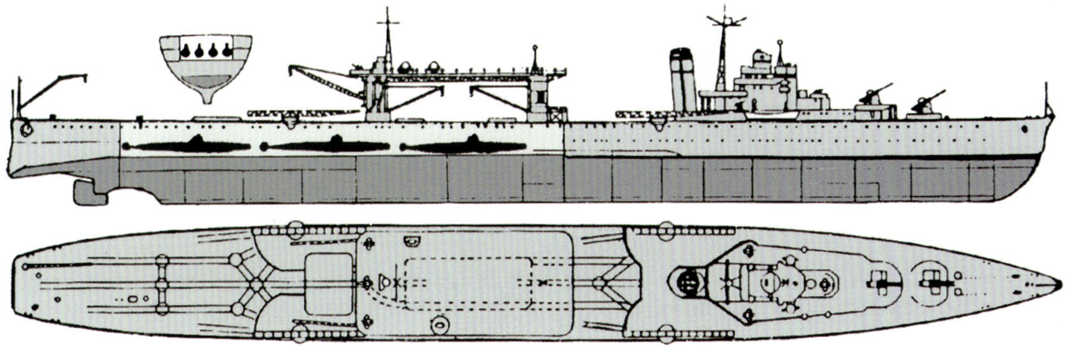

Chiyoda's configuration as a *kō-hyōteki* carrier. The hangar deck carried four rows of three submarines, which would launch, on rails, one at a time through an access hatch cut into the stern of the carrier. This design was based on the original plan of using the midgets in an open sea battle as a small swarm of combatants. That tactic was abandoned for the Pearl Harbor attack and was never used throughout the entire war, although *Chiyoda* did ferry midget submarines to different theaters of war to be loaded onto I-boats. (Burl Burlingame)

Chiyoda's crew poses on the ship in April 1942 before heading to Chuuk (Truk) with the midget submarines intended for the attack on Sydney. (Australian War Memorial, 128884)

was sunk on October 25, 1944, by aircraft from USS *Essex* and USS *Lexington* 235 miles off Cape Engano. *Chiyoda*, damaged on the same day by planes from *Lexington*, *Franklin*, and *Langley*, was sunk by gunfire from the cruisers *Wichita*, *Santa Fe*, *Mobile*, and *New Orleans* 260 miles off Cape Engano.

In the 1937 program of naval construction, the Imperial Japanese Navy decided to build a fourth tender along the lines of *Chitose* and *Chiyoda*. Laid down in November 1938 and launched on November 30, 1939, *Nisshin* was completed on February 27, 1942. Before completion, the hangar was converted to carry 700 mines, with launching rails and stern doors. The platform on the main deck was also omitted. When the decision was made to convert *Chitose* and *Chiyoda* to aircraft carriers, *Nisshin* was modified to carry twelve midgets. She did not survive long, however. *Nisshin* was sunk by US aircraft 17 miles west of Cape Alexander on July 22, 1943.

Vessel Characteristics: *Chitose* and *Chiyoda*

Dimensions: 603.5 feet (183 m) at the waterline × 61.75 feet (18.7 m) × 23.5 feet (7 m)

Armament: twenty-four seaplanes; later twelve Type A midgets; four 5 inch / 40 caliber guns (2 × 2); twelve 25 mm guns (3 × 2 and 6 × 1)

Machinery: Twin turbines (44,000 SHP) and twin diesels 12,800 BHP, four Kanton boilers
Speed: 29 knots

Vessel Characteristics: *Nisshin*
Dimensions: 616.75 feet (182.9 m waterline) 570.5 feet (173.8 m perpendiculars) × 64.5 × 23 feet (7m)
Displacement: 11,317 tons
Armament: 700 mines, twelve seaplanes, later twelve Type A midgets; six 5.5 inch / 50 caliber guns (3 × 2); eighteen 25 mm guns (6 × 3)
Machinery: Six diesels 47,000 BHP
Speed: 29 knots

joined the navy, he was one of three hundred cadets selected from six thousand applicants in April 1937. Even more cadets were weeded out by the rough discipline of Etajima. The cadets faced a grueling regimen that began at 5:30 every morning, 7 days a week. Physical training, drills, and classroom work occupied each 15-and-a-half hour day. Punishment was meted out by officers and upperclassmen who regularly beat those being disciplined. Blows to the face were regularly administered with a clenched fist to enforce the rules, to weed out those who questioned authority, and to punish failure.

The cadets' routine included kendo, archery, rowing and sailing, and intense physical training. During the summer months, the cadets swam for 3 hours in the Inland Sea. An annual "campout" on Miyajima Island ended with a 10 mile swim back to Etajima. Midget submariner Kazuo Sakamaki, recalling his academy days, wrote that "often, when we were rowing our cutter, our hands bled and our *fundoshi* (underwear) were smeared with blood. But we rowed on. We charged our boat into a fierce storm, and if we vomited in anguish, we did not turn back. When we were on land we practiced wrestling, rising up from the floor even when we could hardly breathe through exhaustion" (Sakamaki 1949:27).

Cadets stand in rank as they sing the naval academy anthem at Etajima prior to World War II. The various routines and rituals of academy life were meant to instill a sense of pride, belonging, and obedience. (Burl Burlingame)

Classroom work occupied 36 hours of the week as the cadets studied a regular college curriculum interlaced with naval history, engineering, seamanship, and battle tactics. Throughout this, the academy constantly and relentlessly thinned and honed its ranks. Six of Sakamaki's classmates dropped out; other cadets occasionally committed suicide.

"Perhaps our spiritual discipline was not as rigid," wrote Sakamaki, but "we were taught, and we came to believe, that the most important thing for us was to die manfully on the battlefield—as the petals of a cherry blossom fall to the ground—and that in war there is only victory and no retreat." It was also clear, he felt, that "there was no room for individual thinking and that absolute obedience to our superiors was the only behaviour becoming a

Cadets pose during rowing practice at Etajima. The reality of the training was far more arduous than this image suggests. (Burl Burlingame)

cadet." There was no time to look at flowers or even think of life or death, thought Sakamaki, because "the weight of duty and the sense of responsibility filled my mind" (Sakamaki 1949:27–28).

When Kazuo Sakamaki graduated from Etajima in August 1940, he was commissioned as a midshipman. In earlier times, the midshipmen would have embarked on a worldwide cruise in one of Japan's training ships. As the nation was in the midst of a prolonged war in China and the prospect of conflict with the United States and Britain loomed, Sakamaki's class spent 2 months on maneuvers off China, Japan, and in the Western Pacific. After a month's training in air operations, Sakamaki was posted to the light cruiser *Abukuma*, flagship of the navy's torpedo squadron. Sakamaki served as a gun officer and a deck officer before being ordered to the midget submarine program in April 1941.

Learning the Ropes

Japan's submarine school at Otake faced the Inland Sea. Described by a British submarine officer in 1945 as "large airy wooden buildings" that would accommodate 200 officers and 4,500 men during the 6 month training course, the school included two RO-class submarines, embedded in concrete for training, and two other boats at anchor, also for training. An inspection of the school by the victorious allies in 1945 found that "the instructional models and practical gear are of good quality," including a diesel shop for engineers that housed "full-size editions of all types of engines found in Japanese submarines" and five diving and three attack teachers, or simulators (Lakin 1945).

For the midget crews, training began at the naval base at Kure, where the crews lived aboard *Chiyoda*, studied at the base submarine school, and visited midgets then under construction. By June, the men, split into two-man crews, were training

Imperial Japanese Navy cap badge from World War II. (James P. Delgado)

Three of the *kō-hyōteki* corps: Ensign Masaharu Yokoyama, Petty Officer Second Class Tei Uyeda, and Petty Officer First Class Naokichi Sasaki. They all died at Pearl Harbor. (Burl Burlingame)

at a secret base at Ourazaki, nearly 12 miles southwest of Kure, where the midget submariners learned how to steer, submerge, and navigate their tiny craft. Two midget submarines were moored to a barge in Mitsukue Bay and were towed to Kamegabuki (Turtle Head Cape) near Kure for each day's training exercises.

The men were told that their craft would be used "to attack the enemy's largest ship at the very first moment of an encounter with an enemy fleet," to attack ships "by secretly entering a harbor or naval base," and "to be used as a 'trump card' as occasion might arise" (Sakamaki 1949:31). A captured midget submariner's training notebook provides some insight into the mind-set of these young warriors. The notes stress that "the spirit of loyalty and sacrifice for one's country are the requisite in the hyoteki's battle. It is necessary that crew members further their fighting spirit, work the *hyōteki* sturdily, resolutely, composedly, and keenly, and thus be

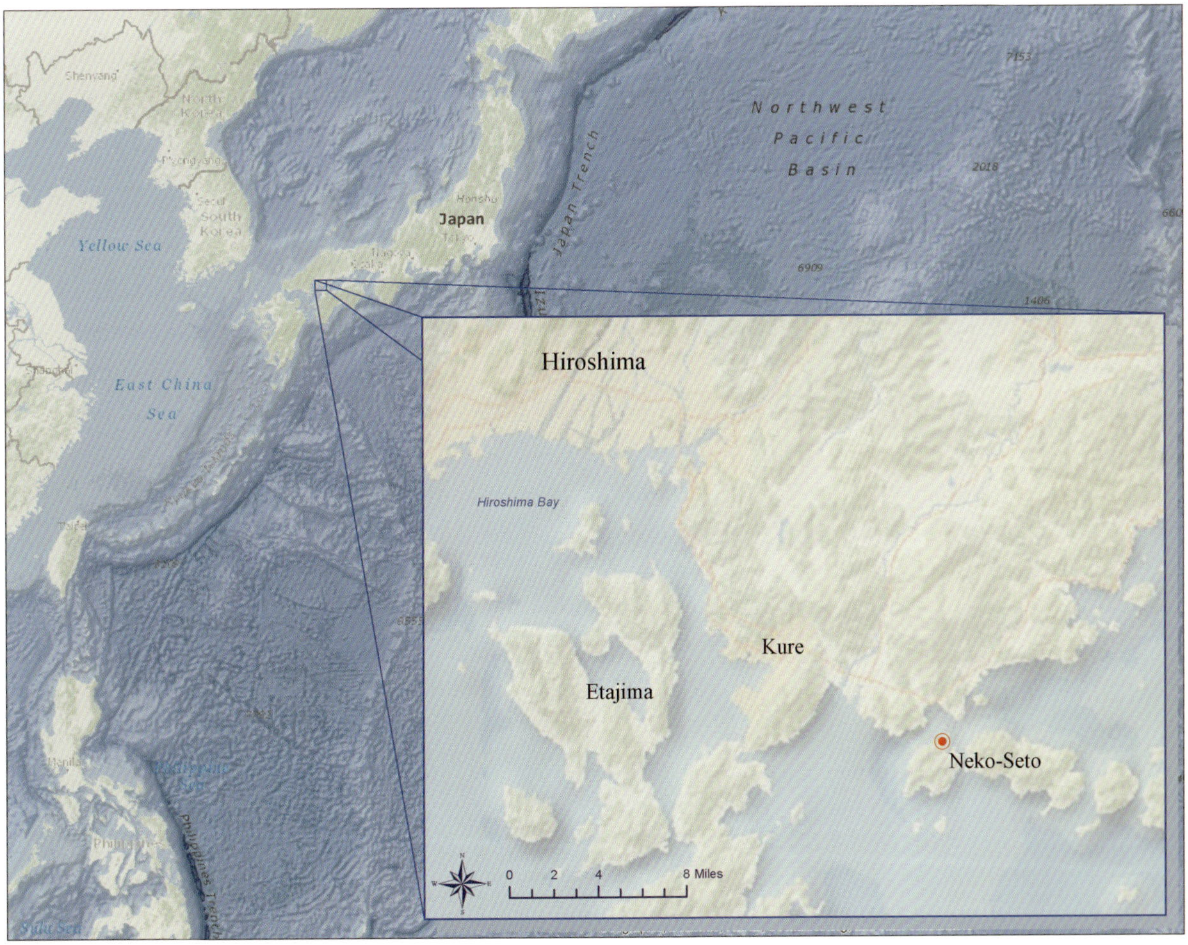

The training area of the *kō-hyōteki* corps. (Tony Reyer/NOAA)

ready to perfect the effectiveness of the *hyōteki* in the battle" (Tanaka 1940–42).[13]

An effective attack occurred when the midget approached the enemy "speedily and secretly," with a direct hit with every shot. "The main point in *hyōteki* operation is accuracy and speed," and therefore each man was encouraged to know his craft, constantly study it, and ensure that "maintenance and adjustment . . . [were] perfect" (Tanaka 1940–42). Classes in the operation of the submarines stressed the importance of maintaining the midget's stability, trim, and buoyancy. Other classes examined the charging and care of the batteries. Others focused on operating the air systems and the computations for aiming and then firing the torpedoes. The crews were warned to wait at least 15 seconds between firing their torpedoes to allow the bow to settle. The loss of weight made the bows rise, which needed to be compensated for. If not, the torpedoes would jump out of the water and give the sub's position away. They were also warned to keep their engine revolutions to a minimum because the gears in the tail section were very noisy at high speed.

Trials drilled the men and stressed that great care was to be taken in the maintenance of the midgets. Midget crews were warned to thoroughly examine the craft prior to launches, "because emergency repair is difficult. The interior of the *hyōteki* is very narrow, equipment is complex and inspections and care are very difficult. . . . Therefore a sense of responsibility and minute observance must be devoted to maintenance." While each submarine had a maintenance and an operating crew, the operating crews were told to cooperate and work with the others, particularly when the operating crew took over prior to launching, when "errors and mistakes in maintenance were likely to occur" (Tanaka 1940–42).

Some of the *kō-hyōteki* corps pose for a photograph on a break during training. In the second row are Sublieutenant Kenshi Chuma and Sublieutenant Katsuhisa Ban, both of whom later died in the attack at Sydney. In the front row are Sublieutenants Shigemi Furuno and Shigenori Yokoyama, both of whom died at Pearl Harbor. (David Jenkins)

Prior to launching, each midget crew went through nine tests. The insulators were checked. The sensitivity of the depth gear and horizontal gear was examined. The emergency valves were then tested, as were the vertical rudders, which had to move left and right equally. The main motor was started and the revolutions checked. At 500 rpm, for example, the motors needed to draw 100 amps. The density of the air inside the submarine was then checked, the trim adjusted, and the seawater pump started. The crews' last drills were the raising and lowering of the radio mast and the periscope.

Ensign Tanaka, summarizing his training with his peers, noted that "the crew are just like blind people as far as the outside world is concerned. . . . They must be informed as to the conditions from time to time." Tanaka also commented that his training showed him that "guts and skill to perform the duty composedly are requisite" (Tanaka 1940–42). They would be needed for the first combat mission of the midget submarine corps. The target was the US Navy's fleet at Pearl Harbor.

CHAPTER TWO

Midget Submarines at Pearl Harbor

THE IDEA OF USING THE *KŌ-HYŌTEKI* IN THE ATTACK ON PEARL Harbor reportedly began in the ranks of the midget submarine corps. Both Lieutenant Naoji Iwasa, the 27-year-old chief test pilot for the *kō-hyōteki*, and Sublieutenant Keiu Matsuo believed that the rise of naval air power had doomed decisive battles between opposing fleets. This, in turn, ended the possibility of the *kō-hyōteki* being deployed in action. In August 1941, as the midget submarine corps continued their training, Iwasa approached Captain Kaku Harada of the *kō-hyōteki* mother ship *Chiyoda*, and proposed shifting their training to attacking enemy ships in protected anchorages. Harada had Iwasa present his plan to Lieutenant Commander Ryunosoke Ariizumi of the Naval General Staff when Ariizumi came to inspect *Chiyoda*. Impressed by the plan and Iwasa's argument that "our weapon can do far more damage to an enemy on his doorstep than in the middle of the ocean," Ariizumi took the idea to Admiral Isoroku Yamamoto and asked him to authorize training the *kō-hyōteki* corps for the planned assault on Pearl Harbor (Orita and Harrington 1976:28). Yamamoto, according to Shigeru Fukudome, Yamamoto's chief of staff, "gave his consent only after his staffs had exhaustively studied the feasibility of rescuing crew of midget subs as well as their chances of survival" (Fukudome 1986:15).

Admiral Isoroku Yamamoto, commander-in-chief of the Imperial Japanese Navy. He authorized the shift from open-ocean assault to stealthy penetration of enemy harbors. (Naval History and Heritage Command, NH 63430)

To assess Pearl Harbor and gain a better sense of what the midget submariners might face, the navy sent two young midget submarine corps officers, Sublieutenant Keiu Matsuo and Sublieutenant Akira Kanda, on the NYK ship *Tatsuta Maru*, disguised as merchant marine navigation cadets. Steaming from Yokohama, *Tatsuta Maru* arrived in Honolulu on October 23, 1941. For the week, the two scouted the harbor approaches, making notes carefully to guide their fellow midget submariners in the event of war. They returned to Yokohama on November 14, via San Francisco. Their intelligence was eagerly accepted, with detailed notes on antisubmarine patrols, nets, and prominent landmarks (Warner and Seno 1986:25–26).

Iwasa desperately wanted to lead the attack. Captain Harada wrote in his diary that he had come to him and "demanded strongly," because "the attack inside the harbour was his plan, and is the tradition of the navy that the person who created the plan should carry out the plan. He demanded he should be put in charge, again and again." Harada did not want to lose him, writing it was wrong to use Iwasa "for this suicide-like mission. There is no need to fight if there are others willing to go" (Association of Midget Submariners 1984:20). In the end, Harada capitulated, but only if his other lead student and trainer, Sublieutenant Saburo Akieda, did not join the attack force.

The initial training of the crews ended in September 1941, and in the following month, training shifted to intense study and preparations for action inside an enemy harbor. Harada ordered the *kō-hyōteki* crews to study maps of Hong Kong, Sydney, Singapore, San Francisco, and Pearl Harbor's waters (Sakamaki 1949:34). *Chiyoda* shifted to the north coast of Shikoku, on the Sea of Aki in the Inland Sea, where the crews practiced entering a narrow inlet at night. Because *Chiyoda* was not suited for a stealth mission, the navy ordered five I-class submarines from Submarine Squadron One to report to Kure Naval Arsenal for the installation of "special fittings." They would carry the *kō-hyōteki* piggyback across the Pacific.

The first to arrive at Kure was I-22, under the command of Commander Kiyotake Ageta, and

The first class of officers of the *kō-hyōteki* corps pose on *Chiyoda* prior to the Pearl Harbor attack. (David Jenkins)

The first class of petty officers of the *kō-hyōteki* corps pose on *Chiyoda* prior to the Pearl Harbor attack. (David Jenkins)

the flagship of Captain Hanku Sasaki, the commander of SubRon 1, the submarine squadron supplying the boats for the Pearl Harbor mission. According to Sasaki, his sub had "no sooner moored at Kure than a dozen technicians came on board. They began making sketches of I-22's after deck" (Orita and Harrington 1976:28–29). Sasaki was worried about the entire operation, later noting "there was too much hurry, hurry, hurry" (as quoted in Prange 1981:338).[1] Modifications to I-22 included installing a cradle to carry the *kō-hyōteki* aft of the conning tower and installing a jack to connect a telephone to the smaller submarine. The submarines I-16, I-18, and I-20 arrived at Kure a few days after I-22 and were also modified. The last submarine, I-24, was new, and after completion at Sasebo, where it had been built, was ordered to Kure for the fitting of its cradle in early November. On November 6, 1941, with modifications complete, the five I-boats were sent to the *kō-hyōteki* factory and base at Kamegabuki. There, cranes lifted each *kō-hyōteki* onto the decks of the larger subs and fastened them to the cradles. The submarines then departed to the Sea of Aki for 4 days of trials.

Despite Yamamoto's go-ahead for training, doubts about the readiness and the probable loss of the *kō-hyōteki* plagued the Japanese planners, and as late as November 14, just 11 days before departure of the attack fleet for Pearl Harbor, the final decision to send the *kō-hyōteki* had not been

A postwar drawing by the Japanese Midget Submarine Association shows the configuration of the I-boats carrying *kō-hyōteki* on their backs. (JMSA / Burl Burlingame).

C1 TYPE SUBMARINE

The submarines selected to carry the first *kō-hyōteki* into battle at Pearl Harbor were all relatively recently completed long-range attack subs known as the C1 (*hei-gata*) type. These subs had a 14,000 nm range when cruising at 16 knots, could reach a top speed of 23.5 knots surfaced and 8 knots submerged, operated to a depth of 330 feet (100 m), and carried a crew of 95 (Carpenter and Polmar 1986:104). The C1 type boats were part of a larger group (the A1, B1, and C1 types) of scouting and attack submarines built by Japan just prior to the outbreak of the Pacific War (Carpenter and Polmar 1986:101–4).

The first C1 boat, I-16, was laid down in September 1937 and was completed on March 30, 1940 (Carpenter and Polmar 1986:104). The next four boats, I-18, I-20, I-22, and I-24, were completed between September 1940 (I-20) and October 31, 1941 (I-24). Larger than the wartime US submarine classes, these I-boats carried eight 21 inch torpedo tubes in two forward torpedo compartments located one above the other (Carpenter and Polmar 1986:104). After their use in midget submarine operations, all these subs were lost during the war, I-16 in the Solomons in 1944, I-18 also in the Solomons in 1943, I-20 in the New Hebrides in 1943, I-22 in the Solomons in 1942, and I-24 off Attu in the Aleutians in 1943 (Carpenter and Polmar 1986:104).

Vessel Characteristics (1941; Carpenter and Polmar 1986:104; Stille and Bryan 2007: 33–34)

Dimensions: 358.6 feet (109.3 m) × 30 feet (9.1 m) × 17.6 feet (5.3 m)

Displacement: 2,554 tons surfaced, 3,561 tons submerged

Armament: Eight 21 inch (533 mm) torpedo tubes, one 5.5 inch (140 mm) gun, two single mount 25 mm guns

Machinery: Two Kampon MK 2 model ten 12,400 hp diesel engines, two electric 2,000 hp motors

I-boats head to sea from Kwajalein in a wartime Japanese propaganda photograph taken during the war. While these are not the Pearl Harbor attack force, a similar scene likely witnessed the departure of those boats in November 1941. (Burl Burlingame)

I-16, the first of the C1 type submarines and a Pearl Harbor strike force, *kō-hyōteki*-carrying craft. (Burl Burlingame)

reached. On November 16, ten of the midget submariners were told they would be sent aboard the five I-class submarines to attack Pearl Harbor. Their force of five *kō-hyōteki* was designated as the *Tokubetsu Kō-geki-tai*, or the "Special Attack Unit." Two days later, they sailed. Just before departure, they met with Admiral Yamamoto, who gave them a simple order: speaking with them aboard his flagship, the battleship *Nagato*, Yamamoto asked them to fulfill their training but stipulated, "You will not complete your mission by dying, so please come back alive after releasing the torpedoes and work another day" (Warner and Seno 1986:18). Despite this, none of the ten expected to return. Kazuo Sakamaki, commanding the *kō-hyōteki* attached to I-24, recalled that as they headed to sea, he watched "the coastal hills disappearing in the deepening darkness" and realized "that this was my last glimpse of Japan. . . . I could not help tears flowing out of my eyes. 'Good-by, Japan,' I whispered, 'Good-by'" (Sakamaki 1949:18).

Kazuo Sakamaki and a fellow officer, Kanda, visit a geisha house near Kure before shipping out to Pearl Harbor. (Burl Burlingame)

The Plan of Attack

The plans for the special attack force called for the five "mother submarines" to fan out and assume launch positions off the entrance to Pearl Harbor. The I-boats would surface at prearranged positions to launch the *kō-hyōteki* under the cover of darkness and then withdraw to Lana'i Island, where they would wait to rendezvous with the midgets at the end of the mission (Shibuya 1952a:14). The *kō-hyōteki* were to stealthily enter the harbor but were ordered not to try to force their way into the harbor. "Everything had to be ideal for them, or else they were to abandon the penetration attempt and retreat to the pickup point," noted Zenji Orita, executive officer on the submarine I-15. Admiral Yamamoto "didn't want to lose the element of surprise just because some young officer became eager for glory" (Orita and Harrington 1976:31). The role of the I-boats was more than serving as delivery and recovery vehicles for the smaller submarines and their crew. In addition to the special attack flotilla, other I-boats were part of a larger armada that ringed O'ahu to catch and sink any American ships attempting to flee Pearl Harbor. In all, there were nearly two dozen Japanese fleet-sized I-boats deployed off O'ahu. In this context, the use of the *kō-hyōteki* was essentially a "stunt," as journalist and historian Burl Burlingame has noted.

The *kō-hyōteki* were to wait for the opportune time, even if that meant after the aerial attacks had ended, and then surface and fire their torpedoes into a capital ship (most of the submariners hoped and planned for a battleship—Sakamaki wanted to sink the battleship *Pennsylvania*),

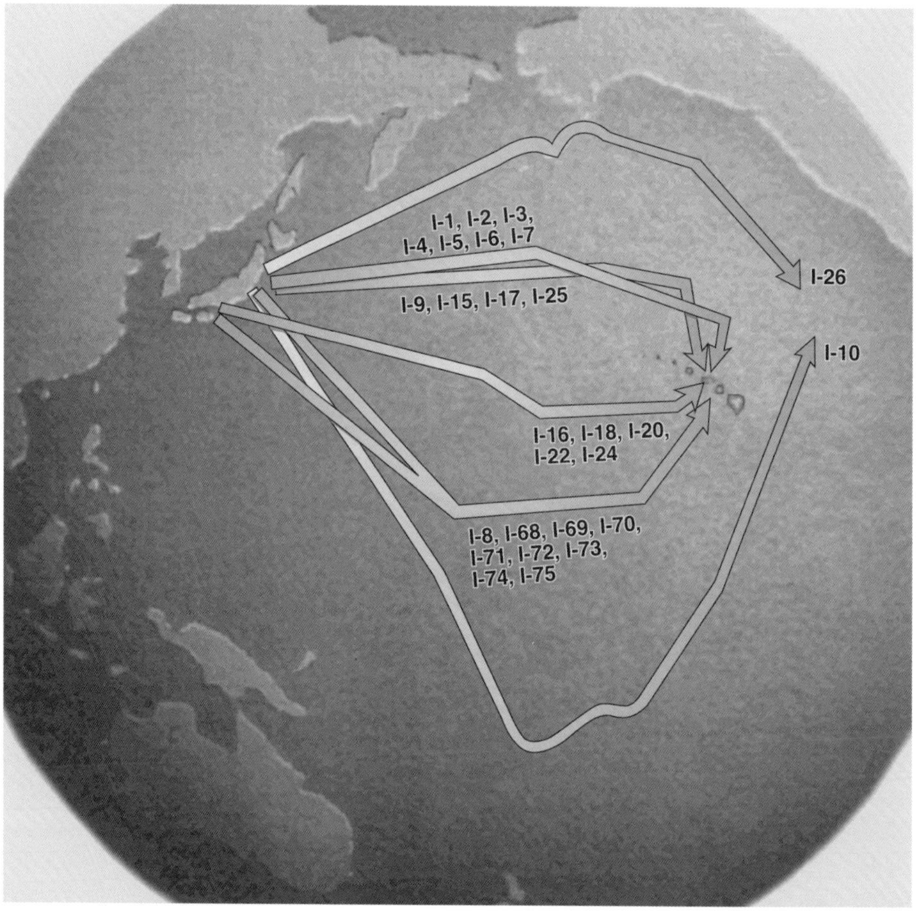

Route of the submarine force to Pearl Harbor. (Burl Burlingame)

I-26. (Burl Burlingame)

before diving and navigating, submerged, counterclockwise around Ford Island and escaping to sea to rejoin their mother subs off the island of Lana'i (Shibuya 1952a:14).

Reaching Hawai'i on December 5 (local time), the five I-boats moved into position for deployment, closing to within 10 miles of the harbor entrance. The lights of the harbor and nearby Honolulu were clearly visible, and the sub's radios picked up local broadcasts, including jazz (Sakamaki 1949:19). On schedule, in the predawn of Sunday, December 7, the I-boats blew their main ballast tanks and rose to the surface, decks awash. The two-man crews for each midget prepared to climb out onto the decks and enter their respective craft. Kazuo Sakamaki, on I-24, had packed his personal effects, written a farewell letter to his father, bathed, and dressed

The interior of a Japanese I-boat, World War II. Already cramped, these craft carried extra crew for the midget submarine missions. (Burl Burlingame)

Tom Freeman's painting of midget submariners boarding their craft in the predawn light of December 7, 1941. (National Park Service)

in a navy-issued flight suit, the "uniform" of the *kō-hyōteki* corps. On his last night in Japan, Sakamaki, along with his classmate Ensign Akira Hiroo, took a walk through Kure. Spotting a bottle of perfume in a store window, Sakamaki suggested they buy it. "Japanese warriors in the old days went to battle attired in their best armor and perfumed, in order to be fit for a sudden and glorious death, like 'cherry blossoms falling to the ground'" (Sakamaki 1949:17). Now he sprayed the perfume on his flight suit as he prepared to leave I-24. "This was the preparation for death" (Sakamaki 1949:20).

The first *kō-hyōteki* to launch was from I-16. Commanded by Ensign Masaharu Yokoyama and crewed by Petty Officer Second Class Tei Uyeda, this midget, known to the crew as I-16 *tou*, or "I-16's boat," left at 0:42. As Yokoyama and Uyeda climbed up the slippery sides of their craft, the I-boat's crew readied to dive. I-16 submerged to 18 meters and at dead slow moved ahead to allow the *kō-hyōteki* to gently launch astern with the turbulence pushing it free as Yokoyama and Uyeda blew their main tanks to rise to the surface and clear the I-boat. Gaining their bearings, they turned toward the entrance to Pearl Harbor, dived to 30 meters, and headed toward shore.

At 01:16, I-22 launched the next midget, this one commanded by Lieutenant Naoji Iwasa and his assistant, Petty Officer First Class Naokichi Sasaki. Prior to the launch, Iwasa and Keiu Matsuo had stood on the bridge of the mother submarine and watched the distant lights of Honolulu. Matsuo, who had taken the ride to give Iwasa the benefit of his previous month's scouting trip as a spy, was to stay behind to relay any lessons learned from the deployment of the craft when I-22 returned to Japan (Warner and Seno 1986:36–37). At 02:15, I-18 launched the *kō-hyōteki* of Ensign Shigemi Furuno and Petty Officer First Class Shigenori Yokoyama. At 02:57, I-20 launched the fourth *kō-hyōteki*,

The official portraits of Masaji Yokoyama and Sadamu Uyeda, the crew of I-16 *tou*. (Burl Burlingame)

The official portraits of Naoji Iwasa and Naokichi Sasaki, the crew of I-22 *tou*, the likely candidate for the submarine sunk by USS *Monaghan*. (Burl Burlingame)

commanded by Ensign Akira Hiroo and crewed by Petty Officer Second Class Yoshio Katayama. Last to launch was 1–24 *tou*, Sakamaki's sub, crewed by Chief Warrant Officer Kiyoshi Inagaki. The craft had been plagued by problems, including a damaged torpedo that had to be carefully pulled out of its tube and then dumped from the pitching deck of the mother submarine; the tube was then reloaded. In addition, Sakamaki had been confounded by what seemed to him to be a malfunctioning gyrocompass (Warner and Seno 1986:35).

It was now 03:33, with each *kō-hyōteki* under way on schedule and headed for Pearl Harbor. The months of training and planning had stressed stealth, patience, and the element of surprise. It was, however, a plan doomed for failure.

First Kill

It is a persistent myth that the Japanese attack caught the US military napping. Such was not the case—for the navy, fearing that war would come with a submarine assault, had intensely drilled and stood vigilant watch with antisubmarine forces and patrols off Pearl Harbor. The Japanese fear that the presence of the midget submarines would be detected before the aerial assault commenced came true. The minesweeper USS *Condor* (AMC-14) spotted a periscope at 03:42 1.25 miles off the entrance buoys to the harbor. The minesweeper radioed their report to USS *Ward* (DD-139), a 23-year-old World War I vintage destroyer on guard duty. *Ward*, commanded by Lieutenant William W. Outerbridge, who had just assumed command of

The official portraits of Shigemi Furuno and Shigenori Yokoyama, the crew of I-18 *tou*, the third submarine launched against Pearl Harbor. The Japanese Midget Submarine Association believes that their submarine is the one discovered in 1960 inside Keehi Lagoon. Raised and returned to Japan, it is now displayed at Etajima. (Burl Burlingame)

The official portraits of Akira Hiroo and Yoshio Katayama, the crew of I-20 *tou*. The Japanese Midget Submarine Association believes that their submarine is that sunk by USS *Ward* and that they lie inside the wreck. (Burl Burlingame)

his ship the day before, searched for just over an hour before securing from general quarters and returning to guard duty, running across the waves in a series of large figure eights.

The next sighting came an hour later and was not in the same area as the first reported submarine, which suggests it was another craft and not the submarine spotted by the crew of *Condor*. At 05:45, the navy cargo carrier USS *Antares* (AG-10) approached Pearl Harbor with a 510 ton steel barge in tow. *Antares* was returning from a mission to the Kanton and Palmyra Islands, where it had delivered personnel and equipment for the construction of an airfield. The crew, awake and eager to reach port, spotted something in the water near the steel cable that linked their unarmed ship to the barge: "The ship was turned slowly to the east at which time a suspicious object was sighted about 1500 yards on the starboard quarter. This object could have been a small submarine with upper conning tower awash and periscope partly raised but it could not be positively identified as such" (Commanding Officer, USS *Antares* 1941). Meanwhile, flying overhead, Navy Lieutenant William Tanner, in a Catalina PBY seaplane, was flying on antisubmarine warfare patrol when he clearly saw what he interpreted as a submarine following *Antares*. The submarine was partially submerged, defying the US Navy's standing orders for any submarine within the waters of the defensive perimeter of Pearl Harbor to remain on the surface.[2] Any submarine within the defensive zone not on the surface was to be considered hostile and sunk. Tanner circled the submarine, dropping smoke pots on the water to mark its location to USS

A top-secret prewar image of the submarine net used to secure the entrance to Pearl Harbor. The steel beams in the shallows were placed there to deter fast boat attacks. (Burl Burlingame)

The prewar defensive zone off Pearl Harbor's entrance was regularly patrolled, as the US Navy believed that the likely source of an attack would come by submarine. On the morning of December 7, 1941, they were partially correct. (Burl Burlingame)

Ward, which was racing to the spot in response to a signal from the unarmed *Antares*. "There is a suspicious looking object on our starboard quarter. Would you please investigate" (*Antares* signal log, December 7–8, 1941). It was now 06:33.

On *Ward*, Lieutenant Outerbridge, a 35-year-old, seasoned officer 14 years into his naval career, but nonetheless new to his role as *Ward*'s commanding officer (his crew described him as "gung-ho" and knew him, behind his back, as "Wild Willie"), sprang into action. As they approached the scene, at 06:37 *Ward*'s lookouts spotted the conning tower of a small, green-painted submarine, covered with moss, running

USS *Condor* (AMC-14), the first US Navy ship to spot a midget submarine off the entrance to Pearl Harbor. That craft may have been I-16 *tou*, the first *kō-hyōteki* launched. *Condor* spotted a submarine off the harbor entrance 3 hours after I-16 *tou* launched from its mother sub. As *Condor* watched, the submarine turned away from the entrance to starboard, and it was not seen again. The submarine may have remained in that location, waiting to fire on ships fleeing the harbor, until it was spotted and fired on by USS *St. Louis* nearly 7 hours later. (Burl Burlingame)

USS *Antares*, returning to Pearl Harbor from Kanton Island, spotted a midget submarine trailing it and also alerted USS *Ward*. That craft was pursued and sunk by *Ward*. (Naval History and Heritage Command, NH 67563)

William Outerbridge, commanding officer of USS *Ward* on December 7, 1941. Outerbridge (1906–86) graduated from the US Naval Academy in 1927. A career officer whose service included time on the China Station, Outerbridge transferred from the destroyer *Cummings* (DD-365), where he had been executive officer, to take command of *Ward* on December 5, 1941. For the actions he and his crew took on December 7, the navy awarded Outerbridge with the Navy Cross. After a stint in Washington, DC, Outerbridge returned to sea in command of the destroyer *O'Brien* (DD-725). Postwar, he served both at the Naval War College and at sea in command of destroyer divisions and squadrons and of the cruiser USS *Los Angeles* (CA-135), worked at the Pentagon, and retired as a rear admiral. (Burl Burlingame)

Tom Freeman's painting of USS *Ward* sinking a midget submarine. (National Park Service)

USS *WARD*

USS *Ward* was one of 114 flush-deck, four-stack destroyers of the *Wickes* class constructed during World War I (Friedman 1985). This class represented a shift, as historian Norman Friedman notes, to designs suited to mass production in response to the navy's need for large numbers of ships (Friedman 1982:39). The Mare Island Naval Shipyard in Vallejo, California, at the northern end of San Francisco Bay, quickly built *Ward* under the supervision of master shipfitter J. T. Moroney in 17.5 days, launching it on June 1, 1918 (Klobuchar 2006:18).

Commissioned on July 24, 1918, *Ward* was too late to participate in the war. Dispatched from Mare Island to San Diego, and then through the Panama Canal to Norfolk, *Ward* served in the Atlantic, assisting in a historic transatlantic flight of new navy flying boats in a demonstration of naval airpower in May 1919. Returning to Norfolk, *Ward* was ordered to the Pacific and arrived in San Diego in August.

After a voyage up the coast to Portland and Seattle, the destroyer returned to San Diego, where it remained at dock for months, occasionally making short voyages (to Mare Island for maintenance) with a smaller crew than needed in wartime, a pattern that continued in the postwar navy. Finally, on June 5, 1922, *Ward* was decommissioned and laid up, joining sixty-seven others that lay idled, in a row, at San Diego (Klobuchar 2006:36).

The outbreak of war in Europe in 1939 and the increasing possibility the United States would become involved pulled *Ward* and many of its sister destroyers out of "red lead row" in 1940–41, and after refurbishing and some refitting, on January 28, 1941, the ship was recommissioned with a crew of navy reservists from St. Paul, Minnesota, and Lieutenant Commander Hunter Wood in command (Klobuchar 2006:48).

After a trip north to Mare Island to load ordnance, *Ward* departed for Hawai'i on February 28, arriving at Pearl Harbor on March 9 (Klobuchar 2006:48). Assigned to the 14th Naval District, *Ward* joined the Pearl Harbor defense patrol as DesDiv80, one of four World War I–era destroyers whose job was "to patrol the channel entrance off Pearl Harbor—a large job for such a small and antiquated force and an important one" as the Pacific Fleet shifted from San Diego to Pearl Harbor to counter the power of the Imperial Japanese Navy (Mooney 1980:101).

After *Ward*'s encounter with the midget submarine and the exemplary actions of its commander and crew, the ship remained with DesDiv through the end of 1941 before being sent to Bremerton, Washington, for modernization into a fast attack transport, emerging as USS *Ward* (APD-16) and heading for the South Pacific in February 1943. Working out of Espiritu Santo, *Ward* served with distinction over the next 2 years, working and fighting in the Solomons, New Guinea, New Britain, and the Palaus. While participating in the actions off Leyte in advance of the invasion of the Philippines, the end came for *Ward* with a kamikaze attack on December 7, 1944. After *Ward*'s crew, a number of them veterans of Pearl Harbor, shot down some of the attackers, one plane angled in and struck the side of the destroyer at the waterline, stopping *Ward* dead in the water and setting the ship on fire. As the flames spread and the possibility of the magazine exploding increased, *Ward*'s commanding officer, Lieutenant Richard E. Farwell, gave the order to abandon ship. Miraculously, none of *Ward*'s crew were killed, and nearby ships picked them up out of the water and from *Ward*'s boats. The destroyer USS *O'Brien* (DD-725) not only stood by the rescue but also fought the fires on *Ward* (Mooney 1980:104).

When it was clear that *Ward* could not be saved, and with *Ward* evacuated, *O'Brien*'s commander gave the order to sink *Ward* by gunfire. It was a difficult order, as *O'Brien*'s skipper was William Outerbridge, who had commanded *Ward* with distinction on December 7, 1941. Gunfire hit *Ward*'s aft magazine, blowing off the stern, and the veteran destroyer sank at 11:30 into 120 fathoms of water in Ormoc Bay. As the ship's historian, Richard Klobuchar, has written, "the name and exploits of the USS *Ward* (DD-139/APD-16) will never be forgotten" (Klobuchar 2006:216).

Vessel Characteristics (1941; Friedman in Gray 1980:124)
Dimensions: 314.4 feet (97.7 m) at the waterline × 30.11 feet (9.1 m) × 9.10 feet (2.7 m)
Displacement: 1,247 tons
Armament: Four 4 inch / 50 caliber guns, two 3 inch / 23 caliber guns, twelve 21 inch torpedo tubes on three quadruple mounts, two roll-off depth charge racks at the stern
Machinery: two shaft Parsons turbines, four White-Forster boilers 24,200 SHP
Speed: 35 knots

at 8 to 10 knots in *Antares*'s wake. At 06:40, *Ward* surged ahead from 5 to 25 knots, racing to the new contact. Outerbridge sounded general quarters, and his crew, many of them as yet-unseasoned new recruits, raced to their battle stations, some at the ship's four 4 inch / 50 caliber guns, others to the depth charge racks at the stern. At 06:45, Outerbridge gave the order to fire. As one of the crew later stated, "Shoot first and ask questions later. That's what the old man did" (Craddock 2006:56).

The first shot missed, but the second, fired from the No. 3 gun, hit. As Outerbridge explained in his after action report, the second shot, fired from a range of "560 yards or less," struck the submarine "at the waterline which was the junction of the hull and conning tower. . . . This was a square positive hit." The round punched into the hull, he noted, and as the submarine heeled over to starboard, Outerbridge noticed it had not gone off, nor did it seem to have exited the hull. "There was no evidence of ricochet. . . . The projectile was not seen to explode outside the hull of the submarine. There was no splash of any size that might results from an explosion or ricochet" (Commanding Officer, USS *Ward* 1941).

As the stricken craft slowed and started to sink, Outerbridge took no chances; he ordered the crew to drop depth charges. Chief Torpedoman W. C. Maskowitz set the depth charges to go off at 100 feet deep, and as *Ward* passed over the sinking submarine, each time the bridge sounded a short whistle blast, a depth charge rolled into the ocean. Six depth charges, including

USS *Ward* (DD-139) before launching at Mare Island Naval Shipyard during World War I. (US Naval Institute)

USS *Ward* (DD-139) after completion, at Mare Island on September 19, 1918. (US Naval Institute)

two from Tanner's PBY, splashed around and on the sinking submarine. As Outerbridge's report noted, "she ran into our depth charge barrage and appeared to be directly over an exploding charge" (Commanding Officer, USS *Ward* 1941). Chief Maskowitz later reported, "I let go the first charge just as the sub starting going under," and then "the second charge was already in the water when the first one exploded. I think the sub waded directly into our first charge" (*All Hands* 1945).

The submarine was gone, leaving as its only trace a bit of oil on the water: "The submarine sank in 1200 feet of water and could not be located with supersonic detector" (Commanding Officer, USS *Ward* 1941). Outerbridge sent a voice radio message that "we have dropped depth charges upon sub operating in defensive sea area," and then modified his report to be more specific. "We have attacked, fired upon, and dropped depth charges upon submarine operating in defensive sea area" (Commanding Officer, USS *Ward* 1941). The message was received at naval headquarters at Pearl Harbor and reported to the officer in charge at 07:12. As the first official report by the Commander-in-Chief, Pacific Fleet (CINCPAC), explained, the response at headquarters was to

> instruct the ready duty destroyer, the U.S.S. *Monaghan,* to proceed to sea; close the net gate; attempt to verify the contact report, with details thereon; and to notify, by telephone, at about 0720, the Commander-in-Chief's Staff Duty Officer. Another telephone call to the Commander-in-Chief, Pacific Fleet, about 0740, from the Operations Officer, Patrol Wing TWO, relayed a report received at 0732 that a patrol plane had sunk a hostile submarine south of the entrance buoy. This was followed by an additional telephone report from the Fourteenth Naval District that the *Ward* was towing a sampan into Honolulu. At about 0755, the Navy Yard Signal Tower telephoned the Commander-in-Chief, Pacific Fleet, as follows: "ENEMY AIR RAID—NOT DRILL". Almost simultaneously, Japanese torpedo planes attacked the battleships. (CINCPAC 1942)

Fortunately for the Japanese, and despite the early warning provided by the sinking of the *kō-hyōteki* in the defensive zone, the aerial attack came as a surprise as the Pacific Fleet began to respond to Outerbridge's report. The CINCPAC report also noted that "during the previous year there had been several reports of

The destroyers USS *Ward* (DD-139) and USS *Chew* (DD-106) visit Hilo on July 22, 1941. This is the configuration and the paint scheme *Ward* carried on December 7. (Burl Burlingame)

WARD'S NO. 3 GUN

The 4 inch / 50 caliber MK9 gun that fired the first shot of the Pacific War, striking and sinking one of the Pearl Harbor midget submarines, survived the loss of *Ward* because it was removed when the destroyer was modernized to become a fast attack transport in 1942. The navy retained the gun because of its historic status, and in 1951, the six-ton weapon was in storage at the Washington Navy Yard, destined for the Smithsonian Institution. *Ward*'s former crew, now known as the "First Shot Vets," began a campaign to have the gun sent to St. Paul, where the crew hailed from, for permanent display. With support from their Congressional delegation and the Veterans of Foreign Wars (VFW), the veterans prevailed, and the gun was shipped by air to St. Paul, installed on the state capitol grounds, and dedicated on May 10, 1958, with all nine of the men who had manned and fired it on December 7, 1941, in their battle-ready positions (Klobuchar 2006:220–21). Well maintained and in excellent condition, the gun remains on display on the west side of the Veterans Service Building.[3] It is noted as being the most significant naval memorial in Minnesota (Merriman and Olson 2010:7).

USS *Ward*'s gun crew pose at their weapon after the destroyer sank a midget submarine outside of Pearl Harbor and "fired the first shot" of the war in the Pacific. The gun crew members were R. H. Knapp (BM2c, Gun Captain); C. W. Fenton (Sea1c, Pointer); R. B. Nolde (Sea1c, Trainer); A. A. De Demagall (Sea1c, No. 1 Loader); D. W. Gruening (Sea1c, No. 2 Loader); J. A. Paick (Sea1c, No. 3 Loader); H. P. Flanagan (Sea1c, No. 4 Loader); E. J. Bakret (GM3c, Gunners Mate); K. C. J. Lasch (Cox, Sightsetter; quoted from the original 1942 vintage caption). This gun was mounted atop the ship's midships deckhouse, starboard side. (Naval History and Heritage Command NH 97446)

submarine contacts, all of which turned out to be false" (CINCPAC 1942).

What had quickly transpired was that a US Navy ship had made the first confirmed kill in the Pacific War that was just beginning. This shot with deadly intent and effect had come only an hour ahead of the main assault on Pearl Harbor, too short a time for the system to react. While fighters and dive, torpedo, and high altitude bombers wrought terrible damage on the US fleet, the remaining *kō-hyōteki* crews continued on, intent on accomplishing their missions and unaware of the loss of one of their own submarines.

The USS *Ward* gun on the grounds of the Minnesota State Capitol, 2015. (James P. Delgado)

Second Kill

The next encounter between the US Navy and a *kō-hyōteki* was at 08:17 when the crew of the destroyer USS *Helm* (DD-388) spotted the submarine hung up on the starboard side of the main channel entrance. The submarine submerged and then popped up again a minute later, apparently with buoyancy problems. *Helm* fired at the submarine, but it submerged again and remained unseen. This *may* have been I-24 *tou*, Sakamaki and Inagaki's craft, as Sakamaki claimed he was fired on by a destroyer that missed. It may have also been another submarine, the craft spotted earlier by USS *Condor* (see chapter 6).

Meanwhile, at 08:30, inside the harbor, the minesweeper USS *Zane* (DMS-14) spotted what it reported as a "strange submarine" 200 yards aft of the moored USS *Medusa* (AR-1); *Zane*'s commanding officer ordered the ship's No. 4 gun loaded and prepared to shoot at it, but the gun would not bear and the nearby USS *Perry* (DMS-17) instead opened up with its gun. *Medusa*, meanwhile, had opened up with its antiaircraft guns at incoming Japanese planes. As the ship's commanding officer noted in his after action report, his crew spotted the submarine near them, bearing some 1,000 yards off *Medusa*'s starboard quarter and about 500 yards astern of the seaplane tender USS *Curtiss* (AV-4):

> I gave orders to open fire on the periscope—shortly afterward the *Curtiss* opened fire. The submarine fired a torpedo at a small dock astern

Plaques on the *Ward* gun speak to its significance and are a source of pride for Minnesotans as well as those in the Minneapolis/St. Paul area. The names of the gun crew are recorded on one of the plaques. (James P. Delgado)

The height of the attack on Pearl Harbor, as captured by a Japanese photographer during the first wave of aerial torpedo and dive-bomber strikes. Despite the ardent wishes of the *kō-hyōteki* corps and their superiors, only one of the five *kō-hyōteki* had penetrated the harbor. (Naval History and Heritage Command, NH 50930)

> of *Curtiss*. The submarine then broached to the surface with conning tower in plain sight. Many shots could plainly be seen hitting the conning tower from both the *Medusa* and *Curtiss*. While being shelled, the submarine appeared by be backing toward the *Curtiss*. About this time the *Monaghan* (DD354) was seen standing down the channel west of Ford Island on course approximately 230° True. She headed directly for the submarine at about 15 knots. The order cease firing was given when *Monaghan* was abeam of the *Curtiss*. She appeared to pass immediately over the submarine and dropped two depth charges. The first charge appeared to drop right on top of the submarine as the volume of water shooting into the air was heavily colored with a black substance. (Commanding Officer, USS *Medusa* 1942)

Curtiss's commanding officer reported that his ship opened up on the submarine at 08:36 from a distance of 700 yards. The first shots missed the periscope, but as the submarine surfaced at 08:40 and the conning tower was visible, as well as part of the bow, *Curtiss* fired twice, reporting they hit the conning tower twice as the submarine fired one torpedo up the North Channel toward the oncoming destroyer USS *Monaghan* (DD-354).

Monaghan's commanding officer, in his after action report, explained that as his destroyer approached the scene, he and his bridge crew spotted the conning tower of the submarine 200 to 300 yards off the starboard quarter of *Curtiss* and that "vigorous fire" from *Curtiss* and USS *Tangier* (AV-8) was directed at it. The ship's captain, W. P. Burford, ordered all engines ahead at

The seaplane tender USS *Curtiss* (AV-4) was a relatively new ship at the time of the Pearl Harbor attack, having been commissioned in November 1940. The ship served in a lengthy career that spanned nearly two decades that included combat duty in the South Pacific and surviving a kamikaze attack in May 1945. After repairs, the ship returned to action and participated in the Korean War, postwar nuclear testing, and an Antarctic mission before being decommissioned in 1957. The government sold *Curtiss* for scrap in 1972. (Burl Burlingame)

The *Farragutt*-class destroyer USS *Monaghan* (DD-354). After the heroic actions of its commander and crew at Pearl Harbor, *Monaghan* served with distinction in the Pacific War, including screening USS *Enterprise* (CV-6) during the Battle of Midway and actions in the Aleutians, in the Battle of the Komandorski Islands, and in the invasions of the Gilberts, Marshalls, Palau, and Saipan. *Monaghan* and two other destroyers were lost in Typhoon Cobra on December 17, 1944, carrying 254 of her crew into the deep after capsizing. Only six men survived. (Burl Burlingame)

flank speed and headed straight for the submarine to ram it, and at 08:43, the destroyer rammed and passed over the submarine while dropping two depth charges. A minute later, both charges exploded aft of *Monaghan* and the submarine disappeared. Another of the *kō-hyōteki* had been destroyed.

Other Encounters

Outside the harbor, other navy vessels were busily depth-charging numerous "submarine contacts." At 10:04, the cruiser USS *St. Louis* (CL-49) reported that as they neared buoy No. 1 near the entrance to Pearl Harbor, two torpedoes

Monaghan's shot through the midget submarine conning tower. (National Park Service)

were fired from a distance of about 2,000 yards that missed and detonated on a shoal. An object the crew thought might be a submarine was fired on but missed. As the commanding officer later noted, "This object was not positively identified as a submarine periscope" (Commanding Officer, USS *St. Louis* 1942). Some historians believe *St. Louis* was attacked by another *kō-hyōteki*. This may have been the craft spotted by both *Condor* and *Helm* earlier.[4] Outside the harbor, USS *Ward* depth charged four separate contacts between 07:05 and 11:27. At 17:15, USS *Case* (DD-370) depth charged another target. Meanwhile, aboard the Japanese "mother submarines," the crews of the I-boats awaited word from their comrades in the *kō-hyōteki*.

The only message received was when I-16 received a faint message they thought was from I-16 *tou*. It appeared to be the coded message for "successful surprise attack" (Chihaya 1991:50). Meanwhile, another I-boat surfaced off Pearl Harbor reported that a "tremendous explosion" in the harbor after moonrise had sent "fiery columns high into the air, scattering red hot splinters. In a few minutes the fiery columns disappeared, whereupon the enemy anti-aircraft batteries went into action" (Japan Times 1942:6). This was seized upon by the Imperial Japanese Navy as proof that at least one of the *kō-hyōteki* had scored an impressive victory inside Pearl Harbor.

On the evening of December 7th, and through the 8th, the I-boats met at the Lana'i Island rendezvous, but none of the *kō-hyōteki* ever returned. The last message was another faint transmission received by I-16 at 01:11 on the 8th, possibly from its own *kō-hyōteki*, commanded by Ensign Yokoyama, that the craft was unable to navigate (Warner and Seno 1986:53). On the morning of the 8th, USS *Ward* depth charged another contact, dropping nine charges at 06:19, and then dropping another two charges at 06:55, bringing an oil slick to the surface. *Ward* also attacked sonar contacts on the 9th, 10th, 11th, 16th, and 17th of December, three times reporting it had brought oil to the surface and twice producing a "large air bubble." By that late date, only one of the *kō-hyōteki* corps was still alive, his craft captured along with him. It was Ensign Kazuo Sakamaki and I-24 *tou*.

USS *St. Louis* (CL-49) sorties from Battleship Row, about to pass the burning USS *California* (BB-44) while en route to an encounter with a midget submarine at the harbor entrance. (Burl Burlingame)

The Misadventures of I-24 *tou* and Ensign Sakamaki

By the 8th, probably only Yokoyama and Uyeda of I-16 *tou* and Sakamaki and Inagaki in I-24 *tou* were still alive out of the entire midget submarine force. While still on board I-24 and prior to launch, Sakamaki had discovered that his sub's gyrocompass was out of order. Defying attempts at repair, the compass was still not functioning when the time came to launch. Lieutenant Commander Hiroshi Hanabusa, I-24's captain, asked Sakamaki what he intended to do. "Captain, I am going ahead," Sakamaki declared firmly, whereupon Hanabusa joined Sakamaki in shouting, "On to Pearl Harbor!" (Sakamaki 1949:21).

As Sakamaki and Inagaki settled into their *kō-hyōteki*, Sakamaki looked out through the periscope and thought that he had "come all the way from Japan within sight of success. How can I quit and return?" Sakamaki thought of the shame that he would face if he returned home. "I cannot fail. I simply cannot fail" (Sakamaki 1949:23–24). After his departure from the mother sub, the crew of I-24 discovered that he did not intend to return. "His hair and nails were found carefully wrapped together with a letter of farewell addressed to his parents. Even the required postage was attached . . . proof of the grim determination of this young officer who did not expect to return alive" (Hashimoto 1954:9).

As soon as I-24 *tou* detached from I-24, it began to sink nose down. As the craft continued down, Sakamaki and Inagaki hauled lead ballast from the bow to the stern to correct the *kō-hyōteki*'s trim. They then surfaced, where Sakamaki took his bearings from Honolulu's city lights, and started for the entrance to Pearl Harbor. Fighting to keep the craft submerged, and navigating in circles because of his faulty compass, Sakamaki finally reached the entrance at 07:00.

It was now broad daylight and too late to sneak in, but Sakamaki told Inagaki they would still go. "Have no fear. Now that we have come this far, it is our duty to do our task. We will somehow break through this guard line and pierce the enemy harbor" (Sakamaki 1949:39). Once inside, he told Inagaki, "We will dare to run on the surface. Then we let our torpedoes go at an enemy battleship. If necessary, let's dash into one of them. That's our mission" (Sakamaki 1949:39).

Still running at periscope depth, Sakamaki threaded past the patrol craft, but running slow, I-24 *tou* was still outside the harbor as the air attack began at 07:55. Watching the smoke fill the sky, Sakamaki laughed and told Inagaki their turn was coming. Then the *kō-hyōteki* hit a submerged coral reef and ground to a halt, partially out of the water. Hard aground, propellers spinning in reverse, I-24 *tou* may have been the craft

The official portraits of Kazuo Sakamaki and Kiyoshi Inagaki, the crew of I-24 *tou*. Sakamaki was the sole survivor of the Pearl Harbor *kō-hyōteki* attack group. His submarine, as a prize of war, had a lengthy career as a traveling trophy, a use never conceived of by a navy that had designed it as a secret weapon. (Burl Burlingame)

spotted by USS *Helm* at 08:17. The destroyer's guns could not get a bearing before the sub disappeared, but 2 minutes later, it again bobbed to the surface. *Helm*'s after action report noted that this time they opened fire: "No hits observed, but there were several close splashes. Submarine appeared to be touching bottom on ledge of reef, and in line of breakers. While still firing at submarine it apparently slipped off ledge and submerged" (Commanding Officer, USS *Helm* 1941). This craft may have also been one of two other *kō-hyōteki* that failed to enter Pearl Harbor that morning, which were found postwar sunk near the harbor entrance.

If this was I-24 *tou*, the submarine was now in deeper water. The two exhausted submariners resumed their increasingly futile efforts to join the battle. Again the two struggled to trim the craft, dragging heavy lead ballast pigs across batteries that were now leaking acid and filling the compartments with chlorine gas. It was also now clear that damage to the bow had mangled the torpedo guards mounted there and the sub could no longer fire. A weeping Sakamaki turned to Inagaki and vowed, "If we can't blast the enemy battleship, we will climb onto it and kill as many enemies as possible" (Sakamaki 1949:43).[5]

The two submariners never had that chance. Instead, I-24 *tou* drifted, with the two unconscious submariners, out of the harbor, and out to sea. Coming to in the early evening, Sakamaki looked out through the periscope to see Diamond

Sakamaki and Inagaki's I-24 *tou* (HA-19), ashore off Bellows Field on the morning of December 8, 1941. (Naval History and Heritage Command, NH 64471)

Sgt. David M. Akui (1920–87), who captured the exhausted Kazuo Sakamaki. A native Hawaiian, Akui served with distinction throughout the war and postwar, including Burma, as one of Merrill's Marauders. In this postwar image, he is shown examining Viet Cong booby traps in Vietnam. (Burl Burlingame)

This historical marker commemorates the site of the "capture" of HA-19 and Kazuo Sakamaki, "POW No. 1." (Pacific Fleet Submarine Museum and Archives)

Head drifting past. Turning on his electric motor, he tried to steer in the direction of Lana'i and the rendezvous and, while watching the stars and weeping, again either passed out or fell into a deep sleep.

In the early morning hours, the batteries failed and the propellers stopped. This woke Sakamaki, who saw they were close to land—a dark mass looming before him—and then I-24 *tou* grounded on a coral reef just offshore. Each of the *kō-hyōteki* had been fitted with self-destruct charges before departing Japan to avoid having the top-secret weapons fall into enemy hands. Sakamaki and Inagaki lit the fuse on the charge, stripped down to their underwear, and climbed out of their craft as it rolled and the surf washed over it.

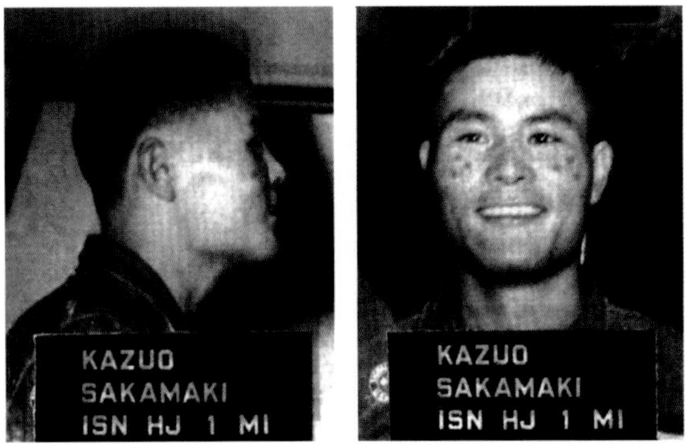

Kazuo Sakamaki's December 8, 1941, "mug shot" as a POW. (Burl Burlingame)

HA-19 being hauled ashore. (Naval History and Heritage Command, NH 91333)

In his memoirs, Sakamaki claimed that was the last he saw of Inagaki (Sakamaki 1949:46). His body, with a massive head wound, washed ashore the next day. Sakamaki leapt into the surf and struggled toward shore, where he began running back and forth across the beach. He had landed in front of the military base at Bellows Field, and Lieutenant Paul Plybon and Sergeant David Akui of the US Army cornered and arrested the stunned Sakamaki at 05:40 on December 8. The hapless ensign had just become US "POW No. 1." His submarine was also captured. The scuttling charge had failed to go off. Wallowing in the surf, it was hauled ashore by the US Navy and loaded onto a truck. Back at Pearl Harbor, it was stripped and unbolted into its three sections. Naval intelligence personnel studied it, drew rudimentary plans, and carefully examined different parts of the craft.

The war was over for Kazuo Sakamaki, the sole survivor of the *kō-hyōteki* corps sent to Pearl Harbor. His failure would soon be known in Japan. While his brother submariners were honored back home as "Hero Gods," he was relegated to a place of shame and dishonor, wiped off the navy's roles, his parents never told he was alive, and his name not mentioned until the end of the war (Doyle 2010:208). I-24 *tou*, however, soon became famous as a symbol not only of the enemy but of the Pearl Harbor attack, as a weapon that exemplified a "sneak attack."

Kazuo Sakamaki's dismantled submarine being documented by the US Navy. (Naval History and Heritage Command, NH 91338)

THE WARTIME ODYSSEY OF KAZUO SAKAMAKI'S SUBMARINE

Kazuo Sakamaki wrote after the war that when captured, he was "possessed by a terrible, uncontrolled shame" not only for being captured but because "through my fault the invaluable secret weapon had fallen into the enemy's hands" (Sakamaki 1949:49). He was right to worry. Sakamaki's midget submarine was quickly assessed by the US Navy, who disassembled and examined it in detail. Damage to the torpedo guards and the propellers from grounding led the navy to take these off the I-24 *tou* and replace them with those from the midget sunk by USS *Monaghan*. The navy was quick to release some details about the craft, although initial reports somehow gave the size as only 41 feet, or little better than half the craft's actual size.[6] A typical response was that reported by the Washington, DC, *Evening Star*'s December 16, 1941, edition, which noted that the "radically designed" submarines "are of such a size that they could be carried on the decks of larger vessels and launched overside by the same cranes and facilities used for handling the ordinary small boats of a combatant ship." The small size of the craft, even when its true dimensions were realized, left a powerful impression on Americans.

While later historians commented that the midget submarine was the "epitome of the Japanese preoccupation with smallness and precision—the mechanical counterpart of a bonsai tree" (Prange 1981:201), contemporary (1941) Americans saw a craft that underscored the notion of a small people who had launched a sneak attack. "People here are wild at the insolence of the little Japs," wrote one correspondent in late 1941 (as cited in Dower 1986:110). *Time* magazine, in its December 30, 1941, edition, noted that the Japanese, "big only in their fury," were advancing in Malaya "in miniature scale" with "tiny one-man tanks and two-gun carriers" (as cited in Dower 1986:111). The other perception, reinforced by the discovery of the self-destruction scuttling charges inside the captured submarines and the complete loss of the *kō-hyōteki* corps at Pearl Harbor, was that of a "suicide" craft. As a report in the Chicago *Daily Tribune* noted in September 1942, "they just shoved those Japs inside with the idea they weren't coming out again" (*Daily Tribune*, September 17, 1942:7).[7]

Sakamaki's *kō-hyōteki* was stripped of its batteries, motor, lead ballast, and much of its equipment, and then shipped to the mainland as cargo on a US merchant ship in August 1942. Landing at Mare Island, the craft was readied by shipyard workers to embark on a nationwide tour to promote the sale of war bonds. Dummy air tanks, a fake periscope,[8] and caps simulating torpedo warheads were installed, along with two mannequins dressed to represent the crew. A set of narrow, 8 by 11 inch rectangular windows were cut into each side of the sub with Plexiglas bolted in place, allowing visitors to peer inside. The finished submarine, freshly painted, was placed on a 94-foot-long trailer with steel walkways and stairs attached to it to allow the government to tow the submarine across the country and into as many towns and cities that could take it (Anadarko [Oklahoma] *Daily News*, November 28, 1943). The submarine was inspected by President Franklin D. Roosevelt on September 24, during a presidential tour of Mare Island Naval Shipyard.[9] A United Press International story on the visit noted that "President Roosevelt looked today with great satisfaction upon two submarines—one Japanese craft captured at Pearl Harbor, the other an American sub with nine Japanese flags painted on her conning tower" ([Pennsylvania] *Franklin News-Herald*, October 2, 1942).

In October, the San Francisco *News* reported that the captured sub was "slated to start backfiring on the Japanese," when on October 27, it would be displayed at the Civic Center "as part of the annual Navy Day celebration. It will be the first public display of the craft in a nationwide War Bond tour, which is expected to produce record bond sales" (San Francisco *News*, October 17, 1942). Visitors were allowed to climb on and peer into the submarine if they made a one dollar war bond purchase; children were allowed if they bought a twenty-five cent war stamp (Anadarko [Oklahoma] *Daily News*, November 28, 1943). In this fashion, HA-19 toured some two thousand cities and towns in forty states for the next 3 years, with notable appearances in Chicago, New York, and Washington, DC, where it was displayed on the Capitol grounds on April 3, 1943. The submarine moved quickly; three days after its display at the Capitol, HA-19 was in Annapolis, Maryland, home of the US Naval Academy (*Baltimore Sun*, April 6, 1943). In San Antonio, Texas, it was displayed at Alamo Plaza where visitors were encouraged to "Avenge Pearl Harbor" while they remembered the Alamo. At the start of the tour, in San Francisco, another patriotic stunt had Chinese-American recruits enlisting by standing on top of the captured craft.

HA-19's tour may not have been unique. A scuttled *kō-hyōteki* from Guadalcanal, raised by USS *Ortolan* (ASR-5) and transferred, stripped empty, to the United States, is now displayed as an outdoor exhibit at the Submarine Force Library and Museum in Groton, Connecticut. The captured German submarine U-505 toured East Coast and Gulf ports to sell war bonds in 1945; laid up at Portsmouth Navy Yard, it languished until saved by Chicago, which acquired the sub in 1954. It came ashore as an exhibit (now housed indoors) at the Chicago Museum of Science and Industry (Wise 2005:97–104). In Australia, the ends of HA-14 and HA-21, raised and meticulously studied after the Sydney attack, were displayed as a single craft in a war bond tour that started at Bennelong Point (where the Sydney Opera House now stands) before being towed on a trailer to various towns where tens of thousands saw it and had a chance to buy souvenir postcards, souvenirs made from glass wool salvaged from the batteries, or small miniature midget submarines cast from the lead ballast recovered from the craft (Jenkins 1992a:61).

After the war, HA-19, its war bond selling days over, ended up on display at the Naval Air Station, Key West. In 1964, it was transferred on loan to the Key West Art and Historical Society for display at their Lighthouse Museum. It remained there until 1990. It was then transported to the Admiral Nimitz Museum, now the National Museum of the Pacific War, in Fredericksburg, Texas, where it has remained on display ever since.

Sakamaki provided his interrogators with a sketch of how his *kō-hyōteki* had been transported to the waters off Pearl Harbor. (Burl Burlingame)

Captured at Hawaii

JAPS LOSE A SUBMARINE IN PEARL HARBOR

News stories featured the "capture" of I-24 *tou* both as a small victory and as "proof" of a sneak attack. (Burl Burlingame)

Workers stripped the captured HA-19 as the navy studied it. Here the forward battery is in the process of being dismantled. (James P. Delgado)

FDR inspects HA-19 at Mare Island Naval Shipyard. With the president are Vice Admiral John W. Greenslade, Commander 12th Naval District, and Rear Admiral Wilhelm L. Friedell, Commandant Mare Island Navy Yard. (Naval History and Heritage Command, NH 47036)

Stripping the bow and cutting into the submarine to access the torpedo tubes. (James P. Delgado)

Sakamaki's sub was loaded on a barge at Pearl Harbor to be shipped to Mare Island. (Burl Burlingame)

HA-19, readied for its national war bond sales tour, is unveiled at Mare Island Naval Shipyard. (US Navy)

Widely reproduced during the war, this image of HA-19 at Mare Island carries a message that was not painted onto the sub but instead was carefully added to the print with airbrushing to make the point about HA-19's new role to sell war bonds. (US Naval Institute)

HA-19 in a small town in America.. This scene was repeated in some 2,000 towns and cities throughout the war years. (US Naval Institute)

A wartime postcard advertised the national tour of the "suicide" submarine. (James P. Delgado)

Advertisements for the war bond tour of Sakamaki's submarine. (Burl Burlingame)

HA-19 on display on front of the Capitol, Washington, DC. (Library of Congress, LC-USZ62-95192)

HA-19 on display in Baltimore. (James P. Delgado)

HA-19 on display at the National Museum of the Pacific War in Fredericksburg, Texas. Photograph by Carol M. Highsmith. (Library of Congress / The Lyda Hill Texas Collection of Photographs in Carol M. Highsmith's America Project, LC-DIG-highsm-28219 [online]; Library of Congress)

CHAPTER THREE

Aftermath

Legend and Reality

On December 19, a despondent Admiral Matome Ugaki, chief of staff for the Combined Fleet, wrote in his diary that reports had been received from Washington, DC, that the United States had captured "some" of the *kō-hyōteki*. Ugaki feared now that Japan's secret weapon was no longer a secret, the United States "will take defensive measures against the use of that type of sub, which was under consideration for use on the western coast of the United States in the future" (Chihaya 1991:58). The previous day, the Japanese government itself had acknowledged the existence of "special submarines" in its official communiqué on the opening moves of the war, noting that five of these "special subs" were missing.

The Imperial Japanese Navy, although it knew of the loss of the *kō-hyōteki* by December 8, therefore only stated they were "missing" and did not announce the actual loss of the subs and their crews until March 6, 1942. The navy promoted the dead submariners as "Hero Gods" who embodied the best of the spirit of Bushido. The *kō-hyōteki* corps was also credited for sinking USS *Arizona*. Japanese aerial reconnaissance had previously not listed the battleship as having been sunk. Instead, the burning hulk, decks awash but not capsized, had been listed by the Japanese as "badly damaged." As reports reached Japan that *Arizona* was lost, proponents of the *kō-hyōteki* seized on the weak radio transmission, possibly from I-16 *tou*, late in the evening of December 7, of a "successful surprise attack" (Yoshida and Boyd 1995:59). That message had to have been reporting the sinking of a battleship, they argued. Eager to find some purpose in the sacrifice of the entire special attack flotilla of *kō-hyōteki*, naval officials agreed with the interpretation. "The instantaneous sinking of a battleship of the *Arizona* class as the result of a night assault by the Special Attack Flotilla was clearly observed" (Japan Times 1942:6).

The interpretation and credit to the *kō-hyōteki* corps did not please the naval aviators who had planned and executed the assault on Pearl Harbor. They had vigorously opposed using the midget submarines and were aware that a high-altitude bomb dropped by Petty Officer First

Japanese wartime image depicts the heroic midget submariners sinking a battleship at Pearl Harbor. (Burl Burlingame)

Class Noburo Kanai from the carrier *Soryu* had struck the fatal blow that sank *Arizona* (Prange 1981:415, 513). They had seen it explode from their vantage point high in the air over Pearl Harbor. The false attribution particularly rankled Commander Mitsuo Fuchida, who had helped plan and then led the aerial assault and "never became reconciled to the idea of submarine participation and made no secret of this views" (Prange 1981:338). Even Yamamoto allowed himself to believe the propaganda. Writing to Admiral Takahashi Sankichi on December 19, he said, "At least it is certain that a radio dispatch saying 'successful surprise attack' was received from one of them and also that a battleship was sunk at a time when there was no aerial attack. When thinking of the fact that those daring young men, including young officers who had graduated from the Naval Academy only less than a year before, penetrated an enemy base in spite of darkness and accomplished such a success . . . This is another point in which I was deeply impressed by this operation" (as cited in Goldstein and Dillon 1993:121).

Vice Admiral Ryonosuke Kusaka, chief of staff for the 1st Air Group, cognizant of the truth of who sank what, nonetheless paid homage to the special attack flotilla's bravery, calling them "those young boys of the midget submarines, to whom our deepest admiration should be paid. Surely even the slightest chance of survival could hardly been seen in their assigned mission" (as cited in Goldstein and Dillon 1993:146).

In press releases, as well as in a book published in English for distribution abroad, the Imperial Japanese Navy's Press Section fabricated a

Even US media were swept up into the myth of the "Hero Gods." This 1942 illustration in *Life* magazine incorrectly depicts the size and configuration of the subs and hints at a deadlier effect than what the brave young men of the *kō-hyōteki* corps actually achieved at Pearl Harbor. (Burl Burlingame)

heroic and victorious role for the midget submariners. Captain Hideo Hiraide, sectional chief of the Press Section, drew his inspiration for these reports from "American sources, and with the aid of my imagination" (Japan Times 1942:8). Hiraide wrote that the special attack flotilla, acting "like one man, perfect, unity of purpose making them one compact whole," had made "nothing of the intricate waterway inside the harbor . . . they proceeded with suppressed eagerness, deeper and deeper into the harbor" (Japan Times 1942:9). There, "some of the submarines came close to the big battleships, taking their position in the center of the lines, and delivered telling surprise attacks, while others discharged their torpedoes at other capital ships, tearing large rents in their sides" (Special Attack Flotilla 1942:9).

"Watching the aerial assault through their periscopes [and] further emboldened by this encouraging sight, they went about their tasks with grim determination, firmly resolved not to leave a single enemy ship afloat" (Japan Times 1942:9). At least one submarine, pushed underwater by destroyer attack, remained hidden on the bottom of the harbor until nightfall, when it surfaced and fired its torpedoes. "The intrepid and daring commander witnessed a big enemy battleship, broken in two, slowly sinking. We can well imagine the ecstasy of the young sailors when they saw their cherished goal finally realized" (Japan Times 1942:11).

As for the fate of the submarines and their crews, well aware of Sakamaki's capture, the Imperial Japanese Navy claimed that all those craft not sunk by enemy action had blown themselves up, and it was this final act that cemented their status as Hero Gods:

> Cases are by no means rare where people seek death, impelled by sudden impulse, but rare indeed are cases where people, like these heroic men, quietly and calmly tread what they believed to be their path of duty, display the highest and purest spirit of self-sacrifice and lay down their lives, satisfied in their conscience that they have done their duty to His Majesty the Emperor and the State. This noble spirit of self-sacrifice is the essence of Bushido; this is the embodiment of the Yamato spirit. Search as one may, he will never find a parallel case in the history of the world. The mere thought of the great deed performed

The Pearl Harbor *kō-hyōteki* corps in a posthumous portrait on silk depicting them as "Hero Gods," minus the captured Kazuo Sakamaki. (Navy Art Collection, Naval History and Heritage Command, NH 86388-KN)

> by these nine men makes our heart throb with deep emotion. (Japan Times 1942:11–12)

The Imperial Japanese Navy published biographies of the nine "Hero Gods" to stress their paths to glory. For Naoji Iwasa, it was his devotion to his country and to his duty. His last letter to his parents was cited, "I am about to venture single-handed into the harbor of the enemy for the justice of Yamato and the welfare of mankind. Forgive me that I was unable to fulfil my duty as a son" (Japan Times 1942:23). Masaharu Yokoyama idealized the hero of the Russo-Japanese War, Fleet Admiral Heihachiro Togo, and his stolid spirit was praised, while at the same time the stubborn dedication of Shigemi Furuno received notice. Shigenori Yokoyama's future was foretold by his childhood nickname, "gambariya no shige-chan," or "never give in, Shige" (Japan Times 1942:33). Unlike some of the other "Hero Gods," Yokoyama was a veteran of Japan's recent war in China.

Yoshio Katayama's last letter home, to his parents, accepted his coming fate: "I take up my pen with a heart full of gratitude for all that you have bestowed upon me—love, kindness, tenderness." He asked them to rejoice and commend him "for the only filial act" of his life. "For what is one man's life when the great objective of this nation lies at stake? From the grave I shall ever be praying for your happiness and long life" (Japan Times 1942:72–73). Sadamau Ueda apologized for not writing for several months and begged his parents not to toil too hard on

The parents of Furuno, Inagaki, and Hiroo, from *Bushido in Greater East Asia* (1942). (Burl Burlingame)

their farm. "You are aware that our country is now facing a grave situation—a period of great emergency," he wrote. "Consequently, we are undergoing intensive training day and night." If he should die, he added, "do not grieve or mourn, for I have dedicated my life in service to his Imperial Majesty. In performance of my duty in the service of the Imperial Navy, I am determined to sacrifice my life" (Japan Times 1942:73–74).

A 2.5-hour-long joint funeral for the nine "Hero Gods" was held at Tokyo's Hibaya Park on April 8, 1942. The navy had posthumously promoted each of them by two ranks. White-robed Shinto priests led a procession of thousands of blue-jacketed naval officers and enlisted men, relatives, and friends into the park. Representatives from Prime Minister Hideki Tojo and Admiral Yamamoto were among the mourners at the first major naval service for war heroes since 1904. Prayers were offered, and Japanese government spokesmen eulogized that

> The lofty, self-sacrificing spirit, which inspired the nine heroes of the Special Attack Flotilla to launch their underwater attack on Pearl Harbour on the first day of the Pacific war as spearhead of the Japanese naval force, deserves

The funeral of the midget submariners at Tokyo's Yasukuni Shrine, from *Bushido in Greater East Asia* (1942). (James P. Delgado and Burl Burlingame)

> to be immortalized for the benefit of mankind, because it has not only revealed the true character of the Japanese spirit, but has once again unbared the soul of Japan's *Bushido*. Their splendid achievements, attained entirely through their unswerving devotion to His Imperial Majesty the Emperor, have perhaps no parallel in the military history of the world. (Hohjo 1942:564)

The navy's disingenuous reports, the funeral, and the heavy media coverage of the "success" of the special attack flotilla at Pearl Harbor encouraged a cult following for the midget submariners and the *kō-hyōteki* corps. Japanese popular culture reflected a new fascination with a formerly top-secret program and weapon with an outpouring of poems, essays, songs, and books (Dorsey and Slaymaker 2010:102–3). Author Toyoo Iwata's novel, *Kaigun* (*The Navy*), was a flowery tale of Masaharu Yokoyama and his single-handed destruction of the USS *Arizona*. In 1943, director Tomotaka Kusaka made a film based on the book (High 2003:386). His effort was followed by Kajiro Yamamoto, Japan's leading war filmmaker, whose *Torpedo Squadrons Move Out* was released in 1944 (High 2003:408, 478, 480). In the film, which tells the story of three young officers sinking a battleship with a midget submarine, dramatic, imaginary scenes pumped up a false impression of not only the battle but the weapons themselves. Like other propaganda efforts, including a song about the subs, "Dai-toa Senso Kaigun no Uta" (the Song of the Navy in the Great East Asia War),[1] all this masked the complete failure of the *kō-hyōteki* at Pearl Harbor (Warner and Seno 1986:58).

WHY THEY FAILED

Masatake Chihaya wrote that the loss of the midget submariners was a tragic and avoidable loss resulting from the misapplication of the submarines:

> Those special submarines had been designed for further uses on the high sea in the "decisive battle" of the navy's imagination. These craft were of high speed and short cruising radius. They were the least fit for such an operation as the attack on Pearl Harbor which would require long periods of secret activities. Directly after the announcement of the attack on Pearl Harbor, a vice admiral who designed that craft said to me in tears, "Alas, I would never have designed such

> craft if they were to be used in such a manner. This is murder of the crews. What a pity!" His voice still remains in my ears. (as cited in Goldstein and Dillon 1993:319)

Another critical view was offered, postwar, by submariner Zenji Orita, who pointed out that part of the Japanese gamble at Pearl Harbor was untested, brand-new craft including the *kō-hyōteki* (Orita and Harrington 1976:31).

For example, the carrier *Zuikaku* had just finished its shakedown cruise 2 months before the attack. Four of the I-boats were newly completed, and one, Hiroshi Hanabusa's I-24, was nearly lost when an untested air valve stuck and the forward ballast tanks could not be blown after a dive. As the submarine sank, Lieutenant Mochitsura Hashimoto was able to free the valve and blow the tanks, saving I-24 and the *kō-hyōteki* strapped to it (Hashimoto 1955:5–6). The modification of Type 97 torpedoes to run shallow in Pearl Harbor and the hasty training of naval aviators to deploy them to effect there was as much a gamble as the rushed training of the *kō-hyōteki* corps to also deploy in the harbor, but the planes and torpedoes were not plagued by being new craft with unresolved problems. Notable in this regard, when Kazuo Sakamaki inspected I-24 *tou* before launch, he noted twenty-five separate deficiencies, including missing lights, bolts, and pins; air, oil, and water leaks; the "broken" gyrocompass; and the fact that his submarine was too heavy, badly trimmed, and hence was hard to handle (Description and Photographs of Japanese Midget Submarine No. 19, 1941).

The issue of lack of readiness would plague the *kō-hyōteki* program for the remainder of the war, but the inherent problem was the navy's self-delusional insistence in using the weapon for a purpose it had not been designed for. The honest assessment of *kō-hyōteki*'s failure discussed postwar by Chihaya and Orita was not voiced during wartime in the right places at the right times. Instead, the needless sacrifice of the *kō-hyōteki* crews at Pearl Harbor was shamelessly exploited to support not only the war but also the continued misuse and sacrifice of additional crews. The end result was not only a continued drain of experienced officers and petty officers (a problem familiar to Japan's naval aviators) but also resources as more *kō-hyōteki* and other midget submarines were constructed, ending in the adoption of the final phase of midget development, the *kaiten*, human-piloted torpedoes from which escape was not an option; there was only certain death.

THE NEXT FAILED DEPLOYMENTS

Japanese options for the first months of 1942 primarily focused on expanding offensive operations. Japanese plans for Australia, a logical base for American and British forces, initially focused on conquering the country, as well as taking action to neutralize naval forces on the southern continent. Ultimately, Japan's plans devolved to striking at Australia's shipping and its morale. In addition, the signing of the Tripartite Pact with Germany and Italy on January 19, 1942, opened the possibility of joint Axis actions in the Indian Ocean. Japan's success in driving the British out of the Pacific had now focused Britain's naval forces in the Indian Ocean (Willmott 1983:40–42).

Japanese naval operations to counter the British buildup in the Indian Ocean and hamper the use of Australia as a base of operations included carrier-based aircraft raids on the port of Darwin, a strategic port on Australia's northern coast, and against the British naval bases at Colombo and Trincomalee, Ceylon (now Sri Lanka). The attack on Darwin damaged shore installations; sank five merchant ships and military transports, HMAS *Mavie*, a naval auxiliary, and the destroyer USS *Peary* (DD-226); and damaged ten other vessels. The attack on Colombo sank the merchant cruiser

Following the Pearl Harbor attack, the *kō-hyōteki* corps returned to training with modifications to their submarines, including a new net cutter at the bow. Here, in an early 1942 snapshot, one of the subs attempts to cut through a net. (JMSA / Burl Burlingame)

In a relaxed portrait, some of the second team of the *kō-hyōteki* corps to sortie pose with their catch. In the front left is Lieutenant Keiu Matsuo, and in the rear left is Lieutenant Kenshi Chuma. (JMSA / David Jenkins)

HMS *Hector* (F45) and the destroyer HMS *Tenedos* (H04). The attack on Trincomalee sank the corvette HMS *Hollyhock* (K64), the escort destroyer HMAS *Vampire* (D68), and the carrier HMS *Hermes* (R95) (Grose 2009; Tomlinson 1976). The Japanese, with fast carrier assaults and submarine attacks, sank twenty-three ships in the Bay of Bengal, six ships off India's west coast, and sank the sloop HMIS *Indus* (U67) off Burma. Japanese carrier aircraft also sank the heavy cruisers HMS *Cornwall* and HMS *Dorsetshire* (Shores et al. 1993, 2002).

The focus on merchant shipping as well as naval forces in the Indian Ocean and the use of submarines in the operation signaled a temporary shift in Japanese submarine doctrine, traditionally focused on supporting the main fleet (Boyd and Yoshida 1995:xii; Carpenter and Polmar 1986:22). As part of the overall plan, the Imperial Japanese Navy decided to deploy *kō-hyōteki* in the Indian Ocean and off the African and Australian coasts. Once again, the plan was to attack using the subs in enclosed harbors, not the open ocean. The initial plan for a second deployment of the *kō-hyōteki* was an attack on ships in the British naval base in Singapore harbor. Plans for a midget submarine assault there were cancelled, with the sinking by aircraft of the cruisers HMS *Repulse* and HMS *Prince of Wales*, the newly arrived backbone of Britain's far eastern naval forces, and the swift capitulation of Singapore after a ten-week campaign. The *kō-hyōteki* program nonetheless forged ahead, preparing another group of submarines for action with modifications suggested by the Pearl Harbor sortie—notably a different form of torpedo guard at the bow and a hatch installed in the bottom of the midgets to allow access to the *kō-hyōteki* through a trunk from inside the "mother sub" I-boat.

Planning and training shifted from Singapore to the Indian Ocean and Australian target harbors in early 1942. The plan at that stage was for a number of submarines, loaded with midgets, to sortie into Far Eastern waters and await the results of a reconnaissance by the submarines I-10 and I-30. Then "areas of attack were to be selected from Aden, Mombasa, Zanzibar, Dar-es-Salaam, Durban, East London, Port Elizabeth and Simonstown. If it was found that major enemy vessels were in port, all submarines were to rendezvous in the area and launch simultaneous attack with midget submarines" (Shibuya 1952a:6–7). At the same time, other subs were to proceed to Australian and New Zealand waters, where I-21 and I-29 would "reconnoiter such proposed areas of attack as Suva, Sydney, Auckland and Noumea" by using sublaunched aircraft. After "confirming the whereabouts of powerful enemy warships," all submarines were to rendezvous and launch midget attacks (Shibuya 1952a:7–8).

The selection of personnel for the second attack drew on veterans of the first training class who had not been chosen to go to Pearl Harbor, some of them being considered too valuable to potentially lose. As Captain Harada noted in his diary on January 19, 1942, this time "will be more difficult than the first attack," and as such, he decided to again hold back Sublieutenant Saburo Akieda, one of the leaders of the class and an eager warrior. Akieda had performed some of the initial tests of the *kō-hyōteki* with Naoji Iwasa, who had died as the senior officer in the Pearl Harbor Special Attack Force. When Harada sent two other midget submariners to tell Akieda he should not go, Harada noted, "he came to me with a serious face demanding he be chosen to go to the front" (Association of Midget Submariners 1984:32). Harada could not refuse, and so Akieda joined the second Special Attack Force. With Akieda was Keiu Matsuo, who had, after helping plan the Pearl Harbor attack, ridden on I-22 with Iwasa to Hawai'i. Like Akieda, he had vowed not to be left behind again. Akieda would lead the group heading into the Indian Ocean; Matsuo would lead the group heading to Australia.

On January 31, 1942, Commander-in-Chief Admiral Yamamoto and his chief of staff, Admiral Ugaki, paid a visit to *Chiyoda* to inspect the loading and launching of the midget submarines and watched a "practice attack." Ugaki was impressed, writing in his diary that the training exercise was "reassuring" because of the great effort expended and the "high spirit" of the crews. "Thus we can hope those midget submarines penetrate into enemy bases and sink major vessels" (Chihaya 1991:81). Deployment was delayed by a training accident that killed three men in early March and by "the remodelling and training" that kept the *kō-hyōteki* at base until mid-April (Chihaya 1991:106). On April 16, 1942, a briefing and farewell on the flagship *Yamato* for officers and crews attached to what was now the "Second Special Attack Flotilla" included a reminder from Yamamoto to only deploy if certain of success and to not "take death lightly or act in a rash manner" (Warner and Seno 1986:91). Admiral Ugaki,

A formal portrait of three of the *kō-hyōteki* corps' second attack flotilla shows Lieutenant Kenshi Chuma (rear), who commanded a midget at Sydney; Lieutenant Keiu Matsuo, who also commanded a midget at Sydney; and Lieutenant Saburo Akieda, who commanded a midget at Diego Suarez (Madagascar), 1942. (Australian War Memorial, 128891)

perhaps with a heavy heart, wrote in his diary that "I wanted to give them a hearty send-off and wish them a brilliant success and the best of luck," especially, he noted, "to those young sub-lieutenants and ensigns of the midget sub crews, being confident of their skill and with firm determination to die for their country" (Chihaya 1991:111).

The submarines I-16, I-18, and I-20, known as the Western Attack Group, or A Force, rendezvoused with the *kō-hyōteki* mother ship *Nisshin* at Penang, Malaysia, and loaded their respective *tou*. Accompanied by I-10 and I-30, each with reconnaissance aircraft, this group headed for the east coast of Africa, where the British were holding out in Madagascar. The Eastern Attack Group, or B Force—I-22, I-24, I-27, and I-28—met *Chiyoda* at Truk (Chuuk) and loaded four *kō-hyōteki*. They then headed south with the aircraft-carrying submarines I-21 and I-29 (Boyd and Yoshida 1995:88–89). Meanwhile, I-30 found no enemy warships in Aden, Djibouti, Zanzibar, and Dar-es-Salaam. The target for the Western Attack Group then shifted to the British fleet anchorage at Diego Suarez (now known as Antsiranana) on Madagascar's extreme northern end, recently wrested from the Vichy French (Shibuya 1952a:12). Worried that the French would turn over the island—a vital base—to their recent Nazi conquerors and the Japanese (as they had done with the Japanese in Indo-China), the British seized the island with a forty-six-vessel task force in early May 1942. After the fall of Madagascar, the invading force departed, leaving behind the veteran (built in 1917) battleship *Ramillies*, two corvettes, three destroyers, and several supply and transport vessels with an occupying force.

A reconnaissance by the aircraft from I-10, flying over Diego Suarez, reported the British ships, and so all three midget-carrying submarines headed to a planned launching spot 10 miles outside the harbor on May 29. All three I-boats had been mauled by heavy seas, and with flooding and engine damage, I-18 was unable to reach the designated deployment point, so only I-16 *tou* and I-20 *tou* launched on the evening of May 30 (Shibuya 1952a:13). I-20 *tou*, commanded by Saburo Akieda and crewed by Petty Officer Masami Takemoto, and I-16 *tou*, commanded by Ensign Katsasuke Iwase and crewed by Petty Officer Takazo Takata, headed out in the darkness for Diego Suarez (Warner and Seno 1986:144–45). The British were waiting for them after spotting I-10's plane and immediately went to action stations (Flag Officer Commanding Force F 1942).

Nonetheless, the two submarines managed to penetrate the anchorage. The first *kō-hyōteki* attack came at 20:25 local time when a single torpedo struck *Ramillies* amidships on the port side, opening a 30 by 30 foot (9 by 9 m) hole and flooding compartments below the main deck. The nearby tanker *British Loyalty*'s crew, roused by the blast, looked out and saw the conning tower and periscope of the attacking sub 3 minutes after the blast (Wastell 1942). As guns opened up on the wakes and the crew caught occasional glimpses of a conning tower and periscopes, a second torpedo, apparently intended for *Ramillies*, hit *British Loyalty* at 21:05, exploding

I-18. (Burl Burlingame)

A wartime Japanese propaganda painting depicts the attack on HMS *Ramillies* at Diego Suarez. (Burl Burlingame)

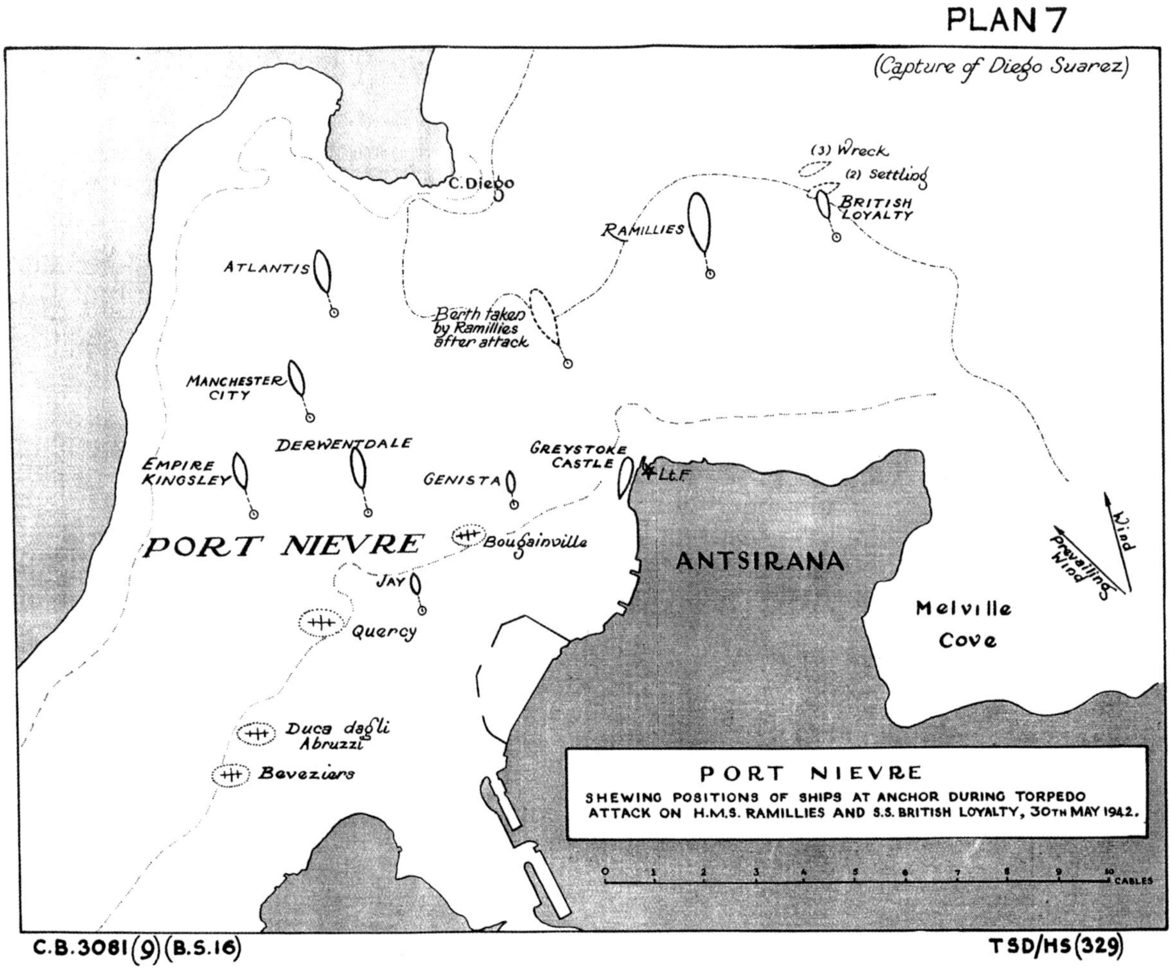

The Royal Navy's confidential chart showing where *Ramillies* and *British Victory* were moored when attacked and their final positions. (The National Archives, Kew)

in the engine room and sinking the burning vessel's stern in 67 feet of water, but with the bow still afloat (Warner and Seno 1986:149; Wastell 1942). During the shooting, it was possible that one of the subs was hit, but no definite trace was found—a search of the harbor failed to find any trace of either attacker.

The following day, on May 31, locals notified the British that two Japanese had been seen in a village 12 miles away. A patrol sent out to search for them discovered the two men on a hill overlooking the site of the rendezvous with the mother subs on June 2, and after a gunfight, the two were killed. According to one account, after one of the men was shot, the second, an officer, drew a sword and charged the British, who shot him down. He died in true samurai fashion. A search of their bodies discovered a series of notes that indicated they were Akieda and Takemoto and that I-20 *tou*, after the attack, had grounded on a reef after their batteries died and they had abandoned the sub after setting its scuttling charge, which failed to go off (Flag Officer Commanding Force F 1942; Warner and Seno 1986:150–51).[2]

Akieda and Takemoto were buried where they fell. No trace of I-16 *tou* was found, but the body of one of the crew washed ashore on June 2 on a beach near Diego Suarez. *Ramillies* was able to depart under its own power for repairs, and the British were able to raise and return *British Loyalty* to service. Another *kō-hyōteki* mission, this time with at least some combat result, had nonetheless ended as a failure and with the loss of the crews and craft (Boyd and Yoshida 1995:89).

The next attack, by the Eastern Attack Group, came at the important Australian merchant and naval harbor at Sydney within a day of the attack at Diego Suarez. After reconnaissance "confirmed the presence of some battleships and cruisers in Sydney," it was designated as the target (Shibuya 1952a:11). Sydney was caught unaware. Australian forces were not notified of the midget submarine sortie in Madagascar because British commanders believed the torpedoing of HMS *Ramillies* had been the work of a Vichy French submarine, and the role of Japan and the *kō-hyōteki* was not known for several days. Australian defenses were, as it developed, capable of meeting the threat.

After arriving 35 miles off the coast and reconnoitering the area with the seaplanes carried by the non-midget-carrying I-boats, the Second Attack Flotilla readied for their mission on the early evening of May 31—another Sunday attack, just as Pearl Harbor had been. The harbor was full of ships, including the heavy cruisers USS *Chicago* (CA-29) and HMAS *Canberra* (D33), the light cruiser HMAS *Adelaide*, the destroyers USS *Perkins* (DD-377) and USS *Dobbin* (AD-3), the minelayer HMAS *Bungaree*, as well as corvettes, armed merchant cruisers, the Dutch submarine K 9, and HMAS *Kuttabul*, a former ferry now moored dockside as a naval depot and barracks ship (Jenkins 1992a). The Japanese were excited to see the large US cruiser, which they presumed was a battleship.

Moving into position 7 miles out and east of Sydney's East Head, five I-boats, three of them carrying midgets, readied their crews for an underwater launch. Newly installed hatches and trunks that connected the mother sub to the *kō-hyōteki* meant the crews no longer had to surface and remain exposed when entering their craft. At 17:21, I-22 launched Lieutenant Keiu Matsuo and Petty Officer First Class Masao Tsuzuku. As the clamps released and I-22 moved forward at 100 feet, Matsuo drove off the stern of the mother sub and then began what planners had hoped would be a quick run at 10 knots into the harbor. I-27 followed suit, launching its *tou* at 17:28 with Lieutenant Kenshi Chuma and Petty Officer First Class Takeshi Omari. At 17:40, I-24 launched its *tou* with Sublieutenant

Keiu Matsuo and Katsuhisa Ban, two of the commanders sent to and lost at Sydney. (Australian War Memorial, 128888 and 128895)

Katsuhisa Ban and Petty Officer Mamoru Ashibe (Jenkins 1992a:202–5).

Heavy currents slowed the progress of the three midget submarines, and it was not until 18:33 that I-27 *tou* passed the Heads, passing the Manly ferry as they readied to run the gauntlet of the antisubmarine net boom that closed off the inner harbor. At 20:05, they were at the net but running too high; Chuman snagged the net, and despite his best efforts to fight his way through the steel cabled barrier, I-27 *tou* was soon helplessly entangled. Alert lookouts noted the submarine caught on the surface of the net, and soon channel patrol craft—most of them smaller boats, some civilian craft pressed into the war effort—approached the stranded midget in the darkness. As they circled and spotlit the midget, inside, Chuman and Omari realized there would be no escape. At 22:35, they set off the midget's scuttling charge, blasting it open in a violent explosion that lit up the night (Jenkins 1992a:205–9).

Meanwhile, an hour earlier, Ban and Ashibe had entered the harbor in I-24 *tou* at 21:48, headed for USS *Chicago*. As Ban made his way, the *kō-hyōteki* proved difficult to handle in the shallows, and it continually bobbed up, exposing the conning tower and at times part of the hull in a harbor that, despite it being wartime, was lit up by ship and shore light. At 22:52, the inevitable discovery of the sub happened when lookouts on *Chicago* spotted the sub. Going to general quarters, gunners opened up with a 5 inch gun and quadruple mount 50 caliber antiaircraft guns. The nearby corvette HMAS *Geelong* joined in, firing more than a hundred 20 mm rounds, but Ban dived and the shots missed. At that same time, I-22 *tou* finally arrived at the harbor entrance, delayed, like the first two subs, by strong currents. Spotted by the patrol craft *Lauriana*, the sub began to dive just as the patrol boat *Yandra* rammed it. The blow heeled the sub over nearly 15 degrees, and as Matsuo and Tsuzuku struggled to right the craft and dive, *Yandra* unleashed a volley of six depth charges. They missed, and the midget slipped away (Yandra 1942).

Back inside the harbor, Ban and Ashibe had hugged the bottom for over an hour. Coming close to the surface at 0:29, they fired a single torpedo at *Chicago*. As they did, the bow bobbed to the surface, exposing them again. The torpedo shot forward but missed *Chicago*'s bow, ran under the submarine K 9, and detonated against the retaining wall dockside where *Kuttabul* was moored. The blast lifted the old ferry out of the water and then sank it, leaving only its upper works awash. In that moment, twenty-one men on board, some still in their hammocks, were either killed by the blast or drowned. K 9, badly damaged by the blast, managed to stay afloat. Steadying his bucking craft, Ban had Ashibe fire another torpedo. This one also missed, running up on to shore side rocks but not exploding. With nothing left to shoot, Ban turned, dived, and started out of the harbor. Australian authorities later determined it was likely that by 01:58 I-24 *tou* left the harbor and headed out to sea, hoping to make its rendezvous with the mother subs off Port Hacking, 18 miles south of the Heads (Jenkins 1992a:211–18). Ban and Ashibe never made it and vanished, with their craft, for decades.[3]

Back in the harbor, I-22 *tou* was moving into position when USS *Chicago*, joined by the corvette HMAS *Whyalla*, steamed out at 02:14, and may have hit the midget a glancing blow. It was spotted again at 03:50, when the armed merchant cruiser *Kanimba* opened fire but missed. The channel patrol boats once again entered the fray. Having been ordered to set their depth charges to go off in 15 meters—a shallow depth but permissible under naval regulations—the craft approached the sub. The patrol boat *Sea Mist* was first to reach it, under the command of Lieutenant Reginald Andrew, a Royal Australian Navy reserve officer fresh out of a 6 week training school and 2 days into his new job. Thinking fast, Andrew ordered a depth charge dropped and then turned to run as it went off. A wall of water lifted and shoved *Sea Mist* forward; it also blew I-22 out of the water, upside down. The sub submerged again and lay on the bottom as *Sea Mist* and the patrol boats *Steady Hour* and *Yarroma* subjected Matsuo and Tsuzuku to a 3.5 hour depth charge barrage. At some stage, the two gave up; Matsuo took his officer's pistol and shot Tsuzuku in the forehead and then turned his gun on himself (Jenkins 1992a:218–20).

The I-boats waited in vain for the three midget submarines and their crews to return and then departed the rendezvous. On the morning of June 1, Australian forces began the task of diving to assess damage and recover the dead from *Kuttabul*. They also dived to I-22 *tou*, lying on the seabed, hull warm to the touch, electric motor still running, and the propellers still slowly turning. The battered but intact sub was raised on June 4 and hauled up the bank, with its stern being torn off in the process. On June 5, the battered remains of I-27 *tou*, still snagged on the net, were cut free and also hauled ashore. The two craft were examined, stripped, and analyzed, and the bodies of the four submariners were autopsied and cremated.[4] Their ashes, returned to the Japanese government in an exchange of diplomats and other nationals in August 1942, were given a formal funeral as their souls were committed to Yasukuni, along with those of the

HA-14 is raised from the bottom of Sydney Harbor in June 1942. (US Naval Institute, James C. Fahey)

HA-21 is raised from the bottom of Sydney Harbor in June 1942. (US Naval Institute, James C. Fahey)

Uniform Tax Bill Passed by Senate—Page 3

LATE FINAL EXTRA

V FOR VICTORY

THE SUN

SYDNEY: THURSDAY, JUNE 4, 1942. PRICE 2d.

"HOLLYWOOD REVIEWER"

2UE

Raid Sirens

"PINEAPPLE" BACON DON'T ARGUE

ONE SHIP SINKS, TWO ESCAPE IN SUB ATTACK NEAR SYDNEY

Action 35 Miles East of Heads, Another in South

From F. R. PETERSON, "The Sun's" Special Representative

MELBOURNE, Thursday.

Enemy submarines attacked three ships near Sydney today — one was sunk, but the others were not damaged.

Two small cargo vessels were attacked 35 miles east of Sydney and the third 225 miles to the south. It is believed all three ships were merchant vessels.

The attack was announced in a noon communique at Allied headquarters and the sinking of the one vessel in a 3.15 p.m. communique.

4 Japanese Subs Sunk In Sunday Raid

FROM OUR SPECIAL REPRESENTATIVE

CANBERRA, Thursday.

Four submarines tried to enter Sydney Ha... on Sunday night, and all were d...

Naval Honors For Victims

Six victims of the Japanese submarine raid on Sydney Harbor on Sunday night were buried with naval honors at Rookwood Cemetery yesterday.

Fired 3 Volleys

Headlines announce the midget attack at Sydney. (Australian National Archives) unaccounted for but obviously dead Ban and Ashibe.

Even with actual damage done to the enemy and a better accounting of the flotilla than was the case for their dead compatriots at Pearl Harbor, the loss of five submarines and ten more Hero Gods again underscored the futility of using the *kō-hyōteki* in the way they were being sent into battle. Wartime propaganda provided glowing, inaccurate accounts of their achievement, however, and for the public, it helped inspire the populace, especially young men. As submarine veteran Mochitsura Hashimoto would later say, "In later years, when the war had taken a different turn for us, the spirit displayed by those who were killed in action at Sydney was an example which ensured ample volunteers for crews for these special units" (Hashimoto 1955:25). The midget submarine program progressed forward to even greater losses and ultimately to a violent end with the *kaiten* program.

YASUKUNI SHRINE

Located in Tokyo's Chiyoda Ward, Yasukuni shrine (Yasukuni Jinja) is a complex of temples, gates, memorials, and a museum dedicated to the *kami* (souls) of Japan's deceased military from the nineteenth and twentieth centuries. In all, the spirits of some 2,466,000 are enshrined and commemorated there (Cybriwski 2011:271). Established in 1869 by the Meiji Emperor to honor those who died in the Bosshin War to restore the Emperor as the head of the Japanese state, Yasukuni grew in response to Japan's several decades of war, including the late nineteenth-century war with China, the early twentieth-century war with Russia, and Japan's subsequent participation in World War I. The largest number of dead enshrined at Yasukuni, however, are from Japan's protracted conflict that began in the 1930s and continued into World War II.

One of the striking features of the shrine is its groves of cherry trees. The "falling blossoms" of Yasukuni were used allegorically during the war by Japan's military, with men about to die noting they would return as cherry blossoms and that they would see their comrades after death at Yasukuni (Ohnuki-Tierney 2002).

The shrine is controversial. Established initially as a state-controlled entity connected to state Shinto, Yasukuni was made private after 1946 during the occupation of Japan. Nonetheless, it remains a hot point of debate due to its symbolic importance to Japan's far right, the enshrinement of 1,068 war criminals convicted in the Tokyo War Crimes Tribunals after World War II, and the occasional visits of prominent Japanese politicians, which ignites criticism, especially from China and Korea (Cybriwski 2011:271).

The museum, known as the Yūshūkan, includes recovered and surviving wartime equipment, including a kamikaze aircraft, a *kaiten* human torpedo, and relics from wrecks and families, including items from the *kō-hyōteki* and the young men who served in them. The shoulder patch believed to come from the uniform of Naoji Iwasa, recovered at Pearl Harbor, is among the artifacts displayed.

The World War I–era veteran HMS *Ramillies* (07) survived its encounter with a midget submarine. It is shown here in an official Royal Navy portrait in 1944. (Imperial War Museum, A.25722)

Yasukuni Shrine's *Haiden* or Hall of Worship, 2009. (Wikipedia Commons)

HMS *RAMILLIES*

When attacked at Diego Suarez, *Ramillies* was a 25-year-old veteran of the Royal Navy. Laid down in 1913 and completed during World War I, *Ramillies* entered into commission with Pennant Number 07 in September 1917 as one of five *Revenge*-class battleships. As part of the First Battle Squadron of the Grand Fleet, *Ramillies* saw little action as the war came to a close but remained in service through the 1920s and 1930s, including a refit. With the outbreak of World War II, the slow and obsolete *Ramillies* was nonetheless of value to the Royal Navy *and* participated in a number of actions during the war.

Ramillies's service included the Battle of the River Plate, when the German pocket battleship *Graf Spee* was destroyed; convoy escort and shore bombardment in the Mediterranean and the North Sea; and two stints in the Indian Ocean, including the invasion and occupation of Madagascar when it was torpedoed and damaged by midget submarine attack at Diego Suarez in May 1942. Repaired and returned to duty after nearly a year, *Ramillies* supported the D-day landings with heavy shore bombardment. In January 1945, the Royal Navy placed *Ramillies* in reserve in Portsmouth. Sold for scrap in 1946, the veteran battleship was broken up in 1949 (Johnston and French 2014). One of its 15 inch naval guns is displayed outside the main entrance of the Imperial War Museum in London.

Vessel Characteristics (Burt 1986:274–76, 281)

Dimensions: 620.7 feet (189.2 m) × 101.5 feet (30.9 m) × 33.7 feet (10.2 m)

Displacement: 30,400 tons

Armament: Eight 15 inch MK1 (381 mm) guns, fourteen 6 inch (152 mm) guns, two 3 inch (76 mm) guns, four 1.9 inch (47 mm) guns, four 21 inch (533 mm) torpedo tubes

Machinery: Two Parsons steam turbines, 40,000 hp engines, eighteen Babcock and Wilkes boilers

Japanese officers and troops visit Yasukuni in the early twentieth century, a time of increased militarism and martial success for Japan. (Library of Congress, LC-DIG-ggbain-21928 and LC-DIG-ggbain-21929)

One of *Ramillies*'s 15-inch guns is displayed along with a gun from HMS *Resolution* in front of the Imperial War Museum in London. (Wikipedia Commons)

HA-14 AND HA-21 ON DISPLAY

Following the wartime, 2,500 mile (4,000 km) bond-selling tour of a "composite" midget submarine made up of sections of HA-14 and HA-21 recovered from the bottom of Sydney Harbor, sections of HA-14 and HA-21 were taken to the Australian War Memorial in Canberra, arriving on April 28, 1943 (Gill 1968:72). The central section of HA-21, not used in the "composite," remained in Sydney at the naval base, on outdoor display for decades. It is now, after restoration, displayed in the RAN Heritage Centre on Garden Island in Sydney.

The Australian War Memorial, which opened in 1941 to honor Australia's deceased World War I veterans, had responded to the new war by expanding its scope, collections, and mission to include the new global conflict. The midget pieces, with viewing holes cut into the hull, were displayed outside the memorial until 1985. Weather and graffiti were a continual problem, and a well-publicized coat of yellow paint applied by two young men in September 1966 to pay homage to the Beatles' "Yellow Submarine" highlighted the need for more protection (Grose 2007:253–55).

The composite "submarine" made up of the parts of HA-14 and HA-21 on display in the Exhibition Gardens in Melbourne, Australia, in late 1942. (Australian War Memorial, P00455.005)

The restored central section of HA-21 on display at the Royal Australian Navy Heritage Centre at Garden Island, Sydney. (Wikipedia Commons)

The submarine sections were shipped to the Royal Australian Navy's base at Garden Island in Sydney in 1985 to undergo a meticulous restoration, which was completed in 1987. They remained there, in storage, until a major exhibition at the Australian National Maritime Museum, "Hitting Home," opened with them as the major exhibits on May 31, 1992, just in time for the fiftieth anniversary of the attack. The exhibition remained open until January 1993.[5] The submarine pieces were then taken back to Canberra in 2001 and placed inside the memorial's ANZAC Hall, where they have been displayed since with artifacts from the submarines and their crew. The exhibit of the midget submarine pieces, adjacent to the restored wheelhouse of HA-21's victim, HMAS *Kuttabul*, tells the story of the attack from both the Australian and Japanese perspectives.[6] The story is also conveyed through a sound and light show that utilizes the submarine pieces: "Sydney under attack."

A boot, glove, and flying helmet belonging to Kenshi Chuma recovered by the Royal Australian Navy from his submarine after raising it from Sydney Harbor. (Australian National Maritime Museum / Jenni Carter)

CHAPTER FOUR

The End of the Midgets

As the I-boats and midget submarines of the Second Special Attack Flotilla sortied to the Indian Ocean and Australia, Japanese naval planners were hard at work assessing the next major fleet operation, a massive naval strike at Midway and the Aleutians, to seize the islands and establish an eastern defensive perimeter for Japan, as well as provide a base for closer strikes at Hawai'i. As part of the planning for Midway, both *Chiyoda* and *Nisshin*, each loaded with twelve *kō-hyōteki*, steamed behind the strike force to establish a midget submarine base at Kure Atoll (Parshall and Tully 2007:48–49, 453; Spennemann 2013). Defeat at Midway scuttled those plans, and the unscathed tenders returned to Japan with their midgets.

While Midway was an unmitigated failure, the feint to the north and the seizure of the western end of the Aleutian chain established garrisons on the islands of Attu and Kiska. Japanese troops waded ashore on Kiska on June 7, 1942, quickly capturing the island's two-man radio station crew. Attu was also quickly taken with no resistance. In the aftermath of the Midway disaster, the Japanese decided to hold their tenuous position in these barren, windswept islands. It was not necessarily a tactical advantage, but it posed a psychologically strategic value. Thousands of troops, materiel, and additional weapons were shipped to Attu and Kiska, each respectively 650 and 800 miles from Japan's northern shores. In the months that followed the seizure of the islands, the Japanese constructed coastal and antiaircraft defenses, a seaplane base, camps, roads, and an airfield (Chandonnet 2008; Garfield 1995).

As part of the fortification program, the navy sent *Chiyoda* to Kiska. The ship carried six *kō-hyōteki* and landed them on the island on July 4, 1942. The midgets augmented Kiska's defenses, which now included a large garrison, five hundred civilian laborers, seacoast guns, and the support of twelve I-class submarines. Naval engineers built a 30-foot-wide, 200-foot-long submarine pen and launching facility for the midgets on the edge of Kiska harbor. It included several buildings—a machine shop, a battery repair shop, an acid storage building (for the batteries), an equipment storage building, and a powerhouse with a diesel generator. The sub pen was set inside a concrete-lined excavation cut into the shore, with two sets of 6-foot-wide narrow gauge track. Steel cradles held the subs, which were winched ashore. The pen was covered by a large wooden truss roof (Payne 1943:34). The first midget base outside of Japan, the new facility represented the navy's return to the original concept of the midgets as shore-based, coastal defense weapons.

However, the *kō-hyōteki* were never used in Aleutian combat. The occupation of the islands resulted in a furious response from the United States, which began a year-long campaign to oust the Japanese. Aerial bombardment and harassment was followed by a naval campaign to interdict the flow of supplies by sea. The midget base was damaged in a September 14, 1942, air raid launched from Adak Island that sank vessels in the harbor and strafed the submarines. Later raids bombed the base, destroying the power plant, and one of the midgets was put out of commission by a fragmentation bomb that peppered and pierced the aft hull. Attu was taken by a joint American and Canadian invasion force in May 1943, and most of the occupation force died in the battle and a last-ditch suicidal banzai charge that saw nearly a thousand Japanese die. In the aftermath of the retaking of Attu, Japan gave the order to evacuate Kiska, and on July 28, under the cover of weather, ships loaded 5,183 men and headed home. The midget corps, before departing, set off the scuttling charges in their last three, relatively undamaged *kō-hyōteki*. When the allied invasion force landed on Kiska on August 15, they found a deserted island filled with abandoned buildings and destroyed equipment, including the wrecked midgets (Coyle 2014:101–10).[1]

Guadalcanal

After the defeat at Midway and the ill-fated Aleutians venture, the Imperial Japanese Navy still hoped that the *kō-hyōteki* could play an important role in the war. In late 1942, the number of *kō-hyōteki* constructed stood at forty-four; of these, at least a third had been lost along with most of the original class of midget submariners. The corps was about to lose more.

The destroyed midget submarine base at Kiska is shown after the US and Canadian landings in 1943. All three craft left behind on their rail-mounted carriages are visible. Only HA-30, the submarine closest to the camera, remains in situ seven decades later. (Naval History and Heritage Command, SC 189261)

In response to the ongoing struggle in the Solomon Islands, where Japanese and Allied forces continued to wage air, land, and sea battles, the navy decided to deploy some of the *kō-hyōteki* to that theater. Admiral Ugaki, while an early proponent of the midget program, was uneasy with the decision, noting in his diary on September 30, 1942, that *Chiyoda* had arrived at Truk from Kure with eleven submarines on board: "According to the skipper who came to report, training and readiness of the craft were still insufficient. I can't help but feeling we called them down too soon, disregarding these points. We shouldn't use them unless success is believed certain. Otherwise, judging from past experiences, sacrifices would only be increased for nothing. I warned the staff accordingly and told them to keep on with their training for the time being" (Chihaya 1991:220–21).

By October, the crews were apparently ready, and *Chiyoda* sailed to the Solomons with six *kō-hyōteki* designated as the Third Special Attack Unit. The commander of the Third Destroyer Squadron argued for placing the midgets at Lunga or Tulagi, while Combined Fleet staff

THE ARCHAEOLOGY OF THE KISKA *KŌ-HYŌTEKI* AND THE MIDGET SUBMARINE BASE

Visitors to remote, isolated Kiska often visit the overgrown remains of the midget submarine base and the rusting hulk of the one remaining more-or-less intact sub, HA-34, which is accessible to entry where it was blasted by demolition charges set by retreating Japanese forces. As part of the first comprehensive survey of the maritime and naval resources at Kiska in 1989, a National Park Service team led by Daniel J. Lenihan, working with the US Navy, the US Air Force, and the US Fish and Wildlife Service, documented the intact submarine and the remains of a second partially buried in beach sands.

The work, part of a larger initiative known as Project Seamark, looked at World War II sites throughout the Pacific. The team also dived on a number of targets in the harbor and offshore, which ranged from the bomb-damaged large submarine RO-65, the transport *Nissan Maru*, and scuttled landing craft probably used to evacuate the garrison when the Japanese abandoned Kiska in 1943 (Murphy and Lenihan 1995). The survey of the one *kō-hyōteki* documented the survival of equipment including racks of batteries stowed in their original compartments, a demonstration of both the preservative effects of the sub-Arctic environment and the remoteness of the place.

A detailed survey of all aspects of the Kiska sites—on land and in the water—was undertaken by a team led by archaeologist Dirk H. R. Spennemann in 2009. Most traces of the midget submarine base have vanished, leaving only the slip cut into the bank above the beach and the rusting hulk of HA-34. The corroded stern of the other submarine, with its machinery exposed, rests at the surf line of the beach and represents the remains of what is likely HA-33, which along with one other submarine was scrapped and cut apart by US forces after the capture of Kiska (Spennemann 2011:89–90, 433–34).

HA-30, now an archaeological resource on Kiska and one of the best preserved Type A *kō-hyōteki* wrecks. (Richard Galloway, US Fish and Wildlife Service, 2015)

The disassembled remains of another *kō-hyōteki* lie on the beach next to the former midget submarine base at Kiska. (Richard Galloway, US Fish and Wildlife Service, 2015)

argued for operating the subs between Guadalcanal and the Russell Islands. Ugaki decided to land the midgets at Guadalcanal, where a base was established for them at the island's northwest tip, near Cape Esperance, at Kamimbo Bay.

A "Tokyo Express" run on October 11 brought the necessary materials for the base in the destroyer *Shirayuki* along with 1,100 soldiers (Frank 1990:321–22). Ugaki remained distressed, because although "consideration to giving them a chance to participate in a battle since they were brought down here can be appreciated, what I am afraid of most is that it will only result in belittling human lives and arms, and sending them to certain death, yet bringing no contribution to the outcome of the operation" (Chihaya 1991:234). Nonetheless, *Chiyoda* delivered eight more submarines in October to Shortland, Bougainville.

A document recovered from a sunken *kō-hyōteki* in June 1943 outlined the strategy for the midgets: "Plan of Attack against Anchored Enemy Warships for the Kō-hyōteki Based at Guadalcanal: The Time for Resolute Action." Resolute action meant acting quickly and decisively: "Upon receiving a report that the enemy has been discovered, the attack will be carried out with the least possible delay. Do not lose your opportunity because you vainly delayed and thereby allowed the enemy to escape into a strongly defended harbor" (Plan of Attack 1943). The orders stressed that two midget submarines were to be deployed against a "powerful" enemy ship and that "four or more will not be ordinarily be used simultaneously at one spot," perhaps because of the possibility of complete loss, as seen in Pearl Harbor, Diego Suarez, and Sydney.

The *kō-hyōteki* were ordered to remain submerged daily from 30 minutes before sunrise until dusk and then make evening attacks. While exhorted to pick out "the most powerful ship or transport" as a target, midget submariners were given the discretion to expend a torpedo on patrol craft. After attacking, commanders were to take a "suitably circuitous route." If disabled or out of power, the subs were to be towed to Japanese-occupied islands; if this was impossible, the subs could be scuttled, but the crews were not to commit suicide. These orders saved the lives of five midget crews at Guadalcanal, who were the first members of the *kō-hyōteki* corps sent into combat who lived to fight another day.

The setting for midget submarine operations in the Solomon Islands was Indispensable Strait between Florida and Malaita islands and Savo Sound between Guadalcanal and Florida islands, with tiny Savo island between them. There, as part of a Japanese plan that deployed RO and I-class submarines to ambush American shipping going up the slot to Guadalcanal, the Imperial Japanese Navy sent I-16, I-20, and I-24, each with a *kō-hyōteki*, to attack American ships anchored off Guadalcanal in early November 1942.

From a position 5 miles off Cape Esperance, I-20 launched a midget commanded by Sub-lieutenant Nobuharu Kunihiro and crewed by Petty Officer First Class Goro Inoue at 02:22 on November 7. Two hours later, while patrolling the Lunga anchorage off the southern end of Savo island, Kunahiro avoided destroyers screening the area and continued to Lunga Point. Just before 09:30, Kunihiro and Inoue fired one of their torpedoes at the destroyer USS *Lansdowne* (DD-486), which was busy unloading mortar ammunition. The torpedo passed astern of *Lansdowne*, which went into action just as the torpedo struck the nearby transport *Majaba* (AG-43) "cleanly amidships on the starboard side" (Commanding Officer, USS *Lansdowne* 1942). Badly damaged, *Majaba* did not sink, as its crew beached it. *Lansdowne*, meanwhile, "slipped her chain and swing around with full rudder and emergency full ahead" and pursued an aggressive depth charge attack on the midget, dropping a total of twenty-two depth charges over the next half hour (Commanding Officer, USS *Lansdowne* 1942). I-20 *tou*, undamaged, retreated, but a faulty gyrocompass led Kunahiro to strand his sub in shallow water off the beach at Malvovo. After flooding their sub, the two midget submariners escaped—the first in the program to do so (Warner and Seno 1986:165).[2]

Over the course of little more than a month, from November 11 to December 13, seven other sorties resulted in the loss of all seven of the midgets. The first was that launched from I-16 and commanded by Lieutenant (j.g.) Teiji Yamaki and crewed by Petty Officer First Class Ryoichi Hashimoto. Yamaki, a veteran of the first training class, had been scheduled to participate in the Sydney attack, but a battery explosion in his *kō-hyōteki* killed his crew member and badly burned him. Now recovered, he was back in action, but his mission was cut short when during the launch from the mother sub, his rudder struck the launch cradle and was disabled. Unable to steer, Yamaki surfaced and scuttled his craft but escaped alive, as did Hashimoto, by swimming ashore (Warner and Seno 1986:165). Another midget, launched from I-20 on November 19, developed an oil leak and was scuttled, but its crew, Sublieutenant Yoshiaki Miyoshi and Petty Officer Kiyoshi Umeda, escaped and swam ashore. Their craft may have been one later raised from some 10 meters (30 feet) of water off Cape Esperance on January 4, 1945, by the coast guard buoy tender *Ironwood* (WAGL-297), which raised and loaded the wreck onto a crane barge and beached it near Hutchinson Creek on Florida island for examination and disarmament by attempting to remove the torpedoes. After what was reported as a "thorough search," with the torpedoes still stuck in their tubes, the sub

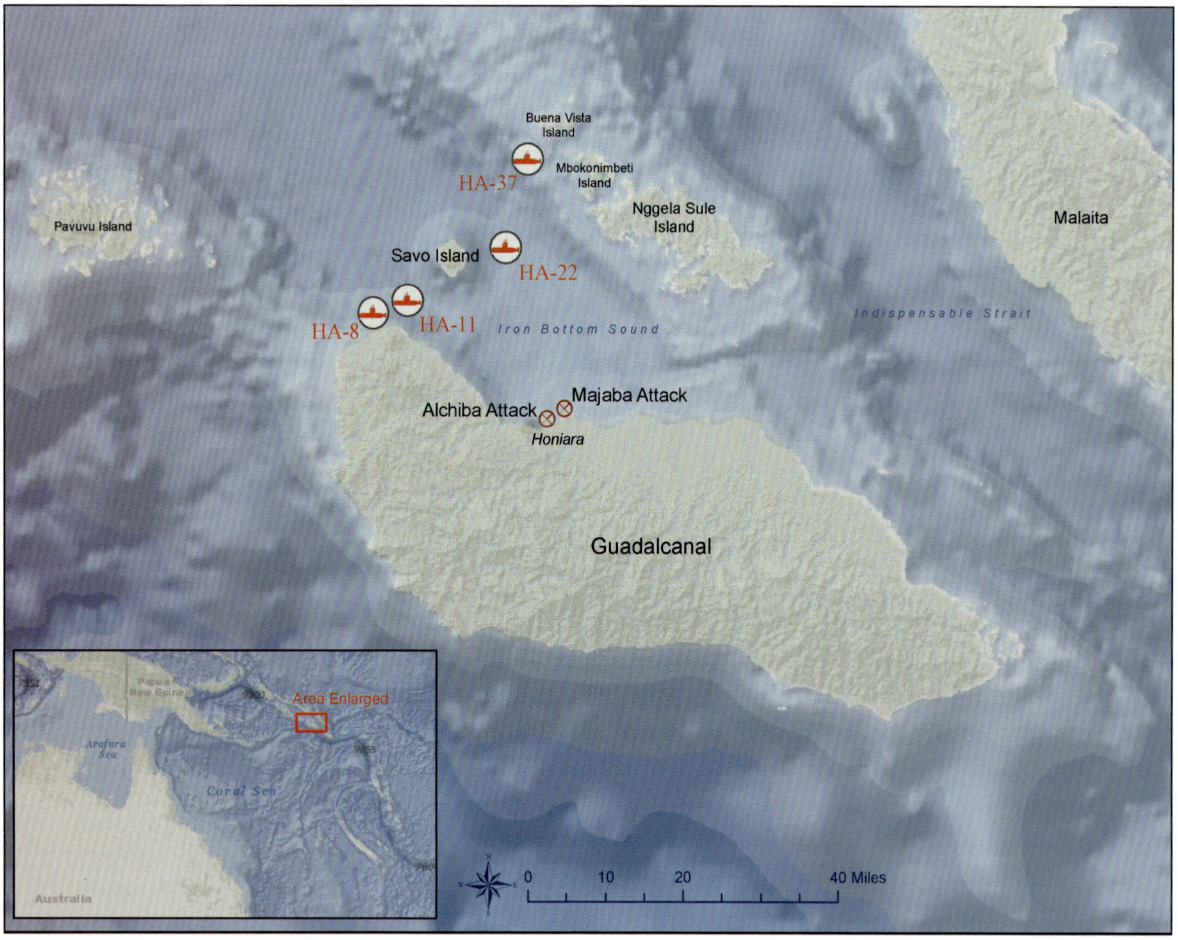

Known Guadalcanal midget submarine operations. (NOAA/Tony Reyer)

USS *Alchiba* on fire after being attacked by Sublieutenant Hiroshi Hoka and Petty Officer Shinsaku Inokuma in I-16 *tou* on November 28, 1942. *Alchiba* survived, but the submarine and its crew did not. (Naval History and Heritage Command, USMC 52795)

was scuttled off to Gavutu island (Commanding Officer, USCG *Ironwood* 1945).

The next midget loss was commanded by Lieutenant Yasuki Mukai and crewed by Petty Officer First Class Kyugoro Sano. Launched by I-24 on November 22, 1942, 14 miles off Cape Esperance, it was never seen again. The fifth loss was I-16 *tou*, launched on November 28 from just 3,000 yards off Lunga Point. Sublieutenant Hiroshi Hoka and Petty Officer Shinsaku Inokuma managed a daring feat, firing through a screen of five destroyers to hit the 6,200 ton freighter USS *Alchiba* (AKA-6). The torpedo tore into the hold, igniting *Alchiba*'s cargo of aviation fuel, bombs, and ammunition. "The impact was followed immediately by an explosion throwing a column of flame and smoke approximately one hundred and fifty feet into the air. Fire immediately seemed to fill number two hold and to spread to number one hold" (Commanding Officer, USS *Alchiba* 1942). The crew managed to beach the burning ship at Lunga Point, where they hastily unloaded ammunition and fought the fire as small arms and ammunition overheated and exploded. The fire burned for days as the heroic crew of *Alchiba*, joined by volunteers from other ships, successfully fought to save the ship. After a month of resting half sunk as a "sitting duck," *Alchiba* was refloated and moved to repair facilities (Tibbets 1996:49–50). *Alchiba* would live to fight another day, but I-16 *tou* and its crew did not return from the mission (Warner and Seno 1986:166).

On December 2, I-20 launched Lieutenant (j.g.) Chiaka Tanaka and Chief Petty Officer Mamoru Mitani. They attacked but missed the freighter SS *Joseph Teal* and then fled, pursued by depth charges. They nearly made it back to base

USS *Alchiba* (AKA-6)

Built under contract for the US Maritime Commission as a standard Type C2 ship by the Sun Shipbuilding and Drydock Company of Chester, Pennsylvania, *Alchiba* was launched under its original name of *Mormacdove* on July 6, 1939. Originally operated by Moore-McCormack Lines, established in 1913 and recently bolstered into a consolidated group of nine shipping companies that worked closely with the Maritime Commission, *Mormacdove* was taken over by the US Navy in June 1941 and converted to military use; it was commissioned as USS *Alchiba* (AK-23) on June 15, 1941, at Boston Navy Yard (Mooney 1970:476).

After serving for the Naval Transportation Command on North Atlantic convoy runs through the remainder of 1941, in 1942 *Alchiba* transited the Panama Canal and entered into Pacific service, including transporting a vital wartime cargo of copper from Chile to New York before returning to the Pacific. As part of the Amphibious Force, Pacific Fleet, *Alchiba* made three runs to the Solomons during the Guadalcanal campaign. It was on the third voyage in November that the ship was torpedoed by HA-10 and HA-38 on two separate attacks. The heroic efforts of the officers and crew saved *Alchiba*, and after temporary repairs at Tulagi, the ship returned to the United States for repair and overhaul at Mare Island Naval Shipyard.

By August 1943, *Alchiba*, now designated AKA-6, was back in service and returned to the South Pacific, serving in the Solomons and New Caledonia through mid-1944, when it was forced to return to the US West Coast for repairs and alterations that lasted through the middle of 1945. After one last wartime voyage, *Alchiba* returned to the East Coast via the Panama Canal and was decommissioned at Norfolk on January 14, 1946. Entering private merchant service in 1948, the former *Alchiba* was finally scrapped in 1973.

Vessel Characteristics (Lane 2001:27–28)
Dimensions: 459.2 feet (139.95 m) × 63 feet (19 m) × 26.4 feet (8 m)
Deadweight Tonnage: 8,794 tons
Armament: One 5 inch / 38 caliber gun, four twin-mounted 40 mm guns, sixteen single 20 mm guns
Machinery: Two steam turbines, 6,000 shp engines, two boilers

but abandoned their craft and swam ashore. The attack was noted by Admiral Ugaki in his diary on December 3, who wrote that he had received a report that one of the midgets had "penetrated Lunga Roads and attacked an enemy transport between capes Lunga and Cori. After confirming two torpedoes [had] hit, it withdrew, submerging deep, and eventually came back to the base at Kamimbo, detouring Cape Esperance, after being attacked with depth charges for one and a half hours. Its crew was all safe, but the boat sank from leaking at 1430" (Chihaya 1991:292).[3]

The seventh loss was crewed by Lieutenant (j.g.) Tomio Tsuji and Petty Officer First Class Daiseiki Tsubokura, who launched from I-24 on December 7. They torpedoed *Alchiba*, still

USS *Alchiba*, c. 1945. (Naval History and Heritage Command, NH 78540)

stranded on the beach from the earlier attack, and flooded its engineering spaces. Two of the crew were killed and six injured, but as noted earlier, *Alchiba* survived (Commanding Officer, USS *Alchiba* 1942). The midget submarine crew did not. They were attacked by a SBD Dauntless dive bomber in an attack coordinated with PC-477 as they withdrew from *Alchiba*. The damaged sub and its crew sank in more than 2,000 feet of water. The last loss was on December 13, when I-16 launched Lieutenant (j.g.) Yoshimi Kado and Petty Officer Second Class Toshio Yahagi. They claimed to have engaged a destroyer before withdrawing and scuttling their sub near Kamimbo. Guadalcanal, like Diego Suarez, proved ultimately to be the finest hours for the *kō-hyōteki* corps, stirring feats of bravery and death at Pearl Harbor and Sydney notwithstanding. Two vessels had been damaged in each attack, although not taken out of the war.[4] *Ramillies*, *British Loyalty*, *Majaba*, and *Alchiba* were all returned to service. The price was eight subs and six trained crew—and the gains purchased by their loss had no real effect. Despite their limited success, the midgets had failed to achieve even a tactical victory. The war had turned against Japan, which after Midway, now lost Guadalcanal.

The Last Campaigns

By the end of 1942, the Imperial Japanese Navy worked to redesign and redeploy the *kō-hyōteki*. Unfortunately for Japan, this effort focused on the technical deficiencies of the submarines instead of focusing on the misuse of the craft

THE GUADALCANAL MIDGET SUBMARINE IN GROTON

On prominent display in front of the museum building of the Submarine Force Museum and Library in Groton, Connecticut (home of the historic nuclear submarine USS *Nautilus*), a Type A *kō-hyōteki* is displayed next to an Italian midget submarine. The craft, locally identified as "no. 8," was raised by divers from USS *Ortolan* (ASR-5) at Guadalcanal in June 1943 and taken from there to Noumea, New Caledonia, where the craft was loaded on a ship for transport to the United States. While some sources identify the craft as HA-10 or HA-30, also known to have been lost at Guadalcanal, documents raised from the craft in 1943 identified it as HA-8 (Office of the AC of 3, G-2 1943). It is I-20 *tou*, the craft of Lieutenant (j.g.) Chiaka Tanaka and Chief Petty Officer Mamoru Mitani that attacked and missed the freighter SS *Joseph Teal* in December 1942 and subsequently sank after being depth-charged. Shipped to the navy's submarine base at Groton in 1943, it remained on the base and was ultimately placed on display at the museum.

The interior of the submarine is stripped, which was probably completed in 1943 prior to shipping, leaving only the shell of what today is one of only six *kō-hyōteki* displayed in the world. There has been some confusion as to whether the Groton submarine also toured the country like HA-19 to sell war bonds. In 1965, in response to a question on the matter from the custodians of HA-19 in Key West, the navy's assistant director of naval history, Captain Kent Loomis, wrote to Key West to report that the navy had asked Mr. J. Mogelever from the Treasury Department's Savings Bond Division, and he replied that there was only one Japanese submarine on tour during World War II and that Mr. Mogelever had personally participated in that tour.

HA-8, as displayed at the Submarine Force Museum and Library, Groton, Connecticut. (James P. Delgado)

and crews on ill-suited missions. Private doubts plagued naval leaders and doubtless some of the veterans of the corps, but the program pushed on. As the last group of Type A submarines was completed, a new sub, numbered HA-53, was designed and laid down in October 1942 and completed in February 1943 with a major difference. Less than a third of a meter (1 foot longer than the Type A boats), its extra space accommodated a 40 hp, 25 kilowatt diesel

One of the scuttled and abandoned *kō-hyōteki* in the shallows in the Solomons, 1942. (Naval History and Heritage Command, NH 74772)

USS *Ortolan* after raising the scuttled midget submarine HA-8. The submarine yielded valuable documents for naval intelligence. HA-8 was the only Type A *kō-hyōteki* retained by the US Navy other than HA-19, Kazuo Sakamaki's craft. Standard practice was to raise, examine, and scuttle any sunken or scuttled midget submarines the navy encountered in the Pacific War. Today HA-8 is displayed at the Submarine Force Library and Museum in Groton, Connecticut. (http://www.navsource.org/archives/11/110204505.jpg)

Intelligence from Scuttled Submarines

In the aftermath of the Pearl Harbor and Sydney attacks, the US Navy turned its intelligence gathering focus from the actual craft to what they carried inside. A 1942 order from the vice chief of naval operations to all commands noted that it was possible with enemy submariners operating close to American shores that they could be sunk and "under favorable conditions an enemy submarine so sunk would present an opportunity for the recovery of documents, personal effects and equipment of the highest intelligence value" (Vice Chief of Naval Operations 1942).

In May 1942, the orders were amended to ensure that all such operations were to be conducted secretly, employing only navy divers, who would enter sunken submarines with waterproof bags "in which papers and documents can be placed for removal, as important enemy papers are often soluble in salt water." Every recovered item would go to the Office of Naval Intelligence. "It is recommended that a suitable and plausible story be prepared which can be circulated, if necessary, to explain any diving operations carried out within sight of persons outside the service. Recovery of documents or other materials must always be denied" (Vice Chief of Naval Operations 1942). Anything found not to be of technical or intelligence value would return to the salvage crews "in consideration of the natural and understandable desire for souvenirs."

These orders were closely followed in the Guadalcanal campaign as the navy raised and inspected more than one of the midget submarines scuttled there. In June 1943, when USS *Ortolan* (ASR-5) raised a midget from Visale Bay at Guadalcanal and recovered the operational plans for midget operations in the Solomons, the work was described in a navy press release as "just fooling around." The raising of selected craft continued, albeit infrequently, through the end of the war—one Type C boat was raised at Guam to become a shoreside souvenir, another was raised and rescuttled at Cebu, and another Type C was raised at Unten Ko on Okinawa and then sunk in deeper water in Buckner Bay to clear another harbor there in 1945. By that time, there was little to nothing the US Navy and its allies did not know about the *kō-hyōteki*.

generator to recharge the sub's batteries, thus correcting the major design inefficiency of the earlier midgets. From this prototype, called an *otsu-gata* (Type B), a new group of *hei-gata* (Type C) boats emerged (Itani et al. 1993:127). These 81-foot-long, 49 ton craft carried a crew of three, the third man serving as the engineer. More complex than their predecessors, the *hei-gata* began to emerge from the factory in the summer of 1943, with five modified *kō-hyōteki*, HA-49, HA-50, HA-51, HA-52, and HA-53 rebuilt as Type C boats.

The Imperial Japanese Navy decided to ship these five submarines to the Bismarck Archipelago (now in Papua New Guinea) to be based at the former Australian base at Rabaul, which was now a heavily built up and fortified Japanese bastion after its January 1942 capture. As supply convoys ferried supplies and personnel and towed a supply and support vessel for the midget submarines, the submarines were readied for towing across the Pacific. Only two of the five would arrive, the first being HA-53, which reached Rabaul on December 16, 1943, under

A navy diver from USS *Ortolan* (ASR-5) in the conning tower of raised sub HA-8 in Visale Bay off Guadalcanal in June 1943. Three divers (W. Crawford, Douglas R. Kemp, and Lt. F. X. Sommer [M.C.] USNR) entered the wreck and removed its batteries, and the lightened craft rose to the surface. They then made a major intelligence coup, recovering the operational plans for midget operations in the Solomons. In keeping with wartime secrecy requirements, the work was described in a navy press release as "just fooling around." (US Naval Institute)

After being raised, a scuttled *kō-hyōteki* at Guadalcanal is about to be entered and searched for documents and any "special equipment" in 1942. (Burl Burlingame)

tow of the merchant ship *Hidaka Maru*. HA-52 arrived under tow of the support ship *Sanko Maru*, which steamed from Palau with the sub on February 12, 1944. Diverted to Kavieng, New Ireland, *Sanko Maru* and HA-52 arrived at Three Islands Harbor, New Hanover, in time for a US aerial assault on February 16 that sent the ship to the bottom. Strafed and straddled by near misses from bombs, HA-52 was scuttled by the crew after the second day of attacks on February 17. The other midgets fared no better. The submarine USS *Seawolf* sank the tanker *Yamazuru Maru*, towing HA-50, on January 14, 1944. The submarine USS *Whale* sank *Tarushima Maru*, towing HA-51, on January 17, 1944. Finally, the ship *Neikai Maru*, towing HA-49, was sunk by aircraft January 28, 1944 (Cressman 2000:205, 208).[5] With only HA-53 at Rabaul, there was to be no effective midget submarine force in the Bismarcks. The base itself, heavily bombed and strafed throughout the first months of 1944, was left cutoff and mauled until the end of the war. When surviving Japanese forces surrendered on September 6, 1945, they scuttled HA-53 in shallow water.

Japan was withdrawing from the South Pacific. A lack of fuel led the Sixth Submarine Fleet to withdraw from Truk in the spring of 1944. The navy sent the beleaguered garrison at Saipan some of the new *kō-hyōteki*. Again, they made no appreciable difference. Two boats out of five towed there were lost at sea, and the other three and their crews vanished in the destruction of Japanese forces who massed for one last banzai charge during the island's invasion. In the aftermath of the battle for Saipan, one of the submarines was discovered in 60 feet of water, raised for inspection, and then scuttled (Commander Surface Squadron Twelve 1944:12). The

THE ARCHAEOLOGY OF THE GUADALCANAL MIDGET SUBMARINES

An ongoing project by Ewan Stevenson of New Zealand has focused on the archaeology of World War II in the Solomon Islands since the early 1990s. A particular focus has been surveys to locate the remains of the midget submarines lost by Japan during the Guadalcanal campaign. With careful research and attention to detail, the project has located *kō-hyōteki* HA-11 in shallow water near Kamimbo, at the site where it was scuttled after the attack on USS *Majaba* (AG-43). The site's future is uncertain, with concerns over possible vandalism and/or scrapping.

The remains of HA-37, which was raised by the USCG *Ironwood* (WAGL-297) from near Kamimbo in January 1945, studied, dismantled, and dumped into the water, was recently relocated and surveyed. HA-22, also lying in shallow waters near Kamimbo, were also relocated and surveyed by Stevenson and his team in 1994.

The remains or presumably intact remains of HA-12, lost in November 1942, have not yet been found. To date, no one has pinpointed the wreck of HA-20, lost after its successful attack on USS *Alchiba* (AK-23). The same is true for two other midgets, HA-30, also lost in November 1942, and HA-38, lost after it torpedoed the beached *Alchiba* in December 1942. HA-38 likely lies between Savo and Lunga Point in 700 meters of water. HA-20 likely rests between Savo and Cape Esperance in 700 meters of water, according to Stevenson, but surveys have not yet located it. Two searches in 1999 and 2011 did not find HA-30, which Stevenson believes rests in waters 900 to 1,200 meters deep.[6] The dedication of Ewan Stevenson and his team is an exceptional example of citizen scientists funding and pursuing the work of discovery and documentation in a distant part of the world where World War II heritage is at risk and rapidly vanishing wherever it can be scrapped or plundered for souvenirs.

USS *Ironwood* beaches the raised HA-37 prior to a detailed search of the craft. It was cut into pieces and rescuttled. (Library of Congress, HAER AK-44-2)

sad legacy of the midget submariners, begun at Pearl Harbor, continued to be one of needless sacrifice.

Ten of the new Type C boats were sent to the Philippines on D-type destroyer transports in 1944. Based in the southern Visayas at Davao, Cebu, and Zamboanga, the midgets were commanded by Captain Kaku Harada, one-time skipper of *Chiyoda* and the "father" of the program. Hammered by American attacks, the

THE RABAUL AND KAVIENG MIDGET SUBMARINES

At the end of the war, Japanese forces surrendered Rabaul to occupying Australian forces, who commenced clearing the wreckage of war from the land and sea. Among the various wrecks in the harbor was the midget submarine HA-53. Scuttled in shallow water in Simpson Harbour, the submarine was raised by the tug *Caledonian Salvor* (BAR-1) and a labor force of Japanese prisoners, some of whom were said to be from the "original crew," who through December of 1945 cleaned up the interior and raised it using empty fuel drums and cables to lift it to the surface on January 17, 1946 (Foster and Stone 1994:122, 126). After being turned over to the naval officer in charge from the Royal Australian Navy, HA-53 was scuttled in deeper water, apparently either when it was discovered the torpedoes could not be extracted from the bow tubes or when the craft deteriorated and could no longer be kept afloat, according to anecdotal information. The intact, scuttled submarine was rediscovered by Fritz Herschied in 1968 or 1969 in 55 meters of water off the Dawapai Rocks (also known as the Beehives) in the center of the harbor and then rediscovered again in October 2011 by a Royal Australian Navy team searching the area for the World War I lost Australian submarine AE1, thought to rest somewhere in the area. The submarine has subsequently been dived by Bob Halstead, but its location is not well known and it is not usually dived.

HA-52 lies some 50 meters off the wreck of *Sanko Maru*, which was partially salvaged after the war in New Hanover's Three Islands Harbor near Tunnung Island. The salvors apparently missed the submarine, which lies in some 22 meters of water. The wreck was discovered by Kevin Baldwin, the engineer of Bob Halstead's dive boat, *Telita*, in 1987 when Baldwin was searching the bottom near the wreck of *Sanko Maru*. The submarine lay intact on the seabed, without torpedoes in the tubes, and the hatch closed but undogged. Baldwin and Halstead opened the hatch and sent a diver in, but the visibility was poor. The wreck of HA-52, festooned with marine growth, is a popular dive site, with a modern guide line connecting the wreck of *Sanko Maru* with its one-time tow, HA-52 (Silcock 2015:14).

bases were abandoned in favor of Cebu, where Harada was located at the end of the war at the 33rd Naval Special Base (Smith 1991:609). There the last of the midgets fought to the close of the Philippine campaign from an advance base at Dumaguete at the southern side of Negros Island, where they sortied to ambush US forces coming through Surigao Strait into the Mindanao Sea.

While the Japanese claimed to have sunk a destroyer with a midget attack on December 8 and two transports on December 18 in Ormoc Bay, the reports were false. Another Japanese claim that a later, newly developed Type D sub sank a cruiser and four cargo ships in early 1945 likewise is not supported by either Japanese or US records. The United States, however, did sink a submarine in Ormoc Bay on November 28, 1944, and while the target was listed as a possible I-boat, it may well have been a midget. Another of the Cebu-based midgets was definitely lost when it was stranded in December (Holmes 1966:398). The Cebu midgets were the last Japanese submarine forces left in the Philippines by February

Japanese prisoners of war working on HA-53, raised by them after being scuttled at Rabaul, 1945. (Australian War Memorial, P09445.004)

HA-53, the prototype Type B midget submarine, was raised after the war and then rescuttled. It is a deep and dark dive in Rabaul Harbor to visit the wreck. (Robert Halstead)

HA-52 lies close to its tender, *Sanko Maru*, in Three Islands Harbour in New Hanover. After an aerial attack sank the tender on November 16, 1944, the crew of HA-52 scuttled the submarine. The wreck is a popular dive site. (Copyright © Don Silcock)

A Type C boat, HA-69, photographed on board Transport No. 5, outside Kure Harbor, August 17, 1944. (Imperial War Museum, MH.6528)

1945. A plan to send the larger submarine RO-43 to Cebu with torpedoes and supplies for the midgets was called off by naval headquarters; the midgets, as always, were expendable.

An attack on USS *Boise* (CL-47) on January 5, 1945, as it approached Luzon by three midgets was met by the destroyers USS *Nicholas* (DD-449) and *Taylor* (DD-468). *Boise* executed an emergency turn and evaded a torpedo by maneuvering "radically at high speeds" (Commanding Officer, USS *Boise* 1945). An escorting TBF aircraft from a nearby carrier spotted one sub, and a well-placed bomb drove it to the surface, where *Taylor* rammed and depth charged it, sending the *kō-hyōteki* and its crew to the bottom (Commanding Officer, USS *Boise* 1945). The other two midgets escaped, reporting back in Cebu they had sunk an American destroyer and one other warship (Rohwer 1983:287). The midgets based at Dumaguete waged a bitter war against the US Navy through March, reporting various unverified successes and one successful attack.[7] In what was likely an attack by a Dumaguete-based midget on February 21, the destroyer USS *Renshaw* (DD-499) was hit with a single torpedo while escorting landing ships and craft through Surigao Strait. The torpedo tore into the destroyer, killing nineteen of the crew.[8] The ship's log reported: "Ship is dead in the water. Examination shows that forward engine room and the after fire room are completely flooded and open to the sea. The bulkhead between the after fire room and after engine room is intact but bulging aft about one foot. There are numerous leaks from bulkhead ruptures where cable pass through the bulkhead that are slowly leaking and flooding the after engine room" (*Renshaw* Log, February 21, 1945).[9]

Drifting without power, *Renshaw* engaged the midget with a 40 mm antiaircraft gun. The midget escaped, and after starting an emergency generator, and with assistance of other ships, *Renshaw* survived.

In March, as troops landed at Cebu, the destroyers USS *Conyngham* (DD-371) and *Flusser* (DD-368) encountered another midget and bracketed it with shells, but it escaped. The next morning, however, the destroyer *Newman* (DE-205) spotted a midget some 7 miles south of the previous day's encounter. Approaching the sub, *Newman*'s crew opened fire with automatic weapons, reporting they had struck the conning tower and possibly sank it (Morison 1963:236). It was the end of the *kō-hyōteki* force at Cebu; the remaining three subs were scuttled, and the base and sub crews joined land forces defending Cebu (Willoughby and Prange 1994:548, n. 72; Vego 2006:298).[10] When the battle ended, the Japanese lost 5,500 men, and another 8,500 troops surrendered (Smith 1991:617).[11]

The summer of 1944 also saw the Japanese send a force of eleven Type C boats to Okinawa. A base at Unten Ko, a small village on the north shore of the Motubu Peninsula, on the northwest shore of the island, housed them in a tiny harbor in the lee of two small offshore islets, Kouri and Yaguchi (Appleman et al. 1948:142–43). The base also housed a torpedo depot and four squadrons of explosive-packed Shinyo suicide boats. The base's presence was known to US forces, and an aircraft carrier strike on October 10, 1944, hit it and sank at least two midgets and the depot ship, the 5,160 ton *Jingei*. A later report claimed that four midgets were sunk in the attack (Appleman et al. 1948:45). This may be true, for by March 1945, only six operational midgets remained, three of which sortied on March 25 to attack TF 54, the Okinawa bombardment force. Only one of the *kō-hyōteki*, HA-67, returned, its crew claiming their torpedoes hit an "enemy battleship." The attack may have been on the destroyer USS *Halligan* (DD-584). On March 26, while patrolling off Okinawa, the bow of the destroyer exploded, with the forward half of the ship literally disintegrating, killing 160 of the 327-man crew.[12] The badly damaged ship drifted ashore and was a total loss. US Navy accounts state *Halligan* struck a mine, but the commander of HA-67 reported he fired two torpedoes at a ship that exploded on that date.[13] If true, it was the only midget submarine success at that stage of the war (Stille 2014:44). On the same day, however, the minesweeper USS *Strength* (AM-309) reported it came under attack from a partially

USS *Snatch*'s late 1945 recovery of a scuttled Type C midget submarine from the captured Cebu base was documented by Lieutenant Louie C. Weed. This report offers the only known closeup views of one of the Philippine-based midget submarines. (US Naval Institute)

TYPE C MIDGETS IN GUAM

At least one Type C *hei-gata* submarine was wrecked at Guam, but there is no specific combat record in Japanese sources, the only documentation being detachments sent to the Marianas and lost en route or at Saipan.[14] Nonetheless, there is a submarine in Guam. Another wreck reported to be a midget submarine may be a submarine-shaped Japanese military cargo tube that was visible for years on the sand bar at the mouth of the Umatac River where it flows in Umatac Bay. It was sighted ashore on July 10, 1944, by aircraft from the carriers *Wasp* and *Coral Sea* during the navy's aerial and shore bombardment support of the Guam invasion, and then investigated and shelled by USS *Halford* (DD-480) with 5 inch / 38 caliber AA rounds (Commanding Officer, USS *Halford* 1944); a spotting aircraft reported "numerous hits" on the craft, which reportedly was "no. 651" (Commanding Officer, USS *Bennett* 1944).

The wrecked craft is a registered territorial archaeological site.[15] The submarine was discovered abandoned offshore in the shallows of Togcha Beach near Talafofo after the invasion and recapture of Guam in August 1944. Hauled out, it was not scrapped, but the interior was gutted. Reportedly, three days after the discovery of the craft, the three crew members surrendered to US forces from their hiding place near the beach, but the account may be apocryphal. In 1945, the navy placed the submarine on outdoor display at Camp Dealey, a rest and recreation facility for submariners, where it remained until 1952, when Camp Dealey closed.

The navy shipped the submarine to Naval Base Guam. The craft remained on display there, with a painted number "51" on the conning tower along with a Rising Sun flag, for the next 50 years.[16] Concern over the condition of the submarine led to a comprehensive survey in 1989 by Naval Architect Don Birkholz Jr.; the craft was also surveyed and documented archaeologically by James Delgado in 1990. The interior retains some fittings, including the torpedo tubes (with their end caps cut off), wiring, switches, valves, the ladder for the conning tower, and the mount and air intake for the generator that charged the batteries.

The craft retained sufficient integrity to be listed in the National Register of Historic Places in February 2000, and the following year, the craft was restored under a navy contract as a significant artifact. In 2008, the submarine, with "51" stenciled on its conning tower, was placed outside the main gate of the Naval Base Guam to form a prominent outdoor display at the T. Stell Newman Visitor Center for War in the Pacific National Historical Park.

submerged midget submarine, which fired its torpedoes but missed. In the confusion of the battle and the loss of most of the Japanese contingent and records, the reality of the role of the midget submarines in the battle for Okinawa will likely never be known.

On that same day, the cruisers USS *Wichita* (CA-45), *Biloxi* (CL-80), and *St. Louis* (CL-49) reported spotting torpedo tracks in the morning. USS *Callaghan* (DD-792) definitely accounted for one of the midgets that day. While screening the battleship USS *New Mexico* (BB-40), the

A postwar view of the Type C midget submarine that washed ashore in Guam, as originally displayed at Camp Dealey until 1952. It is now displayed at the T. Stell Newman Visitor Center in Agana. (James P. Delgado)

The Type C midget submarine on display in 2015. (National Park Service)

The midget submarine base at Unten Ko, Okinawa, under attack. (National Archives)

destroyer's crew noticed "a small periscope . . . about 35 yards to port and abreast the bridge" (Commanding Officer, USS *Callaghan* 1945). The destroyer went hard to port and depth charged the area, blowing the sub to the surface. Rolling on its side, the sub sank. *Callaghan* kept depth charging until an oil slick and pieces of wood from the midget's interior rewarded their efforts (Commanding Officer, USS *Callaghan* 1945).

Another midget attacked the transport USS *Catron* (APA-71) on April 5, but the torpedo missed the ship and exploded on the reef. The following day, the last operational submarine at Okinawa was scuttled, and the base and sub crews joined the naval forces of Rear Admiral Minoru Ota and the land forces of General Mitsuri Ushijima's 32nd Army for a last-ditch fight to the death with the invading US forces. The base at Unten Ko was cut off and isolated on April 7, when the 29th Marines reached Nago and isolated the Motobo Peninsula. The Marines discovered twenty-one sub pens and six destroyed midgets when they reached the base, another tangible reminder of the failure of a once-vaunted program and its craft (Dyer 1972:1100).[17]

After the fall of the island, and the death of most of its defenders, a small group of seven of the

CLEANING UP THE UNTEN KO MIDGET SUBMARINE BASE

With the fall of Okinawa and the destruction of the midget submarine base at Unten Ko on the Motobu Peninsula, victorious US Naval units moved in to clear the area of hazards and to ready the small bay as a typhoon refuge for navy small craft. The minesweeper *Industry* (AMc-86) arrived on July 7th and on the 9th commenced dive operations on "several sunken midget submarines," rigging a bow section of one with the torpedoes still inside it for raising by USS *Mahogany* (AM-23) on July 22. After analyzing it and sending their report to naval intelligence on the bow and the torpedoes, the team from *Industry* then detonated the torpedoes inside the bow with it pulled ashore, resulting in a shower of "flying metal, rocks, and clods with no injuries. Thereafter, it was the custom to explode dangerous ordnance underwater" (Commander, USS *Industry* 1945:2). The war diary of Commander Mine Squadron Four, overseeing the Unten Ko operations, noted that the actual count was "one complete midget sub, one bow section, one amidships section, four torpedoes, four depth charges" (Commander Mine Squadron Four 1945:2).

In early August, divers from *Industry* worked for 2 weeks to ready an intact submarine, which was pulled up by the net tenders *Catclaw* (AN-60) and *Baretta* (AN-41) "for investigation by Naval Intelligence" before being scuttled (USS *Industry* War Diary 1945:3).

USS *Catclaw* (AN-60) and USS *Baretta* (AN-41) raising a sunken Type C midget submarine as part of clearing operations at the former midget submarine base at Unten Ko, Okinawa, 1945. This craft was then rescuttled in Buckner Bay. (National Archives, 80-G-3500054)

kō-hyōteki corps joined fifteen infantry soldiers in an attempt to escape to Japan. Pushing off from Okinawa in a small barge in early August, they drifted through the islands without food and water for 3 weeks, strafed on occasion by American planes. Eight survivors were reportedly rescued on August 18 by an unnamed US submarine (Warner and Seno 1986:194–95).

Desperate Measures

In its final phase, the midget submarine program finally dropped all pretenses and openly shifted to *tokku*, or suicide tactics. The concept, reinforced from the beginning by the response to the disastrous loss of all boats and crews at Pearl Harbor, Diego Suarez, and Sydney, was pushed forward by two of the *kō-hyōteki* corps, Lieutenant (j.g.) Hiroshi Kuroki and Ensign Sekio Nishina (Boyd and Yoshida 1995:168). As part of the *kō-hyōteki* force sent in *Chiyoda* and *Nisshin* to Midway, the two had been frustrated and angered by the defeat and believed that had they been allowed to deploy, they could have made a difference.[18]

Also aware of the limitations of their craft, they proposed modifying torpedoes into fast, human-piloted craft (*ningen gyorai*). The weapon of choice was Japan's highly successful Model 93 "Long Lance" oxygen-driven torpedo. Exceptionally fast, and with greater range than the Allied steam-driven torpedo, the Model 93 was

Lieutenant Sekio Nishina (left) and Lieutenant Yoshinori Kamibeppu, young proponents of the *kaiten* corps. Nishina and Hiroshi Kuroki were essentially the "founders" of the corps. After Kuroki's death in training in September 1944, Nishina carried his ashes with him in a *kaiten* launched against the US fleet at Ulithi on November 20, 1944. Nishina detonated his *kaiten* against USS *Mississinewa*, and the two founders were reunited in death, carrying with them many of *Mississinewa*'s crew. Kamibeppu was killed when I-37, the submarine carrying his *kaiten* and others, was sunk by USS *Conklin* (DE-439) and USS *McCoy Reynolds* (DE-440) off Kossol Roads in the Palaus on November 17, 1944. (Kaiten Memorial Museum, Japan / Michael Mair)

a 6,000 lb, 30-foot-long weapon with a 49 knot speed and a 21 mile range. The "Long Lance" had inflicted tremendous losses throughout the war. Nishina and Kuroki took their rough sketches of how to modify a torpedo to a civilian employee at Kure, Hiroshi Suzukawa, who worked with them to perfect the design and present it. Longer, thicker, and with a small compartment for the pilot (who would crouch inside, peering through a small periscope), the weapon carried a 3,000 lb charge. While slower (now 40 knots), it now had an increased range of 40 miles. Kuroki, Nishina, and Suzukawa named the new craft *kaiten*, or "return to heaven," and believed the weapon would alter Japan's fate (Ohnuki-Tierney 2002:161).

Initially rejected by Navy headquarters when first presented in January 1943, a year later, the weapon and a change in the *kō-hyōteki* program was approved. Recruits from throughout the navy were gathered and told, "Your Motherland faces imminent peril. Consider how much your

Launching a *kaiten* from the cruiser *Kitakami*, near Kure, on February 26, 1945, in test trials. (Imperial War Museum, MH.6529)

Motherland needs you. Now, a weapon which will destroy the enemy has been born. If there are any among you who burn with a passion to die gloriously for the sake of their country, let them step forward" (as cited in Cook and Cook 1992:306). Trained at a secret base at Otsujima, the *kaiten* corps started small, training as bloody campaigns in the Palaus and the fall of Peleliu foreshadowed for Japanese naval intelligence a closing ring that would culminate in the Japanese home islands. One of their ranks was a young man named Yutaka Yokota, who later recalled that when he heard about Pearl Harbor, he was a 16-year-old finishing middle school and was "really impressed by the nine war gods of the midget submarines who were credited by the papers with much of the success at Hawai'i" (Yokota and Harrington 1962:307). A more pragmatic view, offered by Pearl Harbor I-boat veteran Zenji Orita after seeing a *kaiten* for the first time, was "Things must be really bad if we have to resort to this!" (Orita and Harrington 1976:240).

The first sortie of a *kaiten* came just after the initial attack from the sky by the kamikaze corps at Leyte on October 25, 1944. Three I-boats, each carrying four *kaiten*, sailed for the American fleet anchorage at recently occupied Ulithi Atoll in early November (Boyd and Yoshida 1995:169; Orita and Harrington 1976:243–44). One of the mother boats, I-37, never made it, as it was sunk by American destroyers en route (Orita and Harrington 1976:244). But I-36 and I-47 did and launched an incomplete strike just after midnight on November 20 with five *kaiten*, after two became stuck in their cradles and one developed a leak (Orita and Harrington 1976:251–53). Only one *kaiten* made it into the anchorage to strike a blow—a hit on the fleet tanker USS *Mississinewa* (AO-59), which had just arrived laden with 404,000 gallons of aviation gasoline, 9,000 barrels of diesel oil, and 90,000 barrels of navy special fuel oil. Lying at anchor in 23 fathoms near the lagoon entrance, *Mississinewa* was one of more than a hundred ships inside the atoll, including the battleships

I-47 departs Kure with the first *kaiten* to deploy into combat, the Kikusui group, on November 9, 1944. They were en route to Ulithi. (Kaiten Memorial Museum, Japan / Michael Mair)

Lieutenant Sekio Nishina and his fellow *kaiten* pilots salute from the deck of I-47 as they prepare to depart for Ulithi. (Kaiten Memorial Museum, Japan / Michael Mair)

North Carolina (BB-55) and *Washington* (BB-56), the carriers *Essex* (CV-9) and *Ticonderoga* (CV-14), and the cruisers *Salt Lake City* (CA-25) and *Pensacola* (CA-24).

The blast set the ship ablaze, and as explosions ripped through the ship, the survivors, some badly burned, leapt into the sea as flames and a massive, dense cloud of black smoke climbed into the sky. *Mississinewa* sank with 60 of its 298-man crew (Mair and Waldron 2014). When I-36 and I-47 returned to Kure, a postmission briefing for officers and *kaiten* pilots claimed that the attackers had sunk three aircraft carriers and two battleships. The room erupted in cheers, and as one pilot later said, postwar, "The kaiten was now a proven weapon. It had shown what it could do. If luck smiles on me, I too would send a carrier to the bottom of the sea!" (Yokota and Harrington 1962:53). The false claims for the *kaiten* strike at Ulithi followed the same disingenuous pattern set with the earlier midget submarines, encouraging even greater, needless sacrifice as the war entered its final months. The attitude of "joyful self-immolation" that permeated the *kaiten* crews owed its esprit de corps to Pearl Harbor, noted Kennosuke Torisu, late war operations officer for the Sixth Fleet. The strike at Ulithi followed the same doomed pattern set at Pearl Harbor, "expended wastefully against well-protected U.S. anchorages," although, at Torisu's urging, at the end of the war "they [were] freed to attack convoys at sea" (Torisu in Evans 1986:442).

From the end of 1944 through August 1945, the *kaiten* corps carried out ten sorties through the remaining Pacific theater where Japan could contest the Allied push but with increasingly weaker weapons, which ultimately is what the *kaiten* turned out to be (Boyd and Yoshida 1995:170). The stories of *kaiten* valor and success were meanwhile spread throughout the corps. The reality was a grim account of a few hits with a larger number of *kaiten* being caught and detonated by gunfire, depth charged, or simply disappearing. On January 22, 1945, I-48 was caught

USS *Mississinewa* burns and capsizes after the successful *kaiten* attack on November 27, 1944. (Sid Harris)

with four *kaiten* off Ulithi by alert carrier aircraft and sunk in a concerted attack by the destroyer escorts *Conklin* (DE-439), *Corbesier* (DE-438), and *Raby* (DE-698), an even greater loss of men and equipment (Orita and Harrington 1976:259).

Near successes included a *kaiten* at Kossol Roads that came within 40 yards of hitting the USS *Prometheus* (AR-3) on January 12, 1945; spotted and fired on, the *kaiten* raced forward in a hail of 40 mm, 20 mm, and .50 caliber fire that "poured into her" until exploding 50 yards off the starboard beam of LST-225, knocking men to the decks and blowing off the LST's hatch covers (Commanding Officer, USS LST-225 1945). On April 28, the destroyer USS *Ringness* (APD 100) engaged and sank a less successful *kaiten*, which approached at "an unusual high speed" and then submerged after being fired on and depth charged. It exploded "2000 yards from original attack, raising water and debris in air for height of 150 to 200 feet" (Commanding Officer, USS *Ringness* 1945). *Kaiten* from I-53 struck another blow on July 24, 1945, when a convoy of LSTs was attacked while en route from Okinawa to the Philippines. The destroyer escort USS *Underhill* (DE-682) was one of nine escorts and in the number one station ahead of the convoy when a mine was discovered.

Stopping to sink the mine by gunfire, the DE made sonar contact at 13:57; dropping depth charges, it brought up oil and debris. Reporting it had sunk a "midget," the DE was told another sub had been spotted by another escort, PC-804.

DESTROYING THE LAST OF THE MIDGETS

Occupation forces in Japan discovered 115 completed as well as 496 incomplete Type D (*Tei Gata*) *Koryu* midget submarines, including many inside a floating dry dock filled with hundreds of craft at Kure, part of a massive fleet of craft intended to protect Tokyo Bay. Others were at the Mitsubishi plant in Nagasaki. After selecting some for study by the US Naval Technical Mission to Japan, the others were blown up inside the dock in early 1947. One survivor, an extensively "cut-away" *koryu*, was displayed for many years at the US Naval Base, Yokosuka. Other craft were towed offshore and scuttled. The war diary of USS *Molala* (ATF-106) reports that on September 22, 1945, they sank "six suicide boats and seven midget subs. Sinking the midget subs was a little more ticklish than the suicide boats due to the fact that the warheads were still in the subs, and the utmost care was taken in towing them to sea. The subs were sunk by planting small demolition charges" (Commander, USS *Molala* 1945:4). In this fashion, the remnants of the midget submarine force were destroyed or sent to the bottom, leaving a handful of surviving craft as war trophies.

The end of the midget submarine program. Captured Type D midget submarines sit in dry dock before their destruction by Allied Forces, 1945. (US Naval Institute)

Underhill responded and spotted a periscope off the starboard bow. The captain gave the order to ram, and as general quarters was sounded, *Underhill* surged ahead, striking the *kaiten*. Lieutenant (j.g.) Elwood M. Rich, the senior surviving officer, reported that there were two slight jars and then a massive explosion, quickly followed by another, which blew the destroyer in half. "The bow was seen floating, bow up, away from the ship at a distance of about 200 yards" (Senior Surviving Officer, USS *Underhill* 1945). The stern remained afloat, partially filled with water and listing to port as it slowly settled. A small fire was quickly extinguished before it spread on the oil-soaked wreck. Nearby ships recovered survivors and sank *Underhill* with gunfire.

The attack on *Underhill* was the last success of the midget and *kaiten* program. The tenth and last sortie left on I-159 on August 16, 2 days after Japan's surrender, but returned 2 days later with its *kaiten* unfired. Japanese crews began disarming the remaining *kaiten*, draining fuel, and preparing for the arrival of American occupation forces. Thus ended the *kaiten* program. *Kaiten* pilot Yutaka Yokota noted, postwar, that eighty-eight pilots had been killed in action and another fifteen had died in training accidents. Eight larger Japanese submarines and six hundred crew members had been lost while carrying *kaiten*. In exchange, while the Japanese estimated and claimed they had sunk between forty and fifty enemy ships, they had sunk only two. The path embarked on at Pearl Harbor ended as it had begun, with grim and unnecessary sacrifice by young men sent to fight with the wrong weapons, abetted by propaganda and lies.

As Kennosuke Torisu, the veteran who postwar became Japan's foremost scholar on the *kaiten*, noted, "Saddest of all in light of the sacrifices the *kaiten* entailed was their utter failure as weapons of war" (Torisu in Evans 1986:442). The sadness of their sacrifice is underscored even more in the postwar comment by veteran US naval officer Bruce McCandless, who noted that sinkings by *kaiten* "could hardly be called a profitable enterprise. In fact, the Imperial Navy did a lot better with its torpedoes before the human guidance system was added" (McCandless 1962:120). It all began, as did so many other aspects of Japan's defeat in the war, with the mistakes made at Pearl Harbor.

The misuse of the *kō-hyōteki* was a critical mistake. It speaks to the failure of the leadership of the Imperial Japanese Navy to utilize the craft for exactly what they had originally been envisioned as: harbor-based coastal defense weapons. Contrary to the original plan, they were designed as ship-launched submarines and utilized in the middle of ocean-ocean battles, with very little effectiveness and major crew casualties. This was not unique to the midget submarines; as Carpenter and Polmar (1986:11) note, the navy changed submarine tactics six times in 4 years of war, and "it was the Japanese Navy's repeated use of submarines for purposes for which they were not designed that was a major reason for the failure of the submarine force to achieve a creditable combat record."

CHAPTER FIVE

The *Ward* Midget

There are two fundamental aspects to the full archaeological understanding of Pearl Harbor's midget submarines: a nautical (naval) and a maritime (battlefield) aspect. The first focuses on the individual craft—in this case the Type A *kō-hyōteki* employed at Pearl Harbor and, with modifications, at Diego Suarez, Sydney, Guadalcanal, and Kiska. Japanese plans and specifications seem to have disappeared at the end of the war, possibly consumed in surrender bonfires to keep the secrets safe from victorious enemy eyes. What have survived are the plans and photographs made by the allies of captured midget submarines during the war, which offer an array of technical detail, especially when the documentation made by both US and Australian examiners of Pearl Harbor and Sydney's submarines is compared and assembled. That body of documentation, when compared to the archaeological data, serves to better illuminate the specifics of the Type A *kō-hyōteki* than relying on either set of data alone. Such is the premise and promise of historical archaeology.

The second aspect of understanding the midget submarines at Pearl Harbor involves assessing the midget submarines within the parameters of battlefield archaeology. As Conlin and Russell (2006:36) point out, "battlefield archaeology is fundamentally about looking beyond individual sites and small-scale activity areas to larger events." This approach provides the archaeologist with the opportunity to "analyze the progression of the attack and the tactics involved by carefully documenting the material remains." While the historical record of the Pearl Harbor attack and subsequent narratives have examined the conduct and role of the midget submarines, what was missing for several decades was the material record of both the first midget sunk and the last, unaccounted-for, midget submarine.

All the Pearl Harbor *kō-hyōteki* have been accounted for thanks to the research and discoveries of the Hawai'i Undersea Research Laboratory, and we are now able to offer interpretations within the framework of battlefield archaeology to place the midgets within their context beyond the observations made during and immediately after the attack by American participants in the battle.[1] In this, we also see how the battlefield archaeology of the midget submarine attacks at Pearl Harbor not only fits within the universal generalizations of the battle but also offers insight and historical understanding of particular

Pearl Harbor and O'ahu from space. While much of the archaeological study of the attack of December 7, 1941, has focused on what lies in and immediately adjacent to the harbor, the larger battlefield encompasses more of O'ahu, the offshore waters, and even the air—all factors that must be taken into account in attempting to reconstruct the events of December 7, 1941. (NASA)

events (Conlin and Russell 2006:41). The first particular or specific event is the engagement between USS *Ward* and a solitary *kō-hyōteki*.

USS *Ward*'s encounter with the midget was widely reported during and after the war as both the "first shot" of the war as well as the warning not heeded—or at least not quickly heeded. As the years became decades and underwater searches for the midget turned up nothing, the lack of physical "proof" began to plague some of the veterans subjected to later twentieth-century skepticism by a younger "question everything" generation. While these veterans of the encounter were distressed that there were doubts that

Ward's crew had actually sunk the midget, historians joined the veterans in noting that *Ward* had indeed sunk the midget (Warner and Seno 1986:60, along with Prange, Burlingame, etc.).[2] A series of paintings done to capture the key events of December 7, 1941, on the occasion of the fiftieth anniversary of the attack by noted naval and military artist Tom W. Freeman includes one of *Ward* surging forward and firing at the exposed conning tower of the midget (Freeman and Delgado 1991:38–39). Nonetheless, as author John Craddock notes, "since the midget sub had never been recovered, it was natural to wonder whether the event had happened at all" (Craddock 2006:2).[3] Ultimately, the discovery of the sunken midget resolved the question for any and all doubters. As archaeologists know, the material evidence can at times provide definitive proof that what was said to have happened did happen.

The Search for *Ward*'s Midget

Given that the depths of the ocean off Pearl Harbor where the midget lay are on average in excess of 330 meters (1,000 feet), finding the sunken craft lay beyond the practical limits for exploration in the aftermath of the war. The development of side-scan sonar, remotely operated vehicles, and deep diving submersibles during the Cold War that followed increasingly made it possible to find the sunken sub. The discovery of RMS *Titanic* in 1985 and subsequent deepwater discoveries underscored the fact that with systematic surveys modelled on archival and oceanographic data, pretty much anything could be found with sufficient time and funding. There remained, however, the fact that sonar alone did not always definitively identify what had been found as a wreck, as opposed to a pile of rocks arranged in suggestive shapes. Nor did a wreck that was clearly *a* wreck on sonar always turn out to be *the* wreck searchers were looking for. As was the case with shallow water discoveries, an initial sonar or magnetometer target required "ground truthing," or simply stated, laying human eyes on it.

The first search for the *Ward* midget took place in 1988, when as part of the National Park Service's survey of USS *Arizona* and other Pearl Harbor sites associated with the December 7, 1941, attack, a side-scan sonar team from the navy's Explosive Ordnance Demolition Group One (EOD 1) were asked to survey "the 1,000 foot +/– deep defensive perimeter outside the harbor mouth for a Japanese mini-sub reportedly sunk by the destroyer USS *Ward*" (Lenihan 1990:3). Based on a review of historical records analyzed by Pearl Harbor survivor and USS *Arizona* Memorial volunteer Ray Emory and USS *Arizona* Memorial Park Historian Daniel Martinez, EOD 1, under the command of Captain Steve Epperson, conducted two survey tows in 750 to 1,100 feet of water (Lenihan 1989:109). The Klein 521T side-scan sonar, coupled with a Motorola Falcon electronic positioning system, was deployed behind TWR 6 *Ferrett*, under the command of BMC Allan Connelley, and set at 100 meter side-scan scale with deep tows trailing approximately 3,000 feet of cable at speeds of 3.5 to 3.8 knots (Lenihan 1989:109).

On July 1, 1988, the team made a contact on a hard sand bottom in an estimated 850 feet of water that was identified as a "high probability for the Japanese submarine" (Lenihan 1989:115). The computed height of the object was 3.4 meters (11 feet), and the length was computed to be 22.68 meters (74 feet), "well within the expected parameters for the target. Although nothing can be said for certain without visual confirmation, the contact is congruent with the sonar signature expected from a Japanese midget submarine," although it was noted "another possibility is a metal-hulled small craft of similar dimensions sunk in the area" (Lenihan 1989:115).

Based on this, a follow-up survey with a remotely operated vehicle returned to the area in August 1990 but was unsuccessful in locating the

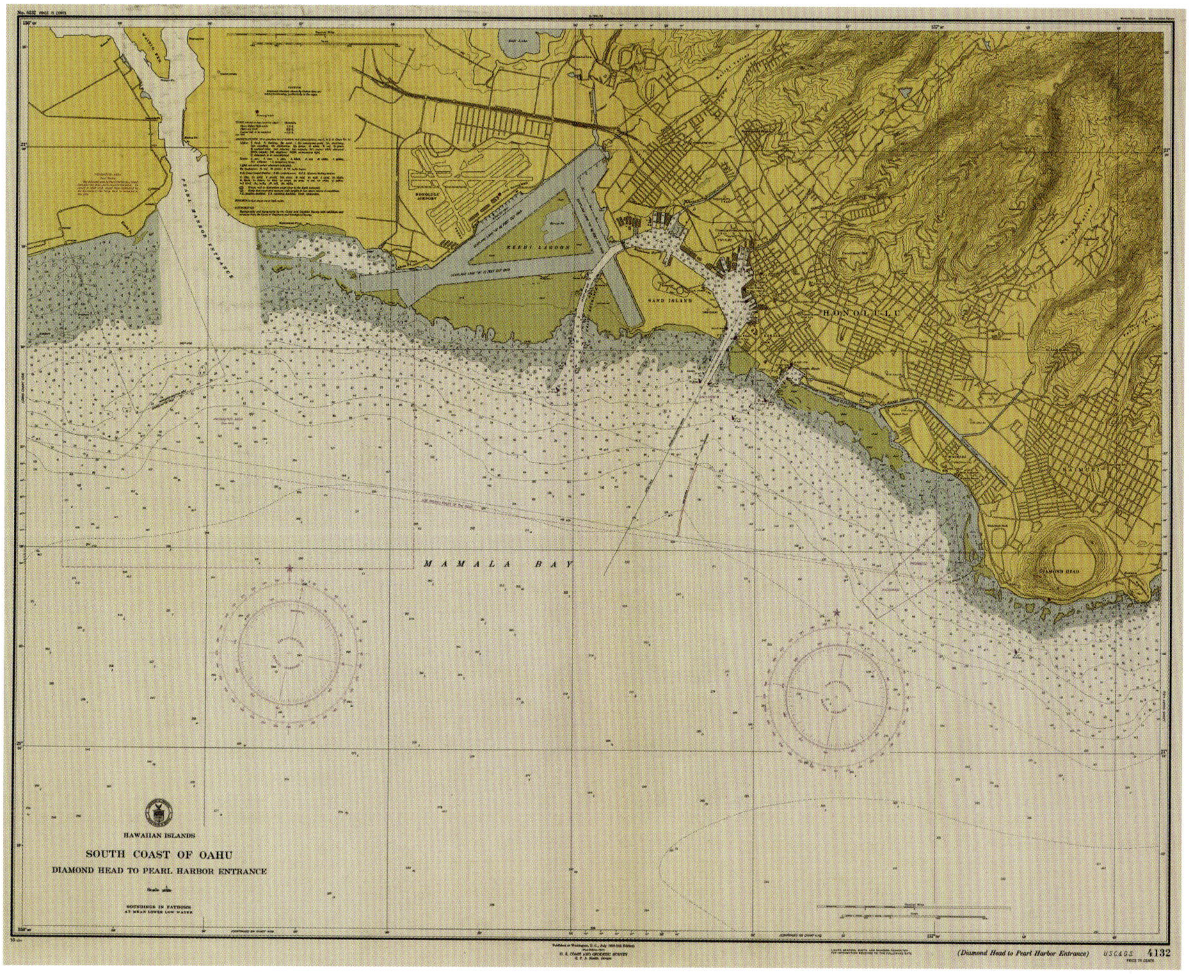

The search zone for the submarine sunk by USS *Ward*, as charted postwar and published in 1950. (NOAA Central Library, Historic Chart Collection, 4132-07-1950)

target. What the ROV instead found was the bottom littered with a variety of artifacts, including vintage naval aircraft, which had been dumped at sea before and after World War II.[4] This frustrating reality was played out on subsequent surveys, including a 1992 discovery of a section of a disarticulated midget dismissed by historians as being part of a Pearl Harbor craft (but now known to be one; see chapter 6), let alone *Ward*'s, and a well-publicized expedition by Robert Ballard in November 2000 that also failed to locate the *Ward* midget. Instead, "we found a bunch of junk," Ballard told his crew (Craddock 2006:195).[5]

The realization that the seabed off Pearl Harbor was a vast assemblage reflecting a century of naval use and discard, and that the submerged "battlefield" of USS *Ward*'s encounter with the midget submarine could be obscured by an array of other wrecks, planes, and dredge spoil, suggested that ongoing survey efforts to find the midget would be difficult and costly in terms of not only conducting sonar surveys but then diving to the 330 meter plus depths where the craft likely lay. The ultimate discovery of the submarine came, ironically, through practice deployments of two deep diving submersibles, albeit focused test dives arranged by dedicated explorers and historians who always kept a "weather eye peeled" in the best seafaring tradition.

The origins of the program that would ultimately discover *Ward*'s midget date back to World War II, when the navy conducted oceanographic research in support of the war effort through work at both Scripps and Woods Hole and postwar established the Office of Naval Research

The NPS search for the *Ward* midget, 1990. (National Park Service / Larry Murphy, James P. Delgado)

(ONR) in 1946 (Knauss 2000:3). The creation of the National Science Foundation (NSF) in 1950 provided a boost to university-supported oceanographic programs that had also benefited from the support of ONR. Starting in the late 1950s, NSF began to surpass ONR as the major supporter of American oceanographic research, especially in marine biological work, and by 1970, at the commencement of the International Decade for Ocean Exploration, NSF had assumed the more prominent role, albeit working closely with ONR as a partner and supporting parallel and joint programs (Knauss 2000:4–5).

Military-funded deep sea research faltered for a while but picked up after the 1963 loss of the nuclear submarine *Thresher* demonstrated a need for deep sea capacity to admirals who hitherto felt money spent on anything deeper than 2,500 feet (the maximum range for a nuclear attack or missile sub) was a waste (Broad 1997:55–64). After *Thresher*, the navy's deep sea program continued with renewed vigor. Significant developments and incredible innovations followed in submersible, robotic, and imaging technology. All of this was done under a veil of secrecy, with the technology and missions classified as part of the Cold War. Deep operations recovered components and intelligence from sunken Soviet nuclear submarines; recovered lost American hydrogen bombs; developed a global system of undersea microphones, the Sound Surveillance System (SOSUS), for listening to Soviet naval activity; and even tapped into Soviet deep sea communications cables. Only with the end of the Cold War in 1991 did some of these assets begin to "surface" and enter the scientific community as well as public awareness (Broad 1997:84–89).

On the unclassified, civilian side of deep ocean science, after a congressional directive to ONR to only fund science with direct military applications also came into play in 1970, the National Science Foundation increased their participation and provided additional funding for deep sea research. Another 1970 development was the merging of various agencies and programs into a new entity, the National Oceanic and Atmospheric Administration (NOAA). It was under NOAA that a new program, the National Undersea Research Program (NURP), began in 1980. Under NURP, NOAA's Office of Ocean and Atmospheric Research leased submersibles and remotely operated vehicles (ROVs) to six regional laboratories throughout the United States in support of oceanographic research.

One of those national laboratories is the Hawai'i Undersea Research Laboratory (HURL) at the University of Hawai'i's School of Ocean and Earth Sciences and Technology at Manoa.[6] Established in 1980 with the birth of NURP, HURL's mission is "to support academic- and government-based science and technology experts in developing solutions to problems facing the Pacific region, NOAA, and the Nation. Preference is given to those projects targeting marine managed areas under U.S. jurisdiction. Ecosystem studies are the largest component of our research program because of the geographic locations we serve, the unique seafloor features and habitats located there, and the cadre of scientists utilizing our submersible assets which are best suited to on-bottom focused investigations and targeted sampling" (HURL 2015).[7]

The principal assets for deepwater exploration at HURL are two veteran submersibles, Pisces IV and Pisces V. Built in North Vancouver, British Columbia, the Pisces craft grew out of a prototype, Pisces I, designed and constructed by three scuba divers who defied conventional wisdom that major manufacturing capacity was necessary to construct deep sea vehicles. Their company, International Hydrodynamics Inc. (Hyco), built eleven Pisces submersibles for government and industry use between 1965 and 1975 (Henry and Dinsley 1998). Pisces IV, originally built for the Soviet Union in 1971, had its export permit blocked by the Canadian government at the request of the United States, which feared the transfer of sensitive technologies to its Cold War foe. The Canadian government instead purchased Pisces IV and operated it for several years. Pisces V, built in 1973, worked in the deep sea oil and gas industry until it was exported along with Pisces IV to the United States for HURL. Upgraded and internally modernized by HURL's Director of Operations and Senior Pilot Terry Kerby and team, and annually inspected and recertified by the American Bureau of Shipping (ABS), Pisces IV and V have been at the heart of HURL's many scientific achievements, including its ongoing maritime heritage work.

HURL commenced scientific diving operations in July 1981 with the two-person submersible *Makali'i*. Built as *Star II* in 1966, *Makali'i* had been donated to the university by its builder, General Dynamics, and had been working for several years, leased to a coral-harvesting operation, Maui Divers. The establishment of NURP in 1980 made *Makali'i* its first asset, and the craft was utilized in the July 1981 mission to Eniwetok Atoll, site of nuclear testing and the first detonation of a hydrogen bomb. The mission took scientists from the Defense Nuclear Agency, Lawrence Livermore Labs, and the Air Force Weapons Agency into the heart of the H-bomb crater, followed by 3 months of additional dives throughout the atoll with scientists from various universities, museums, and other labs. Pisces V, stored in a warehouse in Scotland after its oil and gas exploration career ended, was purchased

Terry Kerby. (HURL)

PISCES IV / PISCES V SPECIFICATIONS[8]

Dimensions: 6.09 m × 3.2 m × 3.35 m
Displacement: 11.7 metric tons
Payload: 113.4 kg
Crew: One pilot, two observers
Maximum Operating Depth: 2,000 m (6,560 feet)
Life Support: 140 hours for three people
Power: Two lead-acid battery systems
Propulsion: Two-side mounted reversible thrusters, tiltable through 100 degrees
Speed: 3 knots for 7–9 hours
The submersible is equipped with the following items and can be configured as necessary to accommodate a variety of mission requirements:

- Insite Pacific MINI-ZEUS HDTV camera
- ROS low-light CCD color camera
- B&W low-light wide-angle CCD
- Digital video recorders
- Two hydraulically operated manipulators
- General purpose science basket
- Applied Microsystems electronic CTD profiler
- Tritech SeaKing digital HD sonar
- Kongsberg-Simrad 1007 200 m altimeter
- Benthos multifrequency pinger receiver
- TrackLink 5000 HA USBL submersible tracking system
- Sonatech long baseline acoustic tracking system
- External lights: Three 250 W, two 500 W tungsten, two 400 W HMIs available
- Two KVH digital magnetic compasses
- Externally mounted temperature probes with internally mounted monitors
- Suction sampler 8-bottle Rosette
- Hydraulic cutters
- Hydraulic rotary saw
- Laser scaling system
- Push core samplers
- Sealable sediment scoops: 4 arrays of 9 samplers, capacity ~1 kg each
- Water samplers: 2 arrays of 6 samplers, capacity ~700 ml each

in 1985, as it could dive five times deeper than *Makali'i*. In 1987, an oil and gas industry support vessel bought at a bankruptcy auction was refitted to become HURL's support ship, *Ka'imikai-O-Kanaloa* (Heavenly Searcher of the Sea), also known affectionately in the deep sea science community as the *KoK*. Pisces IV was purchased from Canada in 1999.

HURL's three and a half decades of ocean exploration undertaken with its submersibles and vessels have resulted in nearly 1,900 dives "representing 9300 hours under water, and a benthic

The bow of Pisces IV. (HURL)

Pisces V. (HURL)

HURL's *KoK* and Pisces IV and Pisces V. (HURL)

ecology database derived from in-house video record logging of over 125,000 entries based on 1,100 unique deep-sea animal identifications in the Hawaiian Archipelago" (HURL 2015).[9] Important projects have included support for a mission that learned that deep sea corals are some of the oldest living organisms on earth; a 25 year study of a submarine volcano, Lo'ihi, documenting the volcanic birth of a new Hawaiian island; studying hydrothermal vent organisms; the first filming of Hawaiian monk seals in nearly 500 meters of water; a 5 month, 14,500

KoK

Built in 1979, the University of Hawai'i's research vessel (R/V) *Ka'imikai-O-Kanaloa*, or *KoK*, is a general oceanographic research vessel designed to operate in coastal and deep, blue-water areas of the ocean. In over two decades, it has ranged throughout the Pacific on its missions from its home base in Honolulu. The heart of *KoK* is its two manned submersibles, Pisces IV and Pisces V.

KoK was specially configured in 1993 to support the subs, but it also supports remotely operated vehicles (ROVs) with its stern-mounted 15 ton capacity A-frame crane and winches. It carries a Seabeam bathymetric mapping system to chart the seafloor to depths of 11 km and an acoustic Doppler current profiler to measure water velocity relative to the ship, and it can also measure seawater salinity and temperatures.

KoK carries a crew of 14 and can accommodate up to 17 scientists and can stay at sea for up to 40 days. In addition to the instruments and submersibles, the ship houses four laboratories—a rock lab to analyze and store samples brought up from the bottom of the sea, a wet lab for chemical sample analysis, a clean lab, and a dry lab.

Vessel Specifications[10]
Dimensions: 223 feet (67.97 m) × 38 feet (11.58 m) × 13.6 feet (4.4 m)
Displacement: 1,779 metric tons
Machinery: Two Detroit diesel engines, 1,350 shp (each)

KoK launching Pisces V. (HURL)

nautical mile research cruise in the central and southwestern Pacific; and "sporting an extended history of technical innovation and operational leadership in support of scientific research and management" while "providing the biggest bang for the buck" by operating its two submersibles with a crew of five specialists "at close to a 100% success rate for over ten years" (HURL 2015).[11]

HURL's first foray into maritime heritage came in 1984 with the discovery of an intact US Navy Dauntless SBD dive bomber. It sparked in the team, especially chief submersible pilot Terry Kerby, the realization that while not a formal part of their mission, making practice and shakedown dives to maritime heritage targets would add a unique element to the program and also resolve questions, as HURL put it, that left "the viewer wondering what exactly its life's story was, and just how and why it ended up in its cold, dark resting place at the bottom of the sea" (HURL 2015).[12] In the next three decades, the list of discoveries made as a result of the research and dives undertaken by Terry Kerby, Steve Price, and Max Cremer of HURL in the two Pisces subs has been an incredible inventory of not only miscellaneous artifacts, ammunition dumps, and lost aircraft, trucks, barges, and fuel tanks but also the US Navy submarines S-4 and S-19 and the postwar scuttled Japanese submarines I-14, I-201, I-400, and I-401 (the largest submarines in the world when they were built as aircraft-carrying craft capable of deploying three airplanes each). HURL has also discovered the prewar gunboat USS *Bennington*, a famous late nineteenth-century navy gunboat involved in the Spanish American War, and the cable ship *Dickenson*, later used in World War II as the USS *Kailua* and then scuttled, as well as amphibious

The discovery of the *Ward* midget. (HURL)

landing craft destroyed in the explosions at West Loch Pearl Harbor in 1944. Significantly, they also discovered two *kō-hyōteki*, which, as we will see, finally resolves the question of where all five of the midgets launched on December 7, 1941, ended up.

Terry Kerby preparing for a dive. Extensive preparations for diving the two Pisces submarines are part of the standard operations of HURL. In addition to dive planning, based on years of research, both Kerby and Steve Price of HURL have extensive knowledge of where some of the submerged history and lost craft likely rest off Pearl Harbor. (HURL)

Discovering *Ward*'s Midget

On what would be the last of a series of annual test and certification dives off Pearl Harbor in the defensive zone's "military debris field" on August 28, 2002, Pisces IV and Pisces V, diving in tandem, discovered *Ward*'s midget.[13] The search was, as HURL noted, the culmination of years of following up on HURL's towed side-scan sonar surveys of the area and following up by diving on the most promising of some 1,000 significant sonar targets. Methodical work, year after year; careful analysis by Steve Price and Terry Kerby; and then diving more often than not to find something else finally paid off. After locating the sub, the HURL team realized that on their first day of diving, August 24, they had missed the sub in 30 foot visibility water by some 90 feet.

Pisces V, piloted by Chuck Holloway and with biologists Chris Kelley and Rachel Shackelford aboard, was the first to spot the sub and guided Kerby, in Pisces IV with Colin Wollerman and Al Kaivaltis, in from 90 feet away where Kerby had paused to change the sub's carbon dioxide filtration pack, a necessary step in a long dive. The sub lay upright in 406.7 meters (1,330 feet) of water, not close to the promising sonar target found by the National Park Service in 1988, which Kerby and team had earlier assessed and discovered to be a provocatively shaped pile of rocks. The *Ward*'s midget submarine lies outside of the 1988 survey box defined by the NPS. The initial target thought to be the submarine in 850 feet of water lies about 1 km (0.6 miles) distant from the wreck. Sonar imagery can be deceptive.

Helping cinch the identification from being a Type A midget submarine to being the one sunk by USS *Ward* was the presence of a single shell hole through the conning tower, exactly where *Ward*'s crew had said they had hit on the morning of December 7, 1941. What had masked the *Ward* midget was not only that it lay in a field of dumped artifacts and debris from Pearl Harbor but also that it also lay on and next to a rock ledge (Wiltshire et al. 2002). One never knows until they go and lay eyes on a sonar target. In this case, the *Ward* midget had never been imaged by sonar and was a truly a discovery made by the unaided eye.

The hull as found in 2002 was intact, articulated and with no distortion, including no evidence of "washboarding" from depth charging or

The bow of the *Ward* midget at the time of the discovery. (HURL)

Conning tower of the *Ward* midget as discovered. (HURL)

Stern view of the *Ward* midget at the time of discovery. (HURL)

Pisces V shining lights at the bow. (HURL)

Pisces V at the stern. (HURL)

crushing from implosion from pressure by sinking unflooded. The only rupture noted in 2002 was the 4 inch shell hole from USS *Ward*'s No. 3 gun at the base of the conning tower on the starboard beam. The shell hole otherwise has no exit point visible, indicating the shell did not detonate inside the submarine but may have punched through the bottom of the hull. The stern dive planes are in the "up" position. Based on his experience in submersible craft and with the currents in the area, one of the authors (Kerby) believes the stern planes, in an upright position, would cause the bow to pitch as soon as it gathered enough speed for the control surface to take effect.

This means the submarine sank in a long, porpoising glide to the seafloor, on an easterly bearing

Profiles of the *Ward* midget. (Terry Kerby/HURL)

The *Ward* midget's glide to the sea bottom as it came to rest, as reconstructed. (Terry Kerby / HURL)

with the westerly current acting as a "headwind" and slowing the descent of the sinking craft. The submarine impacted at a slight angle at the stern where the propeller guards dug into the seafloor as the rest of the craft settled and came to rest. The impact tore free the lower propeller guard. A stern first impact may also explain why the rudder is heeled to starboard. The submarine then sat there, filling with silt, for the next six decades. Change, however, was inevitable over time.

PEARL HARBOR AND THE NAVAL DEFENSIVE SEA AREA (NDSA)

The origins of the US military presence in the "harbor of Pearl Bay" date back to the Reciprocity Treaty established between the US government and the Kingdom of Hawai'i under King Kalakaua in 1876. This treaty essentially opened the US mainland market to Hawaiian agricultural products in exchange for exclusive rights of access to Pearl Harbor, the potential of which had already been noted by surveyors of several European navies. Contention surrounding the treaty, the use of Pearl Harbor in perpetuity, and the ownership of the land surrounding the area became a moot point following the illegal overthrow of the Hawaiian government in 1893 by an annexation clique, backed by the US Minister to the Kingdom John L. Stevens and marines from the USS *Boston*. The islands were formally annexed by the United States in 1898.

Surveys to dredge the bar at Pearl Harbor channel were begun in 1900, and in 1908, Congress passed appropriations for $1,000,000 to develop Pearl Harbor as the primary defensive position of the United States in the Pacific Ocean. By the mid-1930s, approximately $42,000,000 had been spent on naval developments. Pearl Harbor would soon boast a navy yard, submarine base, hospital, air station, seaplane base, Marine barracks, ammunition depot, railway, tank farm, supply warehouses, major ship dry docks, and dozens of buildings for support activities. On May 26, 1939, President Franklin Delano Roosevelt declared, by Executive Order 8143, a Defensive Sea Area around the entrance to Pearl Harbor, extending approximately 6.5 km (4 miles) seaward off the channel mouth and restricting and controlling the entry of all persons, ships, and aircraft due to the strategic nature of the harbor and purposes of defense. The Pearl Harbor Naval Defensive Sea Area remains in place today.

THE ARCHAEOLOGY OF THE "FIRST SHOT"

Following its discovery in 2002, scientific missions to the *Ward* midget in 2003 and 2005 conducted a variety of experiments and documented the craft as part of opportunistic "ride alongs" in the traditional HURL maritime heritage model. These dives focused on retrieving environmental parameters (salinity, dissolved oxygen, pH, temperature, etc.), video survey footage, limited sediment and corrosion samples, and measurements of corrosion potential (Ecorr) at selected positions along the hull. HURL does not have historians or maritime archaeologists in their program but has a long-term interaction with both the National Park Service and NOAA's Office of National Marine Sanctuaries' Maritime Heritage Program. This partnership came into the forefront with the discovery of the *Ward* midget to conduct the archaeological and scientific assessment of the submarine. The National Park Service's Submerged Resources Center has continued to work in and around Pearl Harbor since the initial work on USS *Arizona* in the 1980s and retains a strong interest in the midget submarines as part of the mandate of the expanded World War II Valor in the Pacific National Monument, created in 2008 with the former USS *Arizona* Memorial as a key part of the new monument.[14] NOAA's Office of National Marine Sanctuaries' Maritime Heritage Program has actively worked in

Pisces V shining lights onto the conning tower. (HURL)

and around Hawai'i on a variety of naval and maritime archaeological projects and actively collaborates with the NPS. With the discovery of the submarine, NOAA, NPS, HURL, the US Navy's Naval Historical Center (NHC),[15] and the Office of Naval Research (ONR) met and agreed that protection of the submarine as an archaeological site, in situ, was the preferred approach pending discussions with the Japanese government. Until Japan signaled its wishes, it was also agreed that scientific research on the wreck and its environment was necessary to determine the preferred alternative for long-term management of the wreck. Meanwhile, NOAA sponsored a return visit to the *Ward* midget with the National Park Service in December 2003 to conduct high-resolution digital documentation of the site.

Japan's answer to the US government agreed with the American approach to the management of the submarine, notably protecting it in place as an archaeological site and war grave, but in a surprise twist, Japan transferred its ownership of the submarine to the United States. Japan and the United States jointly agreed to move forward with those principles in place on February 12, 2004, and since then, NOAA and NPS have managed the *kō-hyōteki* and continued research and monitoring of the site. The primary research objective is to collect data on the condition of the wreck and the environment, contributing to the collaborative preservation effort and management decisions.

The next major mission to the sub came in August 2005, to continue to conduct corrosion research, gather environmental data (dissolved oxygen, temperature, pH, and salinity/conductivity), and with that model, oxidation reduction potential. Additional documentation of the sub's exterior was carried out, including monitoring current-caused scouring beneath the craft that might cause it to shift or lose support.

THE MARITIME HERITAGE PROGRAM

The Maritime Heritage Program of NOAA's Office of National Marine Sanctuaries was created in 2002, although an informal program existed from the earliest years of sanctuaries. The first National Marine Sanctuary in the United States, established in 1974, was for the historic shipwreck USS *Monitor*, which rests 16 nm off Cape Hatteras, North Carolina. Since then, the National Marine Sanctuary System has grown to thirteen sanctuaries and one National Marine Monument throughout the United States and extending into the Pacific off Hawai'i and to American Samoa.

Within the system, the vast maritime cultural landscape includes submerged prehistoric sites, as well as other places of special cultural meaning to indigenous peoples, living creatures powerfully associated with those cultures, as well as evidence of human use and interaction from the historic period. That includes thousands of shipwrecks representing international, national, regional and local trade, cultural exchanges, warfare, and a wide range of significant events as well as everyday life for those who have lived, worked, and occasionally died on these waters.

The Maritime Heritage Program works not only with the cultural and heritage resources within the National Marine Sanctuary System but coordinates with other parts of NOAA; other federal, state, and local agencies; and academic, nonprofit, and citizen partners to locate, study, protect, and share the stories of those resources. That includes work outside the system, including occasional projects with resources or sites of exceptional significance outside the United States. One part of the mandate for MHP is working with NOAA's Office of General Counsel and the Department of Justice before the US District Court on matters pertaining to RMS *Titanic*, a shipwreck in international waters but with important ties to the United States.

In addition, a plan was developed to take a look inside the craft through the shell hole to conduct a nondisturbance limited interior survey using a camera endoscope system constructed to assess internal siltation (which, in addition to sealing the sub, would also affect weight distribution and stability of the wreck on the seabed), internal corrosion, and inventory exposed artifacts. The project team included Terry Kerby, Hans Van Tilburg, and David Conlin as well as HURL pilot Max Cremer, archaeologist Kelly Gleason Keogh from the Office of National Marine Sanctuaries, videographer John Brooks from NOAA, Director of the Office of National Marine Sanctuaries Daniel Basta, Director of the Office of Naval Research Admiral Jay Cohen, and archaeologist Barbara Voulgaris from the Naval Historical Center.

The exterior corrosion study used methods similar to those used in an ongoing corrosion study of USS *Arizona*. During the dive, several small segments of marine concretion were recovered from the aft end of the midget sub by the robotic arm of Pisces V. These samples were analyzed in metallurgical and chemistry laboratories at the University of Nebraska–Lincoln, and X-ray diffraction measurements were conducted at the Air Force Research Laboratory at Eglin Air Force Base, Florida. The NPS's Submerged Resources Center, in partnership with researchers at Michigan State University, University of Nebraska-Lincoln, University of New Mexico,

The National Marine Sanctuary System, 2015. (Matt McIntosh / NOAA ONMS)

Off the coast of North Carolina, NOAA divers document the German U-701, lost in combat during the Battle of the Atlantic in 1942. (NOAA)

The Maritime Heritage Program's fieldwork includes diving on sites as well as working in the shallows. Here, in Hawai'i, students with the University of Hawai'i's Marine Option Program study wrecks off Lana'i Beach, a long-established ship graveyard. (NOAA)

and Eglin Air Force Base, has been developing a low impact model for the measurement of steel hull corrosion rates on submerged steel and iron shipwreck sites. The *Ward* midget offered an excellent opportunity to test this model in a deepwater environment. Preliminary results suggest a corrosion rate of 0.05 mm per year, equivalent to a metal thickness loss of 0.9 mm over a 60 year period (original hull material 8 mm cold rolled MS44 steel plate). It must be emphasized that these data are approximations, and the corrosion investigation represents ongoing work (Wilson et al. 2007).

As with many deep ocean projects, annual monitoring and assessments are often contingent on availability of funding. HURL made additional dives to assess the condition of the submarine in 2007 and 2009 as part of their planned training operations. The dives have shown that the submarine's condition has changed in the decade since discovery, reflecting a dynamic marine environment and the fact that the submarine is not in stasis, which may in time suggest a different approach in managing it if, for example, it breaks open and exposes its interior to the open ocean and current.

Changes over Time: The Submarine Site in 2002–14

The *Ward kō-hyōteki* rests 4.81 km (2.6 nm) offshore, in 406.7 m of water (1,330 ft). At that depth (August 2005), the surrounding seawater possesses a salinity of 35 psu, dissolved oxygen

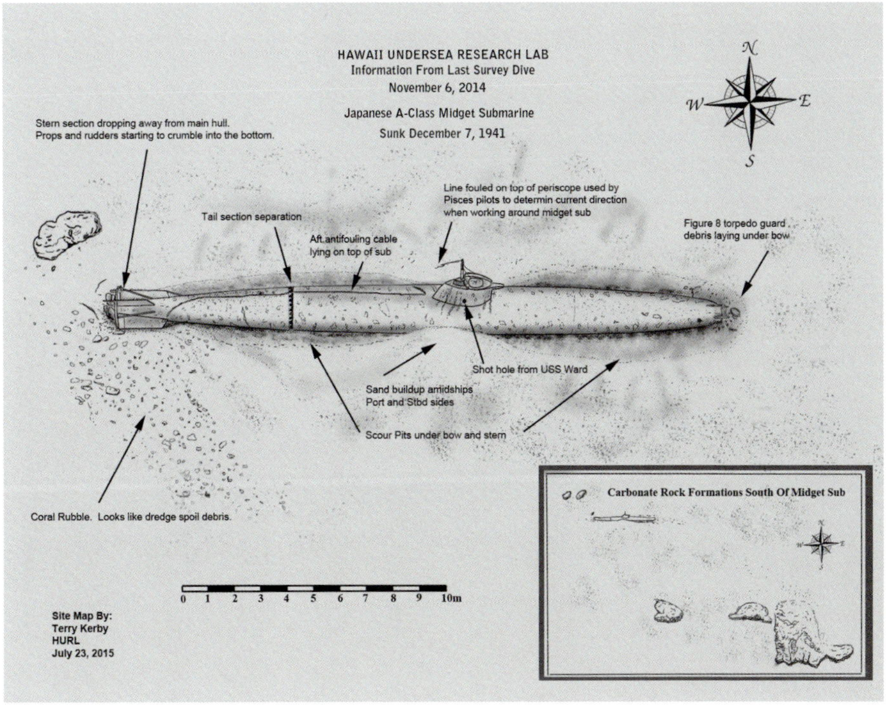

Site Plan, *Ward* midget submarine. (Terry Kerby / HURL)

level of 4.2 mg/L, pH of 8, and temperature that varies between 8 and 11 degrees Celsius over a 24 hour period. Hawaiian ocean currents are very complex. They are the result of large-scale ocean currents combining with coastal tidal currents, wind currents, waves, and coastal topography. The generalized circulation pattern outside Pearl Harbor varies with the tidal cycle. Water moves slightly shoreward during flood tide, while the ebb circulation moves eastward under general prevailing trade wind conditions. Tidal current speeds vary and can be in excess of one knot. The NDSA area is in the protected lee of the island, so effects from the prevailing northeasterly tradewinds are minimal. The bottom currents are westward, but magnitude and variability are unknown (Wiltshire et al 2002:36).

The *Ward*'s submarine lies upright, angled some 12 to 15 degrees to port, on a bottom distinguished by a carbonate substrate and sediment. The submarine lies on an east-west axis.

Scouring at the bow has left a depression underneath the forward torpedo and forward battery compartments, while sediment has mounded up amidships on the port side abaft the conning tower. Scouring at the stern has been dramatic and has wrought significant changes to the sub since its discovery, as over time the stern has dropped onto the harder substrate as sand supporting it washed away, opening a gap in the hull at the joint where the stern section joins the middle section of the sub. The propeller guards and propellers rest in direct contact with

The sub's position on the outcrop. (Terry Kerby / HURL)

The stern of the submarine as discovered. (HURL)

the substrate, which was not the case when it was found in 2002.

A limited interior visual survey was conducted in 2005 via a pole-mounted low-light camera lens held in place by the Pisces' manipulator through the shell hole in the conning tower. The operation was done carefully and slowly, to avoid damaging the submarine or disturbing the silt and obscuring the camera's vision. The placement of the camera pole involved rotating and inserting it in a 10 centimeter (4 inch) hole at the angle the shell entered, from above and at a sharp angle from the hull. The camera's limited range of motion and particulate matter in the water column obscured many of the finer details in the command space.

The interior images revealed some sedimentation, as well as marine life (sponges and crabs), indicating both water and oxygen circulation within the interior. Several features in the conning tower and on the lower port side of the small command space could be made out, including periscope shaft and control cables, the periscope's handles (in the up position, which is odd as it is the stowed position), and the retractable access ladder (folded down in the in-use position), as well as the top of the helm (which is a steel wheel). Comparison to the schematics available from the Australian War Museum's Sydney submarines suggests that the equipment visible in the lower aft space of the compartment may be the vertical rudder gear, and visible portside features were likely the master gyrocompass housing (portside forward) and equipment, possibly control valves, near the helmsman's seat position (portside).

The interior of the submarine's lower central section is filled with silt at least 30 to 45 cm (1 to 1.5 ft) to the level of the equipment on the port side. Whether the silt extends fore and aft into the other portions of the submarine is unknown, though even if the internal hatches are open (limited mobility prevented examination), the amount of possible silt in the forward and aft compartments is likely to be much less than in the central command space immediately below the shell hole and therefore not a major factor in additional weight throughout the submarine. No human remains were observed during the interior inspection.

An even layer of concretion including rusticles covers the exposed exterior areas of the hull. Marine life growing on the underside of the sub suggests that the current scouring at the bow and stern is not a new process. When discovered, it was noted that both Type-97 (mini) torpedoes remained loaded in the forward tubes. The characteristic "figure eight" torpedo guard for the Pearl Harbor attack *kō-hyōteki* was visible and intact without any apparent distortion or damage in 2003, but in 2009, HURL pilots discovered that the figure-eight torpedo guard had fallen off the bow. This was apparently due to the forces of natural deterioration, for the

Degradation in action: the bow, 2002 and 2014. (HURL)

Degradation in action: the stern, 2014. (HURL)

fragile pieces lie directly under the bow, and is not distributed in any pattern indicating forceful removal. During a previous inspection visit in 2007, the torpedo guards had appeared in good condition.

In 2011 during a monitoring visit, HURL pilots discovered that the aft tail section was breaking away (downward) from the central hull section, the gap appearing close to the smooth edge of the bolted flange between the sections.

SUMMARY OF RESEARCH MISSIONS TO THE *WARD* MIDGET SITE

- Discovery by HURL
- Initial archaeological assessment by HURL, NOAA, NPS
- Media coverage for documentaries and archaeological survey by NOAA, NPS, WHOI
- Monitoring survey by HURL
- Corrosion study initiated by NOAA, NPS, ONR
- Monitoring survey by HURL, NOAA
- Media coverage for Asahi TV by HURL
- Corrosion studies and interior survey by NOAA, NPS, NHC
- Monitoring surveys by HURL, NOAA, National Geographic, and Herzog Films

The separation of the hull at the aft joint, 2014. (HURL)

Further observations were made by NOAA archaeologists upon a return to the site in July 2013. The gap, approximately 5 cm at maximum separation, indicated a failure of the hull in a line just aft of the connecting flange (the flange bolts were visible and still in place). Active (orange) corrosion appeared on the lower hull around the flange area, and corrosion product was flaking off where the hull seemed to be "flexing." The stern section now rests its weight on the rudder and fins, which appear to be deteriorating or "melting" into the sediment. The current scour beneath aft section is approximately 1 foot at deepest, at least 5 feet in length, from flange to aft fin section.

In short, following the discovery in 2002, the submarine appeared essentially intact with relatively minor siltation in the interior, despite obvious bottom scouring at both stern and bow, the forward compartments being wholly unsupported. This may have been deceptive, for change over time is inevitable. More recently, monitoring in 2007 and afterward revealed more dramatic changes (i.e., separation of aft compartment flange, loss of bow torpedo guard, deterioration of rudder, hull plate flexing).

RECONSTRUCTING THE *WARD*/MIDGET ENCOUNTER: WHAT ARCHAEOLOGY TELLS US

In a 2015 blog, archaeologist Innes McCartney (McCartney 2015) succinctly explains how "modern" sites like the midget submarine benefit from archaeological study:

> In the popular imagination at least, wrecks of this type could confirm and demonstrate exactly what

Probable degradation and collapse of the submarine. (Terry Kerby / HURL)

> contemporary reports of their sinkings stated. In other words the wreck tends to function as a friendly witness and although interesting is largely incidental to the central historical tale of wreck and loss . . . This is however to fundamentally misinterpret the true interface between archaeology and text . . . these sites can significantly contribute to the understanding of events if the bodies of the wrecks themselves are subject to the forms of scrutiny which seek to go beyond the original historical depiction of the sinking.[16]

In assessing the *Ward*'s midget, the discovery of the wreck raises some interesting questions, notably why the submarine is exactly where it is. The wreck lies approximately 2.77 km (1.5 nm) from where *Ward* reportedly shot it and then depth charged it along with Lieutenant William Tanner and his crew's PBY depth charge attack. Was the original location cited for the encounter not accurate? Or was it accurate and the craft moved that distance? Interestingly, even as a compelling sub-like target was "found" in only 259 meters (850 feet) of water in 1988, *Ward*'s after action report stated, fairly accurately as it would be later seen, that the submarine sank in 396.24 meters (1,300 feet) of water. As the submarine flooded, did it flood rapidly and sink directly to the bottom? Or did the submarine sink gradually and drift away from the scene of the action?

Ward's after action report noted the submarine was moving at approximately 8 to 10 knots when encountered, intercepted, and sunk. "Immediately after being hit the submarine appeared to slow and sink" (Commanding Officer, USS *Ward* 1941). The sub did not sink straight to the bottom, as it was not completely flooded when it went down and the dive planes were in the "up" position. As increased flooding pulled it down, counteracting the dive planes, the submarine proceeded some 1.5 nm from the point it had been hit and descended 0.197 nm; at 10 knots, this would have taken approximately 9 minutes, and at 5 knots, 18 minutes, to traverse not counting the effect of current. "Porpoising" of the bow by the planes would have occasionally pulled the bow up, partially stalling the descent, but not enough to stop a more or less steady glide to the seabed. Deviating from its original course of nearly due north, it was headed 90 degrees off its original course and sank at an angle that was not steep, progressively flooding with water entering initially from the 4 inch diameter shell hole and increasing as pressure built—at 30 meters (100 feet), the water would be entering at 3.17 Bar (46 psi)—as it made a descent to the bottom within 20 minutes of the fatal encounter with *Ward*. It should be noted that this analysis cannot take into consideration any possible changes in course or speed that the crew, if they had survived the initial shell impact, may have made in their final moments.

The burial of much of the lower command compartment in silt, along with the limited range of the interior survey, does not allow for an examination of whether there is an exit hole on the bottom of the hull, or if the hatches are open or closed that separated the central, command section of the craft from the stern, where the motor and some of the batteries were located, and the bow, where the torpedo and other batteries were located. For the sub to sink, however, they would have to have been open and quickly flooded. The craft would have traveled, then, essentially as a "dead stick" past crush depth, which for the *kō-hyōteki* was likely around three times its operating depth of 30 meters (100 feet) or some 100 meters (330 feet) at 10.2 Bar (148 psi).

The placement of the shell hole confirms that *Ward*'s No. 3 gun crew hit the tower just above the juncture with the pressure hull on the starboard side, firing from an angle and with the gun depressed. *Ward*'s log notes: "Fired two salvos. Observed second salvo to be direct hit on enemy submarine conning tower."[17] It was, as historians have noted, an exceptional shot. The shell hole and the condition of the sub conform to Outerbridge's report of the incident: "The shot from No. 3 gun fired at a range of 560 yards or less struck the submarine at the waterline which was the junction of the hull and conning tower. Damage was seen by several members of the crew. This was a square positive hit. There was no evidence of ricochet. The submarine was seen to heel over to starboard. The projectile was not seen to explode outside the hull of the submarine. There was no splash of any size that might results from an explosion or ricochet" (Commanding Officer, USS *Ward* 1941).[18]

The distance between *Ward* and the sub was apparently insufficient for the fuse to detonate the projectile, as was also the case with the shot from USS *Monaghan* that penetrated the conning tower of the submarine it encountered inside Pearl Harbor. Neither shell exploded. Nonetheless, in both cases, and specifically here with the sub sunk by USS *Ward*, it was a deadly shot. The Mark 9 4 inch / 50 caliber naval rifle fired a complete Mark 6 round with a 14.97 kg (33 lb) 40.1 cm (15.8 in) long projectile filled with 0.5 kg (1.39 lbs) of black powder at a muzzle velocity of 884 mps (2,900 fps; Campbell 1985:143). The projectile entered the conning tower angled sideways and down. The projectile entered the conning tower and missed the periscope, which interior examination by camera shows is intact with its handles folded up. The shot angled down. It either stopped inside the central section or punched through the bottom of the hull and exited without exploding.

With this hit, square in the center of the operational heart of the submarine, the impact of the projectile and any shrapnel could have killed the sub commander at the periscope and the enlisted crew member at the adjacent steering wheel. The complete flooding of this space and the loss of the crew could have resulted, as

The fatal shot fired by USS *Ward*, as reconstructed. (Terry Kerby / HURL)

The sinking and flooding of the submarine fired on by USS *Ward*, as reconstructed. (Terry Kerby / HURL)

previously noted, in the sub continuing to operate as a "dead stick" angling down into the depths as its buoyancy went negative, gliding down, the dive planes exerting sufficient thrust to continue to "porpoise" the bows and extend the glide for the distance between the point of encounter and the sub's final resting place on the seabed.

As soon as *Ward* fired, Outerbridge ordered four depth charges dropped, and Tanner's crew dropped two more from their PBY. "She ran into our depth charge barrage and appeared to be directly over an exploding charge. The depth charges were set for 100 feet" (After Action Report 1942). The depth charges reportedly brought the submarine to the surface, after which it submerged. What we believe is that the depth charging, while not adding to the damage that sank the submarine, did reorient it in the water column the approximate 90 degree turn it took on its ultimate glide to the seabed 2.4 km (1.5 nautical miles) away.

The final question to be asked, and for now unanswered without the unlikely excavation of the craft, is which *kō-hyōteki* did USS *Ward* sink, and who is inside the wreck? As Burlingame (1992) notes, various identities have been proposed, but the one most often advanced is I-20 *tou*, with Ensign Akira Hiroo and crewed by Petty Officer Second Class Yoshio Katayama still inside their submarine (Burlingame 1992:418). This theory is also supported by the Japanese Midget Submarine Association. The question of which submarine it is speaks to the role of archaeology. For now, attempts to identify the submarine's wartime designation and crew are speculative. If it were to happen, excavation of the craft would be the only likely means by which to answer that question. If so, one wonders if one of the artifacts buried in the silt inside the craft is a bottle of perfume, as Kazuo Sakamaki would later reminisce about his last night ashore in Japan with Ensign Hiroo.

INVESTIGATING THE SHELL HOLE: TERRY KERBY'S ACCOUNT

When we first inspected the shell hole in the conning tower, we noticed the torn metal from the fairing and pressure hull extending out as though the shell had come through from the other side. This might have been caused by the thin steel fairing covering the pressure hull deflecting back out when the shell punched through the hull, but we could see a flap of the pressure hull deflecting out as well. It was hard to imagine all that water flooding into that one small hole while all the air inside the sub was trying to get out the same hole in time to flood enough water into the sub to prevent it from imploding.

The shell hole in the conning tower. (HURL)

We suspected there must have been a lower exit point that produced a flood port, and the hole in the conning tower was the exhaust port. The force of the air exiting the hole might have forced the metal tear out as well.

In 2004 we were preparing to place a camera inside the hole to inspect the control compartment. We made a survey dive with a small test camera and a 3.5 inch PVC tube to see if it would fit in the hole. We discovered that the best approach with camera and tube was to enter at the same angle as the shell. When we put the test camera and tube in the hole at the shell entry angle, this put it in line with the main cross frame that separates the access trunk and periscope trunk. The test camera did not have any lights on it, so we could not see down inside the control compartment, but we could see that the hole was clear and that we would be able to get a better camera into the control compartment but would have to maneuver it around the periscope and cross frame. The cross frame between the access trunk and periscope trunk was a main support frame and could have deflected the shell through the bottom of the sub.

This would have provided a flood port and vent port. A long pitching descent would have carried the submarine far from the area and provided it enough time to flood so that it did not implode. On August 7th and 8th of 2005, we went back with a dedicated camera to put in the shell hole to inspect the inside of the command center. Placing the camera inside the shot hole was a very delicate operation that required perfect conditions. We could not get the camera into the hole while sitting on the bottom next to the sub without the risk of damaging the hole and possibly getting the camera stuck. We attached a thick rubber pad on the front of the sample basket frame on Pisces V so we could rest on the hull of the submarine and get a clear view into the hole and have better control of the manipulator.

The Pisces submersibles ballast control systems allow us to achieve perfect trim so there is no weight pressure on the hull when the rubber pad is resting in contact with the hull. The current conditions have to be favorable as well. I used a small fan coral on the top of the hull as a guide. If the coral was vibrating, then the current was too strong. We could work in a slight current but it had to be coming from the northeast or north. When we placed the camera into the hole, we could see that the bottom of the control compartment was filled with sand.

The sand level was about 1 to 1.5 feet above the bottom of the control compartment. This could also support the theory that there was a hole in the bottom of the hull. The hole in the conning tower is about 6 feet above the bottom. It is unlikely that this much sand could filter through that hole that high above the bottom, even in 70 plus years. The hull is scoured clean on both port and starboard side right up under the control room. If the center of the sub is resting on the carbonate outcrop, the force of the currents under the hull could have blown sand into the hole and filled the control room up to a certain level before enough sand filled the compartment to stabilize. We could see that the periscope handles were in the up position. Will Lerner said he saw the periscope turn and seemingly look right at him just before the shot was fired. In the lower right hand image, there is a circular object in the upper right hand corner in the right position to be the helm. If this is the helm, that means the level of the sand is below the helm.

Terry Kerby maneuvering the video camera-equipped probe to enter the *Ward* midget's conning tower. (HURL)

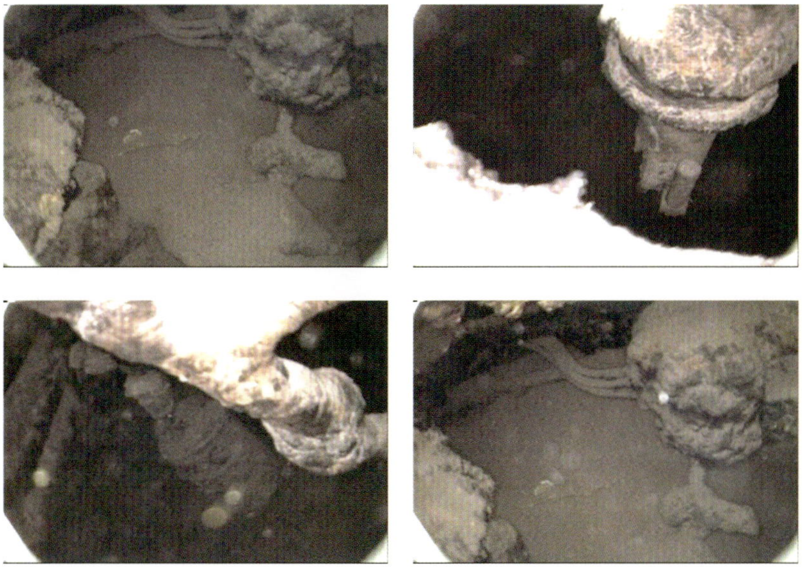

These murky images are from the first and only interior inspection of the control room of the *Ward* midget. (HURL)

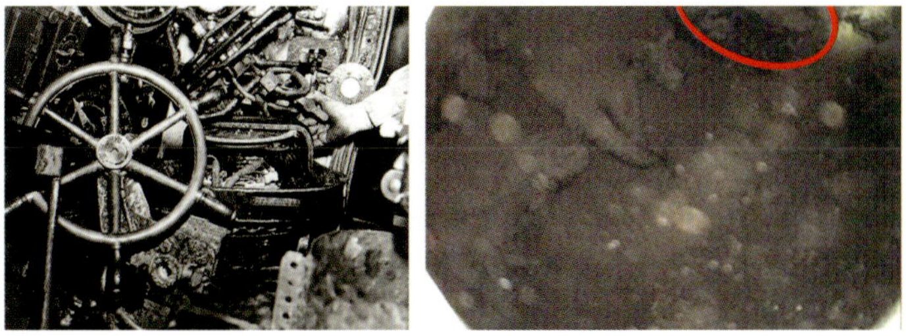

The partially buried helm of the "*Ward* midget" compared with that of HA-19. (HURL/U.S. Navy)

CHAPTER SIX

The Three-Piece Midget

By the morning of December 8, three of the midget submarines had been encountered by US forces: the craft sunk by USS *Ward*, the craft sunk by USS *Monaghan*, and Sakamaki and Inagaki's I-24 *tou*, which lay awash on a coral reef on the opposite shore of Oʻahu with Sakamaki in custody as "POW No. 1." The position of the submarine sunk by *Monaghan* was charted and navy divers rigged it for recovery within a few weeks of the attack. A heavy lift floating crane lifted the submarine from the bottom and placed it on a barge for inspection on December 21. Navy explosive ordnance disposal experts boarded the barge and found "the upper part of the front end (the torpedo tube section) was completely gone. There was nothing left of the tubes or their torpedoes. Below the tubes the hull seemed to have been blown outwards to where it was almost flat" (Eigell n.d.:45).

The torpedoes, they surmised, had exploded in their tubes, "destroying the upper forward section of the midget submarine hull" (Eigell n.d.:45). The examination noted other damage, including ramming damage to the aft hull; "it appeared that the sub had been rolled completely over and the rear end of the boat had been bent badly out of line. Overall the body of the boat showed the wrinkles and indentations typical of exposure to heavy explosions underwater" (Eigell n.d.:45). The conning tower "clearly showed the path of a five-inch projectile completely through the conning tower" (Eigell n.d.:45). They also noted the stench of the rotting remains of the two crew, "firmly locked inside the wreckage" (Eigell n.d.:45). With nothing to disarm, the EOD team left and the barge was moved to the sub base, where construction of a new pier provided a burial site for the craft and crew. Marine Lieutenant Cornelius Smith Jr., visiting the base, saw the submarine there and commented that "the conning tower is tiny, with room enough for one man to steer the craft. He's still in there. One of our ships rammed him, broadside, and he's caught, dead, with his legs hanging out; I guess they'll have to cut him free with a blowtorch. I suppose the torpedoman inside is dead, too" (Smith, in Stillwell 1981:224).

The bodies did not remain in the submarine for long. According to Doyle L. Northrup,[1] who was apparently sent along with others to inspect the submarine by Naval Intelligence after the craft was landed, he was sent into the wreck "because I was the smallest one there . . . the only one in the party that could get through the conning tower. . . . I went in and got the two crewmembers and pushed them out through the conning tower, their bodies, and got the chart case and all, anything else that was of intelligence value" (Northrup 1973). Once this was done, naval personnel stripped the sub of parts to repair Sakamaki's damaged craft. Paul Baham, assigned to the task, reminisced in 1986 that "We used almost all the *Monaghan*-midget external parts to put on the Bellows sub . . . There were no bodies or papers or maps on either sub when we were assigned to cannibaling [*sic*] the two. The man that worked with me was Victor E. Bello, Half Moon Bay, CA. We did go inside both subs. I got a lot of souvenirs, but they were later stolen" (Baham 1986).

When this work was done, a crane barge "dumped the wreckage along the back edge of the pier where they were filling in to level the shoreward edge of the pier," and the sub was then covered with landfill as the pier site was completed (Eigell n.d.:45). The dead crew were buried in Honolulu at the Nu'uanu Cemetery. Their identities were either not known or went unreported at the time. A clue as to who they were comes from the fact that in March 1947, a Japanese naval lieutenant's shoulder patch was repatriated to Japan by the US Navy and was said to have come from the dead submarine commander. The insignia suggests to the Japanese that this craft was that of Lieutenant Naoji Iwasa, commander of the Special Attack Flotilla and of I-22

The raised hulk of the midget submarine sunk by USS *Monaghan* prior to burial, December 1941. (Naval History and Heritage Command, NH 54302)

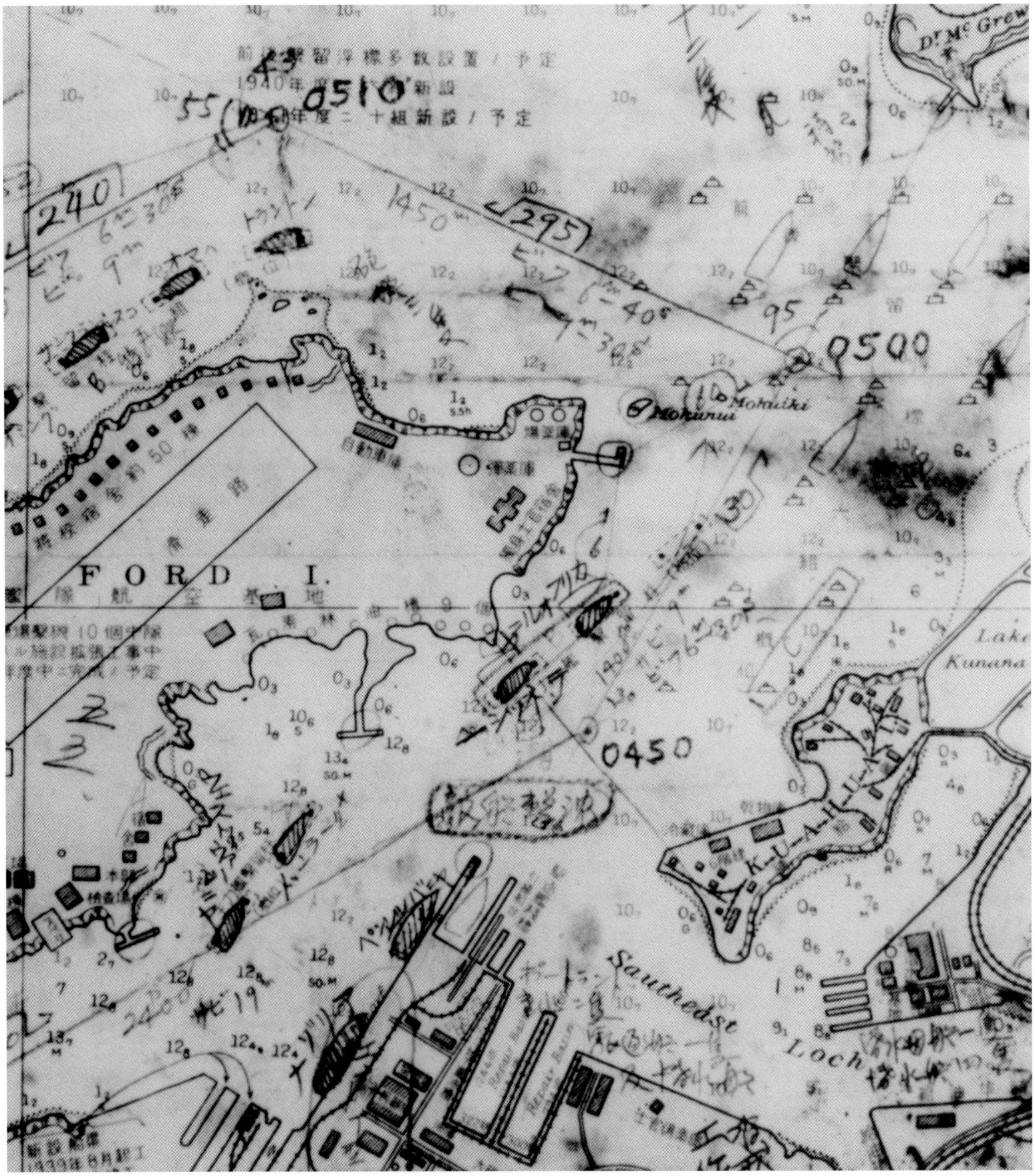

One of the intelligence recoveries from the "*Monaghan* midget" was this chart of the harbor with a course laid out that circles Ford Island. Often identified as coming from Sakamaki's *kō-hyōteki*, it does not. The notations of the course and timing make sense for a craft that entered the harbor before the attack, circled and reconnoitered the scene, and then surfaced to attack as the aerial assault commenced. After the attack, intelligence personnel entered the raised submarine, removed the bodies of the crew, and recovered papers including this chart. (Naval History and Heritage Command, 80-G-413507).

tou, which was crewed by Petty Officer First Class Naokichi Sasaki. The patch is now preserved at the Yasukuni Shrine as a *memento mori* of Lieutenant Iwasa.[2] The ostensible I-22 *tou* resurfaced briefly in 1952 when workers improving the quay wall at the sub base hit the buried midget with a dragline while excavating landfill to drive new sheet piles. After digging a deeper trench alongside the exposed hull, they rolled the boat over and reburied it to clear the work area (Bronson in Stillwell 1981:195–96).

Thus at the end of the battle in 1941, two of the midget submarines remained unaccounted for.[3] The mystery of where one of those two lay was partly resolved in 1960 with the discovery of a fourth Pearl Harbor *kō-hyōteki* in the shallows of Keehi Lagoon by US Navy diver SK/1 C.F. Buhl during a long distance training dive on June 13, 1960 (Stewart 1974:61). The sub was resting in 76 feet of water with torpedoes still in their tubes, and as it was later learned, the crew hatch undogged. A US Navy salvage vessel, USS *Current* (ARS-22), raised the submarine on July 13, 1960. It was inspected and found to have experienced depth charging as evidenced by "bent piping, a door twisted off its hinges, her large electric motor torn from its mountings, and much shattered glass" (Stewart 1974:62). No

The midget submarine sunk in the encounter with USS *Monaghan* was carefully and quietly studied by the US Navy and other military intelligence officials before being buried. (US Naval Institute)

Workers prepare to bury the *Monaghan* midget at the Pearl Harbor Submarine Base in early 1942. Sakamaki's dismantled submarine can be seen in the background. (Burl Burlingame)

human remains were encountered, but the demolition charge and the still live torpedoes gave naval officials pause. The bow section, with torpedoes, was unbolted, taken to sea, and dumped (Riley and Delanoy 1961; Stewart 1974:62).

The submarine was slated for return to Japan at the request of the consul general in Hawai'i, and it was transferred, minus the bow, to the Japanese LST *Shiretoko* on June 19, 1961 (Riley and Delanoy 1961:127). In Japan, the recovery and analysis of some artifacts, including a boot, a flying suit (the "uniform" of the midget crews), and tools, as well as a glove, led the Japanese Midget Submarine Association to determine it was likely I-18 *tou*, commanded by Lieutenant (j.g.) Shigemi Furuno and crewed by Petty Officer First Class Shigenori Yokoyama. A number of American destroyers reported submarine contacts and actively depth charged them in the same general area where the wreck was found, and so it is probable that a damaged and out of condition I-18 *tou* was abandoned by its crew, who may have survived but most likely died after leaving their flooded, sunken craft (Burlingame 1992:426–28). Once in Japan, the battered *kō-hyōteki* was refurbished as a land-based exhibit,

The Keehi Lagoon submarine as discovered. The location of the sunken craft off the port outbound lane of the Pearl Harbor entrance essentially mirrored the unannounced, earlier find of another *kō-hyōteki* discovered and quietly disposed of in 1950 off the starboard outbound lane. The position of both submarines underscores the fact that in addition to plans to attempt to penetrate the harbor and attack ships, the *kō-hyōteki* corps were also part of a larger submarine armada whose job was to sink ships fleeing the aerial attack. (Burl Burlingame)

Raising the Keehi Lagoon submarine on July 18, 1960. (National Park Service, PR-106)

The Keehi Lagoon submarine is landed and readied for inspection. (Naval History and Heritage Command, KN-2589)

Because corrosion had sealed the torpedoes into their tubes, the navy made the decision to remove the bow of the submarine and dump it into deep water. It has not yet been relocated during deepwater surveys. The remainder of the sub, as shown here, waited under guard until loaded on a Japanese LST for transportation back to Japan. (Burl Burlingame)

complete with a newly constructed mock-up of its missing bow. Dedicated on March 15, 1962, in a special ceremony, the midget has been displayed ever since at the former Naval Academy at Etajima, outside of Hiroshima, in front of the Naval Tactical School.

Thus it could be argued, even without physically relocating the submarine sunk by USS *Ward*, that as of 1960, there remained only one last, unaccounted boat from the Pearl Harbor special attack force. The Japanese Midget Submarine Association, following on the wartime conclusions of a final broadcast suspected to have come from I-16 *tou* hours after the raid, believe that to be the identity of the "last midget."

Final Broadcast: December 7–8, 1941

After the war, Shigeru Fukudome, one of the naval officers who had helped plan the Pearl Harbor operation, noted that the "erroneous opinions" of midget submarine successes during the war were all based on "the fact that one of our submarines on watch outside the harbor entrance the night of 7 December observed a huge explosion inside the harbor at 2101 Hawai'i time, and also on the fact that [a] secret message that stated 'succeeded to make attack' was received from one of the midget subs at 2241 that night" (Fukedome in Evans 1986:34).

As noted earlier (chapter 2), it was in the early morning hours of December 8 that I-16 received a faint message at 01:11, possibly from its own *kō-hyōteki*, commanded by Ensign Yokoyama, reporting the craft was unable to navigate. At that stage, only one or possibly two of the midget submarines were left (if the boat later found at Keehi Lagoon in 1960 was not yet on the bottom).

The mysteries that remain seven decades later focus on the matter of exactly what the 22:41 signal meant in regard to a successful attack. Japanese naval and political leaders seized on the message as a sign of midget success and, as noted earlier, credited the *kō-hyōteki* corps with the sinking of a battleship. Did that message reflect on a successful mission by the reporting crew in their *kō-hyōteki* or on a sense of the operation overall? More than likely, it meant the reporting submarine had penetrated Pearl Harbor's defenses and fired their torpedoes, and with the last message received at 1:11 the following morning, that submarine's crew now faced a difficult choice, likely resting on the seabed somewhere in or around Pearl Harbor, out of battery power, running out of air, and according to their code and their beliefs, with only one task remaining before them—to destroy their craft and themselves.

In a poignant letter home, written before the Pearl Harbor mission, Yokoyama told his mother that he intended to follow his brother, who had died earlier in the war in China, to a glorious end: "I will render as distinguished a service to the State as my eldest brother and meet him in Yasukuni Shrine, Japan's Pantheon. I think that you will become a typical mother in a country engaged in war, when you rejoice over sacrificing your two sons for the sake of the State" (Hohjo 1942:579).

As wartime Japanese propagandists noted, "the idea of returning alive was not in their minds. It has been ascertained that a number of special submarines of the flotilla were sunk by enemy warships, and others destroyed themselves" (Hohjo 1942:466). Sakamaki's failure to set off his charges in I-24 *tou*, and the fact that the suspected I-18 *tou*, when discovered in 1960, had also not been purposely destroyed and contained no bodies inside, does offer an alternate theory that the last crew may not have detonated their craft in a suicidal end to their mission. However, a subsequent discovery made in 2000 argues that at least one team deliberately chose to meet their fate at their own hands. It remained unclear for close to a decade, however, that this find actually related directly to the Pearl Harbor attack and was indeed a key piece of evidence—notably, part of the fifth and final missing *kō-hyōteki*.

Rediscovery and Controversy

Following a second National Park Service mission in 1991 to try and locate *Ward*'s midget, another opportunity for dives off Pearl Harbor came through Terry Kerby and HURL, who allowed Gary R. Larkins and George Carter along on one of the annual test dives so that they could search for and document discarded 1930s era Douglas PD-1 flying boats.[4] They were present on July 27, 1992, when Kerby discovered the stern section of an apparent *kō-hyōteki* in 480 meters (1,575 feet) of water approximately 3 nautical miles off the coast. The wreckage was cleanly separated from the rest of the submarine (which was not observed) and appeared at the time to be "neatly sheared off at the bolted joint" (Honolulu *Star-Bulletin*, July 29, 1992:A-1).[5] Initial media accounts suggested the sunken submarine section was from one of the Pearl Harbor attack midgets. The university's leadership, as well as Kerby and his team, were surprised to learn that subsequently, on August 11, an attorney acting for the Institute of Aeronautical Archaeological Research filed an unsuccessful admiralty claim against the wreck requesting salvage rights and an award. The case will be discussed in the next chapter. Unfortunately, the tracking system was not working on the dive, so there was no record of the exact location of the old submarine wreckage.

Disagreement over exactly what the find represented—a Pearl Harbor attack sub, a later wartime capture, or a postwar prize dismantled and dumped—continued. Kerby's diligent searching on cruises of opportunity discovered the middle section of a *kō-hyōteki* during another Pisces V dive on September 5, 2000. This find, in 400 meters (1,312 feet) of water, was in the same general vicinity of the previously sighted stern section, which remained at that time still lost. The middle piece was heavily damaged, Kerby noted. In addition to the missing bow and stern sections, it appeared to have suffered a catastrophic explosion aft of the conning tower. Two months later, in November, the middle section was again relocated and filmed by a National Geographic / Robert Ballard film team searching for the *Ward*'s midget, but most experts dismissed the possibility of this wreckage relating to the Pearl Harbor attack.[6]

The third and "final piece" of the puzzle was discovered by Kerby and HURL on August 29, 2001, while on a dive to resurvey the middle section. On approach, they observed and documented the bow section of a *kō-hyōteki* in 400 meters (1,312 feet) without torpedoes but with the empty openings, surrounded by the distinctive figure-eight guard. Believing that the stern section seen in 1992 must be nearby, Kerby searched for and relocated it. Clearly the three pieces came from one craft. All appeared to have been dumped into the sea, one at time, in close proximity. Holes punched in the hull and steel cable choked and looped around the stern showed that the individual sections had been deliberately rigged for easier handling, either for recovery or for dumping.

The thought that the craft could represent a Pearl Harbor attack midget, but definitely not *Ward*'s midget (which was found the next year), continued to plague Terry Kerby and Steven Price

The "mystery" of the submarine discovery of 1992 was compounded with the discovery of the mid or central section of a Type A *kō-hyōteki*, albeit with one end damaged by what appeared to have been an explosion. (HURL)

Terry Kerby's painting of the discovery of the "three-piece" central section. (Terry Kerby / HURL)

The bow section of the "three-piece" midget and the last section of the submarine to be discovered. The figure eight torpedo guard / net cutter is intact, and there are no torpedoes in the tubes. (HURL)

of HURL, and a follow-up mission was planned. The *Ward* midget discovery, and the various missions to it after 2002, however, delayed any return to what was now called the "three-piece" midget. The realization that the various pieces fit into one complete submarine, meanwhile, fed into an ongoing controversy dating from a study by Autometrics Inc., a Washington, DC–area[7] advanced imaging company that closely worked with the defense industry, including utilizing a variety of images from various sensors to assess underground nuclear tests. Inspired by the supposition that at least one of the *kō-hyōteki* had made it into Battleship Row during the attack and fired its torpedoes (Burlingame 1992:199), Autometrics analyzed two negatives of the same photograph—an aerial image taken by the Japanese at the start of the assault on Battleship Row, which had ended up in American hands (Autometrics 1994:2).

The image, shot by a rear seat observer in one of the Japanese torpedo bombers, captures the moment when the initial torpedo strike hit the battleships USS *Oklahoma*, *California*, and *West Virginia*, as well as the cruiser USS *Helena* (CL-50) and the minelayer USS *Oglala*, between 08:01 and 08:03 hours (Autometrics 1994:4–5). An object in the photograph, noted as rectangular, appears in the midst of torpedo tracks, with what the analysts determined were "rooster tails," which they equated to splashing. Their conclusion was that the object was a "certain sub" and likely the fifth, unaccounted for *kō-hyōteki*, which had fired its two torpedoes at USS *West Virginia* and USS *Oklahoma*. They further speculated that when struck by shock waves from warhead detonations, the midget had partially surfaced, and its counterrotating propellers had created the "rooster tails" in its wake (Autometrics 1994:14). Autometrics concluded by noting the submarine had likely not escaped Pearl Harbor and possibly lay in the channel entrance, caught and sunk while trying to leave (Autometrics 1994:17). The Autometrics study, with revisions, was published in *Naval History* magazine in December 1999 (Rodgaard et al. 1999).

The study and subsequent article and its assertions were controversial, and a variety of forums have debated the matter in print and online since. A 2005 letter to the editors of *Naval History* by a group of military officers and historians (Zimm et al. 2005) noted what they felt were critical faults with the theory of the "rooster tails," in the photographic interpretation: "It cannot be conclusively proven the marks on the photograph are plumes of water. If they are plumes, they are curious, as they cast no shadows on the water that we could see. Alternately, the marks might be shell splashes, drifting smoke, AA shell bursts, or even just imperfections on the film" (Zimm et al. 2005). They also pointed out how the Autometrics study did not match the historical record in that later in the day a torpedo attack was made on the cruiser USS *St. Louis* (CL-49) by a "baby" submarine that fired two torpedoes that missed their intended target. Both schools of thought have their passionate defenders as well as critics.[8] Finding a midget submarine, albeit in three

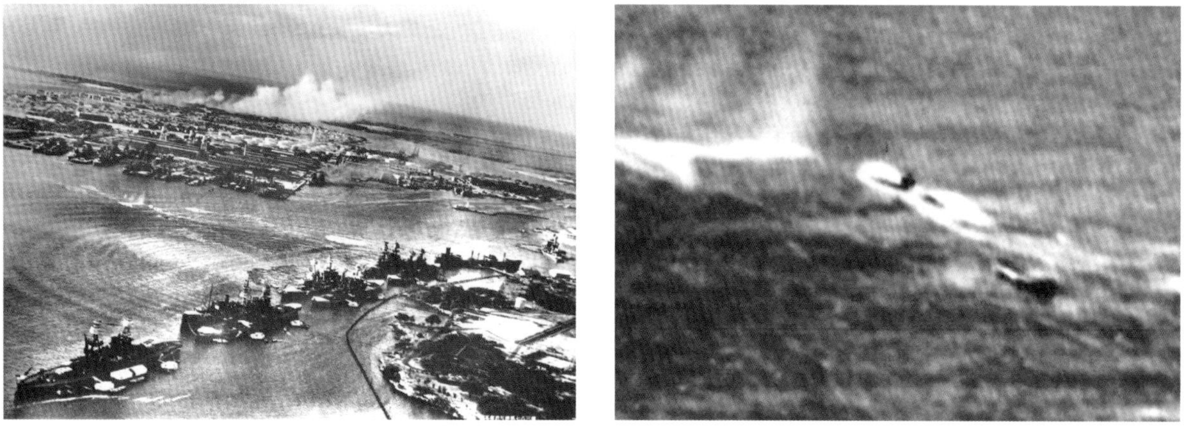

The Autometrics-analyzed image said to depict a midget submarine firing its torpedoes into Battleship Row on the morning of December 7. Controversial and not accepted as fact by some Pearl Harbor historians, nonetheless this image was seized upon as visual proof of a successful penetration and attack by at least one of the *kō-hyōteki* corps other than the sub sunk by *Monaghan*—and perhaps even being the craft discovered in pieces by HURL. (Autometrics / Burl Burlingame)

pieces, without two torpedoes, focused even more attention on the controversy. Key questions now arose concerning whether it was indeed a Pearl Harbor *kō-hyōteki*, and if so, how did it end up dismantled, in three pieces, 3 miles outside the harbor in deep water? In addition, if it was a Pearl Harbor attack sub, and the fifth and final midget to be accounted for, could it offer any additional evidence on the controversy?

But if a second attack sub was within Pearl Harbor, what happened to it following the attack? One possibility holds that, following the release of its two torpedoes, the *kō-hyōteki* crept into the shallow back waters of Pearl Harbor, such as West Loch, and unable to escape, the crew detonated the scuttling charge. Other hypotheses exist.

In response to the discovery of the three-piece midget sub, and in the aftermath of the legal attempt by private parties to seize control of the submarine, NOAA, the National Park Service, and HURL returned to the three-piece wreck site in 2009, 2013, and 2014 to conduct additional research. The February 2009 mission included one day of filming by Lone Wolf Productions for an episode of the PBS television program, *NOVA*. Lone Wolf brought along retired Japanese naval officer and wartime midget submariner Vice Admiral Kazuo Ueda. After making a dive to the three-piece midget, Admiral Ueda declared the craft to be, in his expert opinion, one of the five *kō-hyōteki* sent to Pearl Harbor.[9]

The Fifth *Kō-hyōteki*?

The primary objective of the 2009 scientific mission as designed by HURL, NOAA, and the NPS was to positively identify the three-piece sub site, confirming (or denying) that the sub was one of the five *kō-hyōteki* involved in the December 7, 1941, attack (Kerby 2008). Possible identification focused on two questions:

> 1) Was the sub disassembled from the interior (indicative of a captured and intact sub carefully studied and prepared), or was it disassembled from the exterior (indicative of wreckage crudely salvaged and discarded)? The connecting flange joints of each section were easily accessible. Investigators theorized that if disassembled from the inside, there should be empty holes where bolts were removed from the interior to take the submarine apart. If disassembled from the outside, there should still be sheared off bolts remaining in the corresponding holes on the flange joint.
>
> If the submarine was disassembled from the outside it is conceivable that there was no access into the control room. Assessing the bolt holes of the flange joint would require only light scraping of corrosion product by the Pisces manipulator arm, in order to expose a small patch of bare metal. This corrosion sample would provide further information about the site (see Secondary Objectives below).
>
> 2) Did the sub have one or two air bottles situated at the forward end of the mid-section? Standard Japanese two-man submarines had one air bottle placed in this area, while the five *kō-hyōteki* involved in the attack had a second air bottle specially fitted to this location. In order to survey this area, first it is necessary to determine if loose debris which obscures the hatchway into this area can safely be moved out of the way with the Pisces manipulator arm, debris which obscures any view of the air bottle(s) immediately beyond the hatchway. Debris, for this purpose, refers to any unsecured non-structural element which is not in its original fixed position, but loose fallen material. If the debris can be cleared safely and two air bottles are found to be present, this could help confirm the identity of this section being part of the fifth Pearl Harbor sub. (Kerby 2008)

Secondary objectives defined for the 2009 survey included analysis of the concretion/corrosion samples obtained by mechanical scraping of the flange with a Pisces manipulator arm. The samples were sealed in the care of the NPS

Submerged Resources Center. NPS, with the University of Nebraska Lincoln (UNL) and Eglin AFB, utilized direct chemistry as a means of determining total iron content of the collected concretion product. A standardized method for chemically analyzing iron in concretion has been developed, and UNL scientists and NPS researchers have combined concretion thickness, density, and total elemental iron content to derive an expression for corrosion rate, as was also done with the *Ward*'s midget. Data obtained from this small study has added additional breadth to the existing studies of marine biofouling and its iron content and provided valuable information concerning the relative preservation of this particular midget submarine as well as other deepwater wrecks from World War II.

The 2009 mission successfully achieved the first goal of its primary objective; the scraping showed the craft had been cut apart externally with a cutting torch severing the bolts at the flanged ends that linked the three component pieces together. It proved impossible to safely approach the submarine and penetrate the forward battery compartment with a camera, or to clear any of the loose batteries that blocked access through the hatch. Four years later, during the 2013 mission, additional corrosion and new openings in the hull were observed, which suggested a return might allow for camera access through one of the holes. At the same time, supplemental research addressing questions beyond the presence or absence of extra air flasks was undertaken in an attempt to reveal the sub's ultimate identity. First, the hull was assessed for evidence of the blanking off of the forward navigation light on the conning tower, yet another modification specific to the Pearl Harbor mission.

The 2013 survey team was on the lookout for design changes made in the *kō-hyōteki* after December 7, 1941. These changes included not only alterations to the torpedo guards but the presence of a counterweight inside the craft to help trim it after firing its massive main weaponry and the addition of an access trunk through the bottom of the craft. Later Type C boats were known to have received a separate recharging motor in the after battery compartment. For the subsequent 2014 mission, supported by Herzog and Company as part of a future television documentary intended to coincide with the seventy-fifth anniversary of the Japanese attack, the focus was primarily on camera penetration of the forward battery compartment in an effort to determine if there were high pressure air cylinders mounted overhead, a specific Pearl Harbor modification, as noted previously.

The Three-Piece Sub Site

The submarine lies on a sediment-covered seafloor in the midst of a field of scattered ceramic dishware, aircraft parts, unexploded ordnance, and eight LVT-2 "Water Buffalo" tracked

HURL operations assessing and determining the three pieces were cut apart by a torch. (HURL)

landing craft. The three pieces of the submarine are oriented in a row, on a NE-SW line bearing 250 degrees. They are separated by 140 meters (460 feet) from the bow to the middle section, and 65 meters (213 feet) from the middle section to the bow.

The bow and stern sections both have flanged joints at the edges where they would have bolted to the center section. Each flange is clear—there is no distortion or bending, nor are there any exposed bolts or bolt surfaces. Scraping the end of a center section in 2009 revealed that the bolts were cut with a torch, severing the craft into its three component pieces. At the proximal end of the bow and at the aft end of the center section, the steel hull plating has been punched in from its external face, leaving a concavity of some 25–35 cm. At the bottom of each of these depressions, a length of steel wire cable was looped through holes measuring approximately 10 cm by 15 cm wide.

The stern retains diving planes, rudder, and counterrotating propellers, along with the single-ring steel propeller guard. More steel cable is looped around the rudder/propeller area and runs across the main body of wreckage. This suggests that the stern was cut, lifted, and, still wrapped with the wire cable used to lift it, dumped from whatever platform it was loaded on. The shell plating at the stern is beginning to deteriorate, and holes have opened in the hull. Remains of an electric motor, with controls and attendant electrical wiring, are visible at the stern's exposed forward end.

The stern section, as discovered, while seemingly "salvaged"—as evidenced by it being severed from the rest of the then still-missing submarine and looped with cable apparently used to lift and perhaps dump it at sea—nonetheless contained its unsalvaged motor. (HURL)

The after end of the bow section, showing the intact torpedo tubes and firing mechanisms, and the same section of HA-19. (HURL / Navy History and Heritage Command)

The bow section consists of two (empty) torpedo tubes, each of which retains an intact figure-eight guard center mounted on a stud bolt and the shackle for a forward net-cutting wire is still in place. Sealed 18 inch torpedo tube doors dominate the interior space at the open after end, which is also crammed with the firing valves, a ballast tank, two high pressure air tanks, and two impulse tanks still in place. Lead pigs for ballast can be seen lying scattered about inside.

The center section is badly damaged and rests at an approximate 45 degree angle to port on the seabed. At this angle, it is possible to observe the bottom of the hull and determine that there is no access trunk or hatch present (as would be the case for post-1941 *kō-hyōteki*).

The conning tower/sail is mostly intact, with the hatch shut. While shut, it is not known if the hatch is dogged (i.e., sealed) or unsealed. When discovered in 2001, the periscope was still in

The post–Pearl Harbor fitted access hatch in the bottom of HA-21 after the wreck was raised from Sydney Harbor. There is no hatch on the bottom of the three-piece midget submarine off Pearl Harbor. (Australian War Memorial, 305013)

place, but as of 2013, the upper portions of it had detached and come to rest on the sediment to the port and below its original position. The conning tower also retains a vertical black rubber coated radio antenna, which is in a stowed position inside with just the tip visible. The tower mounts the remains of U-frame periscope sheers and a battery ventilation exhaust. An aft navigation light, visible on the conning tower in 2001, had fallen free of the tower by 2013 and lay in the sediment adjacent to the periscope.[10] There is no navigation light visible on the forward edge of the conning tower; the light in this position appearing to have been blanked off (as was done for all five of the Pearl Harbor attack subs). Above it is a pulley for the net, cutting wire that once ran the length of the center section to the tip of the bow. The wire is in place and hangs loose from the front of the conning tower.

The forward end of the center section retains a clean flange and the bulkhead leading into the forward battery compartment remains intact. Twin racks of wet-cell batteries are stacked, with some having come loose, filling the compartment, so that visible access to the interior is not possible through the open hatch. However, a hole has formed and grown through corrosion on the starboard side, which allowed a small specially rigged camera to penetrate the compartment in 2014. As the camera entered the wreck, images transmitted back to the Pisces crew revealed an interior piled high with loose battery debris almost to the level of the entry point. Further exploration was blocked by a large metal object bolted or hanging from the overhead, which upon comparison with I-24 *tou* appears to be the side of a high pressure air flask.

The after end of the center section is exposed as the result of an internal explosion that destroyed the aft battery compartment, leaving the control room open to fill substantially with sediment. Visible just beyond the partially intact aft bulkhead is what may be the periscope well. The aft battery compartment is largely empty except for detached battery buss bars and a tangle of electric wiring, along with fragments of other loose batteries, which have fallen out of the wrecked submarine section to lie on the seabed nearby. There would have been 136 batteries in this compartment.

The metal of the hull in this location is twisted and buckled from explosive force. Approximately 6 meters (some 14 feet) of the center section is missing, as are most of the batteries that would have been in this compartment. The damage suggests that this craft was initially scuttled deliberately by setting off the aft demolition charge. The Pearl Harbor midgets carried an explosive demolition charge of 300 pounds in the aft battery of the center section. The damage to the hull in the center section is similar to that observed in the forward section of one of the *kō-hyōteki* lost at Sydney, where the hull plating thrust out and tore through the overhead of the compartment, leaving the mangled lower hull in place. This is exactly the type of destruction seen

The forward end of the central section, showing deformation and how it relates to the same area of HA-19. (HURL)

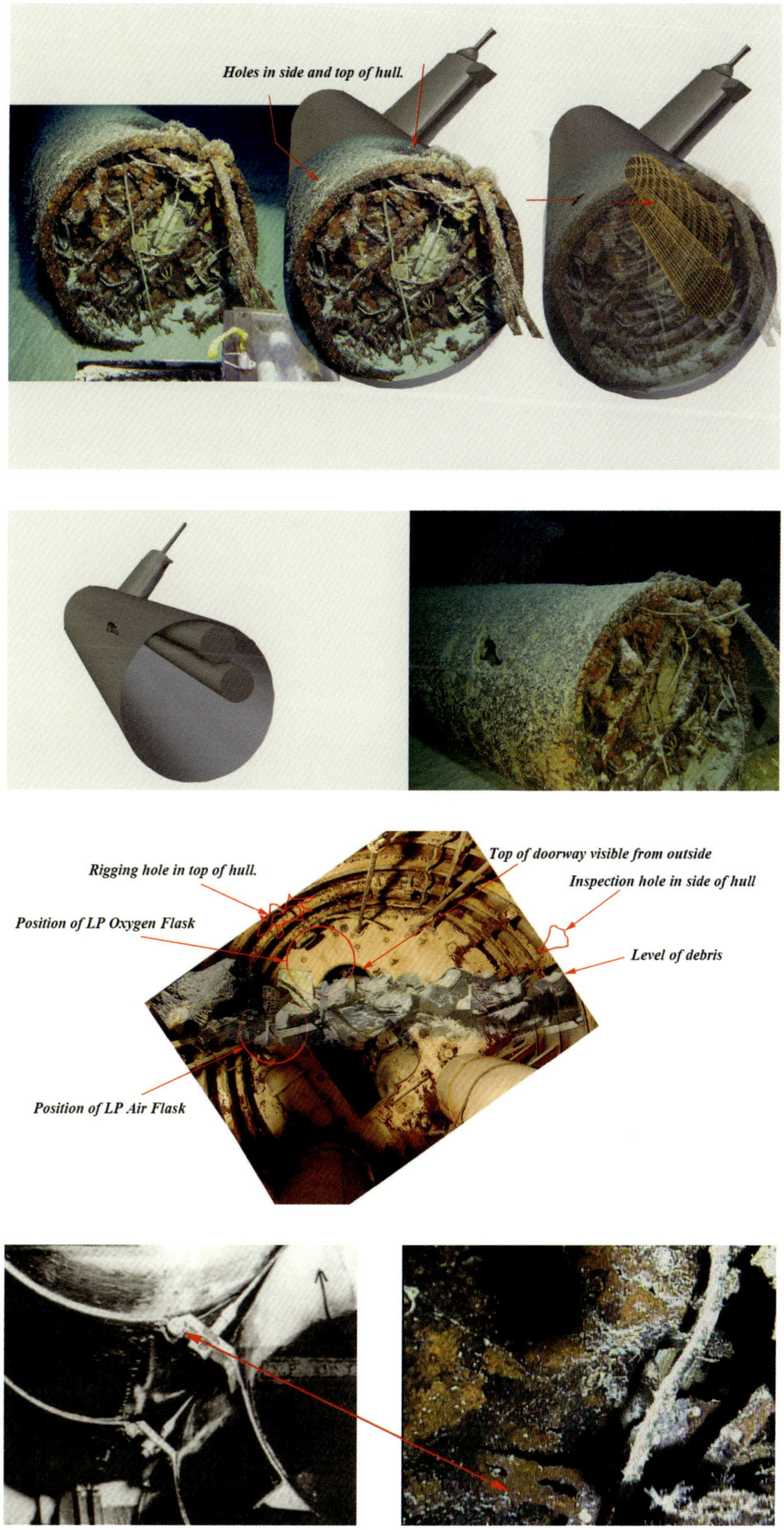

Penetration camera operations, 2014.
(HURL/Herzog)

In situ storage of the conning tower light fixture. (NOAA)

The forward battery of the central section of the submarine, showing the tumble of batteries that have fallen from their racks and blocked access into the interior of the compartment. (HURL)

The surviving area of the after battery. (NOAA)

in the three-piece midget. Jagged ends of metal from the blasted section were apparent when the submarine wreck was first discovered in 2001, but over the course of the following 12 years, the damaged ends deteriorated and fell free of the hull, now giving an impression of a much cleaner break than was initially observed.

At the conclusion of the 2014 mission, multiple directions of inquiry and multiple pieces of evidence clearly indicated that the three-piece midget is indeed the fifth and final *ko-hyōteki* from the Pearl Harbor attack.

In summary, first, the craft is definitely a Type A *kō-hyōteki*. In all, fifty of the Type A boats were built by Japan. These craft, hull numbered from no. 3 through no. 52, are not all accounted for in the historical record. But what is known, thanks to the detailed research of Bob Hackett and Sander Kingsepp in the midget submarine section of http://www.combinedfleet.com, is that four of these subs (nos. 49–52) were rebuilt into Type C boats, and HA-49, 50, and 51 were sunk at sea in deep water and never recovered. HA-52's wreck lies off Kavieng, and HA-53's wreck lies off Rabaul. Midget HA-53 was the prototype for the Type B *kō-hyōteki* (and the sole Type B), leaving forty-six submarines as potential candidates for the identity of "three-piece" midget if solely sorted as a Type A. Of those forty-six, ten were lost in attacks on Pearl Harbor, Sydney, and Diego Suarez. While not all hull numbers are known for the ten, HA-14, HA-19, and HA-21 were lost in those operations according to analysis of the recovered wrecks by US and Australian forces. Japanese sources (as tabulated by Hackett and Kingsepp) note that HA-5 and HA-13 were in Japan at war's end, where they were scrapped. HA-8, 10, 11, 12, and 30 were known to have been lost at Guadalcanal. Additionally, HA-28, 29, 31, 32, 33, and 34 were lost at Kiska.

One Type A (variously identified as HA-8, 10, or 30 but now known to be HA-8) was

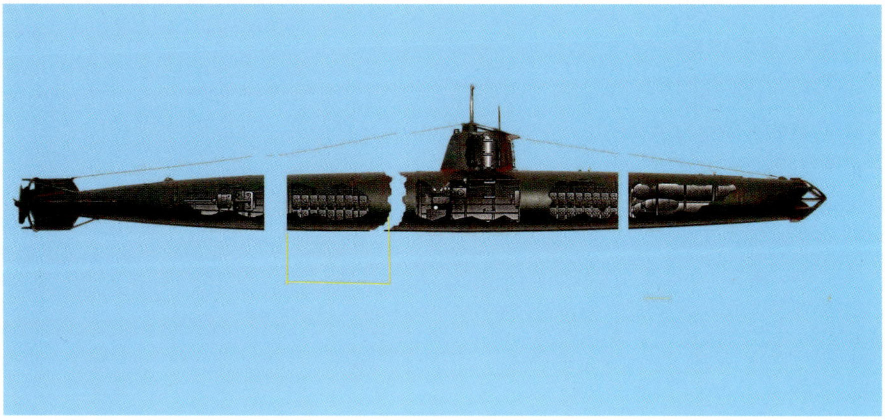

The three-piece midget submarine reconstructed, showing the mission section where the scuttling charge disintegrated the majority of the aft battery compartment. (Terry Kerby / HURL)

SCUTTLING CHARGES AND SHIMOSE POWDER

Analysis of the unfired charges found in I-24 *tou* found them to be Shimose blasting powder shaped into trapezoidal charges. Shimose powder (*kayaku*) was developed in the late nineteenth century by Japanese inventor Masachika Shimose. Also known as picric acid, it is a trinitrated derivative of phenol or trinitrophenol (Lacroix 1997:763). The Imperial Japanese Navy adopted Shimose powder in 1893 and commenced manufacture of it in naval facilities after 1897. It was a highly effective, powerful explosive with greater effect than TNT. A common artillery shell filled with 1.70 kg of Shimose exploded with an effective radius of 18 meters (Lacroix 1997:239). The empirical formula is $C^6H^3N^3O^7$, and Shimose generates 826 l/kg in explosive gas volume, with the heat of explosion being (H_2O, liquid) 822 kcal/kg = 3437 kJ/kg (H_2O, gas), 801 kcal/kg = 3350 Kj/kg, a specific energy of 101 mt/kg = 995 kJ/kg, a specific heat of 0.254 kcal/kg = 1/065 kJ/kg, and a deflagration point of 300°C = 507°F (Meyer et al. 2002:256–57).

recovered from Guadalcanal and ended up on display at the US Navy Submarine Force Library and Museum in Groton, Connecticut. One other midget, raised by USCG *Ironwood*, was broken into three pieces and dumped back into the ocean. It and the others remain submerged in the Solomon Islands as archaeological resources, as do the Kiska craft (save one that rests ashore). In all, Hackett and Kingsepp list the ultimate disposition of twenty-one numbered Type A *ko-hyōteki*. When that figure is combined with the unknown numbered craft lost in action at Pearl Harbor, Sydney, and Diego Suarez, it means a total of twenty-eight Type As have definitely known fates, leaving an additional twenty-eight Type A boats unaccounted for. It should be noted that the forensic evidence is clear that the three-piece midget is not a later Type C variant. There is no trace inside the sunken craft of an additional generator to recharge the batteries, which was a distinctive feature of the C class.

Second, the sunken three-piece sub has specific features common only to the Pearl Harbor *ko-hyōteki*. One modification of major interest that the 2014 interior camera inspection encountered was an overhead mounted high-pressure air flask inside the forward battery compartment. This is a significant diagnostic feature. The Pearl Harbor submarines were all fitted with four high pressure air flasks and an oxygen flask inside the forward battery compartment, necessitating the removal of thirty-two battery trays to accommodate them on the overhead (Itani et al. 1993:121). The oxygen flask was there to provide additional life support for an extended mission, while the high-pressure flasks were added to give sufficient compressed air to control the rudders and diving planes. After Pearl Harbor, further modifications suggested by the operational experiences gathered during training and launching of the Special Attack Unit commenced as early as December 11, 1941, and continued through May 1942 (Itani et al. 1993:125). Rudder and plane control was changed from high pressure air to hydraulic transmission and so "no battery trays had to be removed and the fitting of additional HP air and oxygen bottles was not necessary" (Itani et al. 1993:125).

In 2009, Vice Admiral Ueda based his positive identification of the "three-piece" midget as a Pearl Harbor attack boat on the characteristic "figure-eight" torpedo guard at its bow. This design was too easily misshapen and blocked the torpedoes from firing, so they were subsequently removed and replaced with "runners [to] enable the boat to creep along the sea-bed" (Itani et al. 1993:126). The only *ko-hyōteki* ever to possess the "figure-eight" guards, as Admiral Ueda, a veteran of the *ko-hyōteki* corps, well knew, were the five boats taken to Pearl Harbor. Additionally, the forward navigation light is blanked off, as was done with the other midgets in the Special Attack Unit.

There is also no access hatch at the bottom of the hull in the center section, a modification made to Type A craft after Pearl Harbor. Initially it was done for those sent to Sydney and Diego Suarez, and then after May 1942, "all *Kohyōteki* were prepared for the fitting of access cylinders" (Itani et al. 1993:126). These features specifically date the three-piece midget not only before May 1942 but to December 1941. Only four other submarines possessed the characteristics present at the three-piece midget site, and they are HA-19 in Fredericksburg, Texas, the "*Ward*'s midget," the Keehi Lagoon midget now at Etajima, and the buried midget sunk by USS *Monaghan* on December 7, 1941.

Third, the craft was destroyed, intact and presumably operational or nearly operational, by an aft scuttling charge. All the internal fittings were in place at that time and remain so other than those that were in proximity to the explosion. Likewise, the periscope, radio antenna, motor, forward batteries, hydrophones, and other fittings and equipment are still present on the craft; there appears to have been no stripping to facilitate study or transportation, as is the case with other wartime recovered *ko-hyōteki*. It made no sense to lift and transport the full weight and sheer bulk of a completely fitted, lead acid battery-loaded submarine thousands of miles if this craft had come from Guadalcanal, Rabaul, Okinawa, or Japan. This is especially true when one considers the risk of batteries leaking acid or chlorine gas in transit.

While there is the possibility of an unfired charge remaining in the forward battery compartment, it is worth noting that the Pearl Harbor midgets carried only one scuttling charge in the aft battery. After its self-destruction, the evidence indicates this craft was found, cut externally into its three component pieces, roughly rigged to be raised (presumably onto a barge), and then dumped, one piece at a time in close succession just outside the 3 mile limit of Pearl Harbor. In applying Occam's razor, it would seem the simplest answer is that the three-piece midget was found not far from where it now lies. Why haul an intact, unstripped, explosively damaged craft thousands of miles for disposal? This craft must have been found close by, raised, cut apart, and dumped without any obvious attempt at salvage, study, or stripping. Apparently this was all done quietly without ever being discovered by the media or the public until 1992–2001.

Fourth, while naval records are not complete, wartime recovery of midget submarines was a rare occurrence. I-24 *tou*, the two Sydney craft, one of the Guadalcanal *kō-hyōteki*, and one Type C boat at Guam, were not only raised but recovered and are today museum pieces. Other craft were brought up and examined but then scuttled and left close to their fields of battle, such as the craft at Guadalcanal, Kiska, and Rabaul, and also at Cebu, Saipan, and Okinawa. Because of this wartime policy of examination and abandonment of midget submarines that had been captured or raised, there are several *kō-hyōteki* wrecks that remain submerged or on the beach at Kiska, Guadalcanal, Papua New Guinea, the Philippines, Saipan, and Okinawa. One of the authors believed in 1992 that the discovery of what would come to be known as the "three-piece" midget was likely a postwar recovery (perhaps the Type C raised at Okinawa, which recent research shows was rescuttled in Buckner Bay). Years of subsequent research and detailed observations of this wreck have ultimately led him to conclude that it is actually one of the five Pearl Harbor attack subs. It makes no sense to take an older Type A craft to Pearl Harbor anytime after 1942, especially one that is so severely damaged. By 1942, thanks to the analysis of I-24 *tou* and the Sydney midgets, the Allies knew all they needed or wanted to know about these craft. Instructions to gather only intelligence material from inside raised midgets applied after 1942.

Finally, as to the questions of how the fifth and final *kō-hyōteki* came to rest in the deep waters off Pearl Harbor, and whether it is I-16 *tou*, there is a hypothesis developed by HURL.

The HURL Scenario

HURL's Kerby and Price believe the sub in question is one sighted by, fired upon, and fired back at by USS *St. Louis* (CL-49) outside Pearl Harbor's entrance on December 7, 1941. They feel it is unlikely that any midget sub made it all the way to Battleship Row. First of all, these craft were notoriously difficult to control at periscope depth. They did not have bow planes, and the stern planes were very small and ineffective. Both *Ward*'s midget and the midget submarine rammed by USS *Monaghan* were spotted running with the conning tower exposed. The submarine sunk by the *Monaghan* had barely made it into the harbor before it was detected and fired on by several shore batteries. After weighing the various arguments around Autometrics's analysis of the Battleship Row photograph, the HURL team believes it does not show the fifth midget firing torpedoes. The HURL explanation for the identity of the "three-piece" craft is that it is a submarine at the harbor entrance that fired its torpedoes at USS *St. Louis*.

At 09:31, in the midst of the Japanese raid, *St. Louis* got under way and stood out for sea via Pearl Harbor's South Channel. When just inside the entrance buoys, according to commanding officer George Rood, "two torpedoes were seen approaching the ship from starboard from a range between 1,000 to 2,000 yards," but before striking their target, they hit a reef "to westward of the dredged channel and exploded doing no damage" (Commanding Officer, USS *St. Louis* 1941). Some of the *St. Louis* crew reported seeing a portion of the attacking submarine: "At the source of the torpedo tracks a dark gray object about 18" long was seen projecting above the water about 8'. At the time, it was not positively known that this was part of a 'baby' submarine but the Commanding Officer has since seen the one on display at the Submarine Base and is positive that the object sighted was the top of the periscope fair water of a 'baby' submarine" (Commanding Officer, USS *St. Louis* 1941).

St. Louis opened up on her suspected attacker with the starboard 5 inch gun battery

USS *St. Louis*. Despite the doubts of some who believe *St. Louis* did not encounter and shoot at a midget submarine off the entrance to Pearl Harbor on the morning of December 7, 1941, the authors believe that they did and that the craft they encountered was the same one spotted by USS *Condor* several hours earlier and subsequently scuttled by its crew after their engagement with *St. Louis*. Rediscovered and quietly raised and cut into pieces by the navy in 1951, it is now further offshore in deep water and is known as the "three-piece" midget. (Burl Burlingame)

for 3 minutes, and the gunners believed they made hits as the "submarine very shortly (30 seconds approximately) disappeared from view" (Commanding Officer, USS *St. Louis* 1941). Not in favor of this argument, author Burl Burlingame, citing after action reports from USS *Condor*, believes that *St. Louis* shelled an Oropesa Minesweeping Paravane Float from USS *Crossbill* (AMC-9). Burlingame believes that the "three-piece" midget may have penetrated the harbor, fired torpedoes against Battleship Row, and then exited the harbor and not been spotted (Burlingame personal communication, November 5, 2015).

Reassessing the Role of the Midget Submarines in the Battle

Into the mix of an attack on *St. Louis* by a midget submarine outside the entrance, one has to also consider the actions of USS *Helm* (DD-388) that morning. Before *St. Louis*'s encounter, *Helm* was fired upon and counterattacked a midget submarine in the same area, just outside the harbor entrance. *Helm*, heading out of the harbor, spotted the submarine hung up on the starboard side of the main channel entrance at 08:17. The submarine submerged and then popped up again a minute later, apparently with buoyancy problems. *Helm* fired at the submarine, but it submerged again and remained unseen. *St. Louis*, at 10:04, was fired on by torpedoes they claimed came from starboard. The timing and the same area—off the main channel entrance buoy, to starboard, or off Tripod Reef (which *Helm*'s commanding officer specifically referenced in the after action report)—within a less than 2 hour period suggests that a midget submarine was in the area, unable or unwilling to attempt to penetrate the entrance or, as Burlingame argues, having escaped the harbor after firing its torpedoes.

Alan Zimm (2013) notes that from the two reports it is clear that "a midget submarine was operating just off the entrance to Pearl Harbor in waters right up to (and perhaps on) the coral reef, and expended both torpedoes" (Zimm 2013:331). Zimm then goes on and carefully, thoughtfully discusses this scenario and, we believe, thoroughly discredits suggestions to the contrary, asserting that, other than the craft encountered by USS *Monaghan*, no other midget submarine made it into the harbor (Zimm 2013:331–53). If the evidence of the insignia reportedly recovered from the wreck of that submarine sunk by *Monaghan* when it was raised in December 1941 is correct, that craft was piloted by Lieutenant Naoji Iwasa, the most experienced of the submariners and the leader of the attack group. The chart makes sense coming from a craft commanded by an experienced submariner who followed a ship entering the harbor. This is the tactic employed unsuccessfully by the craft following both USS *Condor* and USS *Antares*. It *was* successfully achieved only by Iwasa in his midget submarine.

As for the other four submarines, one was sunk by USS *Ward* before entering the harbor. Kazuo Sakamaki and his submarine failed to enter the harbor. And the Keehi Lagoon submarine, when rediscovered, lay outside the entrance in relatively shallow water, torpedoes unfired, scuttled without its charge having detonated and apparently without its crew on board. It also failed to enter Pearl Harbor. Taking the evidence into account, this could not be the submarine *Helm* and *St. Louis* encountered, and it is also unlikely that *Helm* encountered I-24 *tou*. That leaves only one candidate, the "three-piece" midget. There are, as previously noted, hypotheses that it entered Pearl Harbor, fired its torpedoes at Battleship Row, and then escaped to West Loch or out of the harbor. What may have actually happened may be simpler. It may have never made it into the harbor. While there is disagreement over whether *St. Louis*'s officers and crew fired at a severed mine-sweeping paravane, we believe that they did encounter a submarine outside the entrance. The action and short combat career of that craft all took place in close proximity to Tripod Reef, off the inbound port side buoy, outbound starboard side buoy of the Pearl Harbor entrance channel.

We here suggest that after firing both torpedoes, the midget sub sat on the bottom and waited. Admiral Ueda opined in 2009 that it would have been unlikely the crews could have survived after being submerged all day, though Sakamaki and Inagaki were certainly still alive that night and survived all the way around to Bellows Beach on the east side of O'ahu.

By nightfall, the Japanese submariners in the "three-piece" craft would have been in their sub for about 17 hours. The crew were probably exhausted, confused, and near death from asphyxiation. After their encounters with *Helm* and *St. Louis* and sitting on the bottom all day listening to explosions and ships overhead, they may have decided to try to surface, risking detection. Death was a certainty anyway if they did not come up for air. If this craft surfaced and was I-16 *tou*, that event occurred around 22:41 hours, when the garbled message of a successful attack was received by I-16.

Whether it was I-16's midget that sent the transmission, for now, no one will know for sure, although the Japanese Midget Submarine Association and a number of historians believe it was. Only more detailed archaeology, including excavation, recovery, and study of components or personal items from the three-piece midget would offer any opportunity to assess personal effects to see if they matched those of I-16 *tou*'s crew and perhaps add new details to help answer this question empirically.

In support of this scenario, Vice Admiral Ueda, who personally knew the Pearl Harbor midget submariners, did not think the crews possessed sufficient knowledge of the local conditions to have the strategic forethought to plan a move through the winding passage to West Loch in Pearl Harbor. However, if the midget sub commander had no idea where he was going and simply chose the route where there was the least amount of activity, the craft could very well have ended up there. If indeed West Loch was the sub crew's final destination, then the submarine would have been hidden in the backwater of the harbor. Once there, out of battery power and having no other options following the 01:11 broadcast stating they were unable to navigate, there would be no honorable choice left but to submerge and detonate the scuttling charge. In this best-estimate scenario, then, the final "battlefield map" of the midget submarines at Pearl Harbor would place one wrecked sub offshore (*Ward*'s midget), one inside the harbor (*Monaghan*'s midget), one craft on the opposite side of the island (Sakamaki's midget), and two craft that failed to enter Pearl Harbor in shallow water on either side of the main channel entrance.

Fitting the Three-Piece Submarine into This Scenario

Today, the "three-piece" midget submarine lies in a field of discarded ammunition, miscellaneous debris, and eight LVT-2s that one student of the submarine attack, Parks Stephenson, suggests could be from the clean-up of the West Loch disaster, explosions that damaged multiple amphibious landing ships (LSTs) and amphibious assault vehicles (LVTs) in 1944. The LVTs are all the same type, he argues, and damaged (although the damage may be from decades of submersion and deterioration), and their close association indicates they were all dumped together. They lie in close association to what appears to be a trail of material that could have been shoved off a moving barge running on a course of 250 degrees. While this suggested to Stephenson the possibility that the three pieces of the midget submarine were removed from West Loch, placed on the same barge, and dumped at the same time as the LVTs, it is

THE WEST LOCH DISASTER

On Sunday May 21, 1944, intensive preparations for the invasion of the Marianas Islands were under way. Hanaloa Point at West Loch was the staging area for amphibious ships during World War II. Due to limited facilities at Pearl Harbor, twenty-nine large landing ship tanks (LSTs) were crowded together during these operations, side-tied in rows or "nests." Soldiers from Schofield Barracks were transferring ammunition and aviation fuel from the landing craft tanks (LCTs) stowed on the decks of the larger LSTs. At 15:08, a large explosion ripped through LST-353, second from the end of TARE (berth)-8. The initial explosion originated near the bow of LCT-963, stored on the deck of LST-353. The exact cause of the initial blast was never determined. Burning debris showered down around gasoline drums and equipment onto a fleet of twenty-nine waiting tank landing ships. Burning oil on the water set nearby ships ablaze, and hot debris thrown into the air swept through the Loch. The inferno and subsequent detonations of shipboard ammunition raged for the next 24 hours, sinking 6 of the LSTs, destroying 17 amphibious tracked assault vehicles (LVTs), and killing 163 men. Another 396 were injured (Cressman 2000:229; Salecker 2014). The disaster, later termed a "second Pearl Harbor," was immediately classified as top secret, and a rigid press blackout kept the events of May 21–22, 1944, quiet until 1960. Recommendations followed that LSTs no longer be berthed in tight nests, but due to the limited facilities available, nested moorings were deemed a calculated risk that had to be accepted. The planned invasion was ultimately delayed by only a day, but the salvage of the sunken ships and clearing of West Loch continued for months and into 1945.[11]

The salvage of damaged and destroyed ships from the West Loch disaster of May 21, 1944, at Pearl Harbor has been suggested by some as a possible scenario for an initial discovery of the three-piece midget submarine. The authors disagree but present all sides to the argument. Here, an official navy aerial photograph shows LSTs burning at berths T-8 and T-9 while others maneuver to escape the inferno. (Navy History and Heritage Command, 80-G-276907)

impossible to discern the sequence of dumping. The submarine pieces could have been deposited on the seafloor before or after the ostensible dumping of the LVTs.

Arguing against that is the archaeological study of the West Loch disaster, which suggests that in the aftermath of the disaster, clearance of damaged material focused on the ammunition loading dock area and the nests of LSTs, and that other areas of West Loch were not subjected to salvage or clearance. The area closest to the dock, and hence an area least likely for a submarine to "hide," was what was quickly cleared out as preparations for Operation Forager remained in full swing. Any damaged material was likely pushed ashore at Hanaloa Point, which is where the archaeological survey of West Loch in 2007 noted the sunken presence of mooring camels, the stern of one LST, and the more intact remains of LST-480 (Van Tilburg and Conlin 2007).

The LVT salvage and dumping in the defensive zone area, if associated with West Loch, may have come postwar, and there is no archaeological evidence to suggest that the LSTs in proximity to the three-piece midget wreck are in fact damaged or simply deteriorated after decades of submergence.

Stephenson's argument stems from a December 2006 best guess in which HURL initially suggested that the submarine could have been located by accident during the cleanup after the West Loch explosion. That work began with the salvage of all that was possible to save after the disaster and continued through 1945. The work continued after the war, and it was then, in this scenario, that one of the salvage crews digging through the thick silt to clear wreckage from the LSTs and LVTs would have uncovered the damaged and sunken sub. (What is uncertain is when—and if—all the LVTs were removed or as previously noted, simply pushed out of the way into the mangrove swamps at Hanaloa Point opposite the magazine loading dock.)

After soaking in the stagnant waters for at least two and a half years, the old boat would have held no intelligence value. To announce its discovery at that time would have also compromised the secrecy surrounding the disaster and salvage. It would then follow, in this hypothesis, that the salvors probably lifted the wreck onto a crane barge and then cut it apart with a torch at the flange joints to make the sections more manageable for disposal (just as examination of the three sections in 2009 indicated the submarine had been disassembled from the outside).

The bow and mid sections were then each rigged in a similar manner, with a hole punched through the forward end near the flange joint and a wire cable looped through the crude opening. The stern section simply had a cable choked around its tail. Packed in among damaged LVTs and other debris stacked on the barge, the remains of the last Pearl Harbor attack sub would have been quietly and unceremoniously disposed of 3 miles out to sea.

That is not an unreasonable hypothesis, particularly given the lack of specific salvage records regarding West Loch. We believe, however, that there is another simpler explanation, which again returns to the submarine encounters of USS *Helm* and USS *St. Louis*. Undamaged by the return fire, the submarine dived and sat on the seabed outside of the harbor entrance throughout the remainder of the day on December 7. As previously discussed, the radio transmissions received by I-16 would have come from this submarine, as HURL and later Stephenson have argued, but it was after a brief surfacing outside the harbor, not in the West Loch. The demolition charge would have been lit, the crew taking to the water or remaining inside, and the craft then sunk at the harbor entrance in the early morning hours of December 8.

What helps support this hypothesis is, for now, hearsay—but from a reliable source. On June 13, 1956, Captain Roger Pineau,[12] then working for Admiral Samuel Eliot Morison at the Office of Naval History, wrote to Charles Osborne of *Life* magazine[13] about the fate of the last two as yet "undiscovered" midget submarines from the Pearl Harbor attack. In the letter, Pineau noted that in or "around 1950–1951," a scientific expedition sponsored by George W. Vanderbilt III[14] had discovered the wreck of a midget submarine at the entrance to Pearl Harbor "west of the port hand sea buoy."[15] The craft was broken into two pieces, which lay about 2 to 3 feet apart. The discovery was kept quiet, and the Commander-in-Chief, Pacific Fleet, ordered the submarine "destroyed." Pineau also noted that the location was close to where, on December 12, 1941, a Japanese body was found with a sword strapped to his back.

If Pineau's recollection was correct, the body discovered on December 12 could have been a crew member from this submarine.[16] The three-piece midget could be his craft, which was then "destroyed" by cutting it into three pieces and then dumping it in deep water, in the usual dumping grounds, in proximity to the scuttled LVTs and ammunition, whose presence would only serve to confuse later researchers. In this scenario, again applying Occam's razor, the simplest explanation may be the correct one: The fifth, unaccounted for Pearl Harbor midget submarine never made it into the harbor, sank off the main channel, outside the buoyed entrance, and was missed for years because no one ventured outside the dredged channel until the Vanderbilt scientific expedition essentially stumbled across it in 1951 while trawling for fish samples or conducting dives. It was then quickly and quietly cleared and taken a relatively short distance for disposal at sea. Could it have been missed in the shallows near the entrance until then? The answer is yes. The Keehi Lagoon submarine, on the other side of the entrance

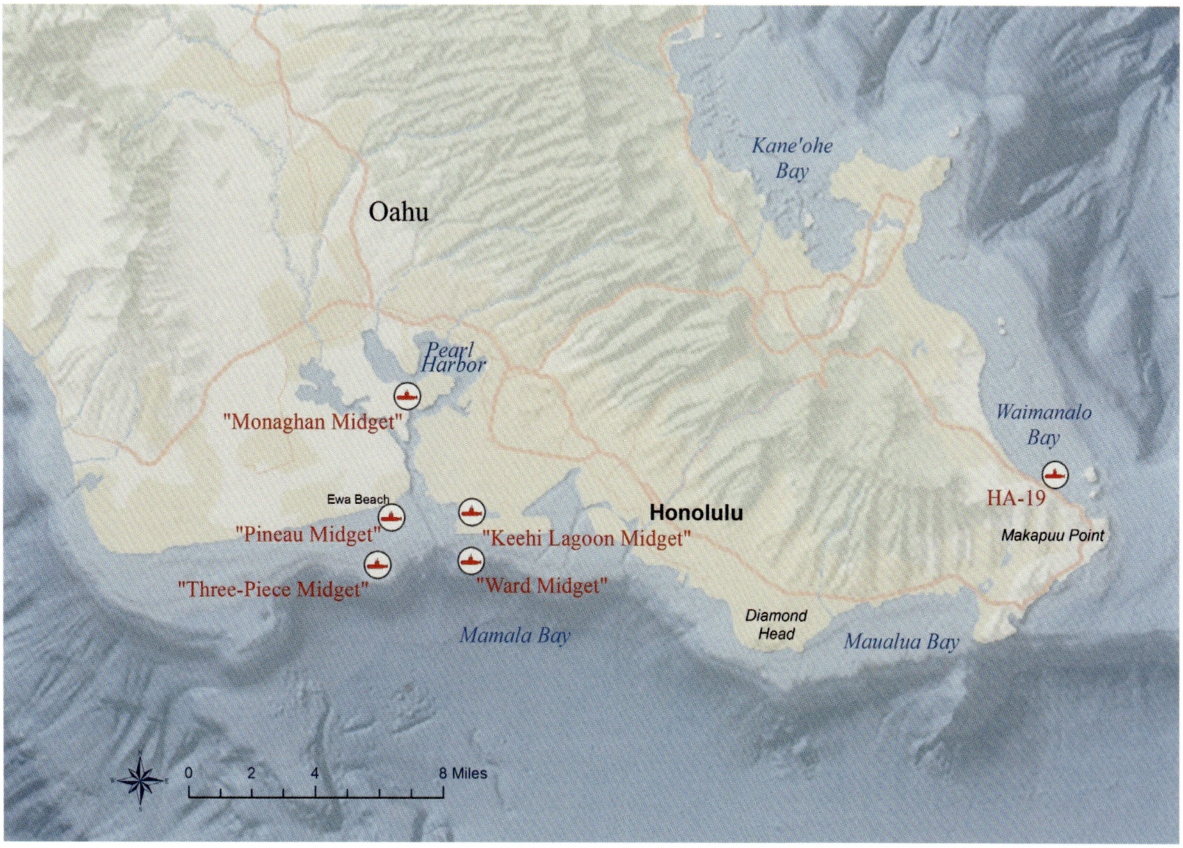

Final dispositions, known and surmised, of the midgets lost at Pearl Harbor. (NOAA/Tony Reyer)

channel, was also missed until rediscovered by a navy diver on a practice dive in 1960. The Naval Defense Sea Area around the entrance to Pearl Harbor was then, and remains today, a controlled area closed to the public. Regardless of which hypotheses one chooses to accept, the attack sub at West Loch or at the entrance channel entrance, or neither, one thing archaeology has clearly demonstrated through forensic analyses of the wreck is that the three-piece midget submarine is the so-called fifth and final craft associated with the *kō-hyōteki* corps' attack on Pearl Harbor. All that remains under discussion is where it lay from December 1941 until dumped in deeper water in a quiet, unannounced disposal. As to why it would have been found in 1951 and disposed of in this quiet manner, unlike the Keehi Lagoon discovery of 1960, also remains an open question as yet unresolved in the archives.

CHAPTER SEVEN

Archaeology, Memory, Management, and Protection

This book began with a discussion of how historical and maritime archaeology expanded its frontiers in the late twentieth century to embrace battlefield archaeology and how battlefield archaeology in the early twenty-first century has grown to include naval battlefields. At Pearl Harbor, this has been reflected by the transformation of the initial project of the early 1980s documenting the wreck of USS *Arizona* into, within a few years' time, a comprehensive study of all aspects of the attack and battle of December 7, 1941. The "frontier" this study ultimately faced was the question of assessing the extensive landscape of that battlefield and the archaeological signature of the battle.

The "frontier" was the challenge posed by the extension of the study into the deepest part of the battlefield, in waters hundreds of meters deep. "Deepwater" maritime archaeology is a relative term. Some of this team worked, using scuba, on sites in water 60 meters deep at Bikini Atoll at what was then a "frontier" of "deepwater" archaeology, while other colleagues conducted an 11 year excavation of the Uluburun site in Turkey at similar depths at the same time. The availability of technology to extend the range of the archaeologist beyond scuba diving depths was already apparent in the discovery of *Titanic* in 1985, when the *Arizona* project began. Between 1992 and 2002, the use of that technology to range deeper at Pearl Harbor and ultimately discover the last two unaccounted for and archaeologically undocumented *kō-hyōteki* makes the deepwater frontier not only one in which archaeology is possible at several hundred meters but one in which the archaeologist must adapt to in order to conduct meaningful work remotely.

The extension of battlefield archaeology to offshore waters, the broadening of the maritime frontier, is a timely and critical initiative, and one that allows us to understand the full context of the Japanese submerged archaeological sites. It would be very difficult to overstate the importance of the Hawaiian Islands to the US military, particularly during World War II in the Pacific. More so than any other location in the United States, the social, military, and economic changes spurred by World War II forever changed the nature of Hawai‘i.

The Pacific War propelled what had been a sleepy backwater location into a major strategic military stronghold and, in time, a full-fledged state. The critical role of Pearl Harbor as the home of the Pacific Fleet, a strategic location that some have referred to as the "Gibraltar of the Pacific," was, after all, the reason for the December 7, 1941, attack. Japan's bold and daring operation and America's immediate entrance into the conflict had enormous consequences at the local, national, regional, and international levels. This accounts for the significance associated with the stories of a relative handful (five) of small submarines and ten Japanese crewmen, and the attention paid to two submerged deepwater sites off O‘ahu's south shore.

The sites of *Ward*'s midget sub and the three-piece sub lie within the vicinity of the Naval Defensive Sea Area, seaward of the entrance to Pearl Harbor. This area was also used in the past as a deposition area, a dumping ground for a wide variety of materials and vessels from Pearl Harbor; it has literally become a submerged "museum," reflecting not only the moments of the attack but also the changing presence of the US military in Hawai‘i over the decades. Early bi-wing flying boats, aircraft from Patrol Squadron One in the 1930s, rest on the seafloor near numerous barges, landing craft, AMTRACs, and even military vehicles. Though not directly associated with the 1941 attack, these sites contribute to our understanding of the physical context of the submerged battlefield as it exists today. For instance, two World War II–era US Navy coastal patrol vessels currently rest in the vicinity of the *Ward*'s midget sub location, PC-578 (500 meters northwest) and PC-594 (800 meters southeast). Both are 173 foot, 450 ton PC-461 class submarine chasers, ordered in 1941 and launched in 1942. Both were intentionally scuttled in the years following the war, now ironically bracketing the then-unknown location of the very prey, the Japanese attack submarine, they were designed to hunt.

HURL is directly responsible for the discovery of many of these other deepwater submerged aircraft and military vessels found near O‘ahu. Multiple landing craft and aircraft in shallow waters, specifically the areas adjacent to World War II beach training areas in Hawai‘i, have also been the subject of a series of ongoing archaeological site investigations in recent years, joint agency surveys conducted by NOAA and the University of Hawai‘i Marine Option Program. These surveys add to our understanding of the broader military cultural landscape in Hawai‘i and the way the military has changed, and been changed by, these islands.

The concept of the maritime cultural landscape, refined by Westerdahl in 1992, provides greater context for understanding major historical events like naval battles than individual and isolated single-site studies. As noted in the introduction, this concept played a clear role in expanding the early studies of the USS *Arizona* wreck site into a larger study of the archaeological landscape of the Pearl Harbor attack. Strictly interpreted, battlefield archaeology should then reflect, in Hawai‘i, three possible battlefield landscapes for the three times that the greater Hawaiian Islands were attacked: Pearl Harbor on December 7, 1941; the subsequent flying boat reconnaissance known as "Operation K" on May 4, 1942; and then the Battle of Midway off the northwestern Hawaiian Islands, June 4–7, 1942. Numerically, though, submerged noncombat related military sites in Hawai‘i far outnumber the lost remnants of the actual battles themselves. The many months and years of intensive and hazardous training above, on, and under the sea have left a legacy of submerged historic properties. The NOAA report "U.S. Navy Shipwrecks in Hawaiian Waters: An Inventory of Submerged Naval Properties"

(2003) documents more than 80 US naval vessels and 1,485 US naval aircraft lost around the Hawaiian Islands, most during training and noncombat operations.

This raises the question of the definition of "battlefield" archaeology; what is the scope of that frontier? Certainly the progression of technical innovation and tactics can be interpreted from the numerous naval aircraft and amphibious vehicles in the oceans around Hawai'i. And the noncombat loss of lives may be no less tragic. There is the accidental West Loch explosions on May 21, 1944, during preparations for the invasion of Saipan, resulting in 163 soldiers killed and 396 wounded (Cressman 2000:229; Salecker 2014). There is also the loss of several LCTs on May 15, 1944, in foul weather, lost over the side from the decks of larger LSTs transiting to Maui for amphibious training, resulting in five wounded and nineteen dead or missing marines (Johnson 1986:12).

Nonetheless, as is clear with the attack on Pearl Harbor, the consequences of battles do generally outweigh the consequences of accidents during training and are therefore properly accorded greater significance. But from the perspective of the military cultural landscape and the numerous properties themselves, the submerged archaeological sites in Hawai'i have just as much to tell us about the war on the home front as they do about the battlefields.

Whether on a battlefield or within wartime combat training areas, the methods used to investigate these archaeological sites remain the same. Over the last decade, and as shown in this book, archaeology can and does happen in any environment, at any depth. Just as important as the archaeology is the responsibility that comes with any public resource and the involvement of public agencies. The responsibility in this case is to ensure maximum public benefit, as well as to protect sensitive and significant resources like historic artifacts that are also archaeological sites and war graves with international implications and meaning to two nations that once fought a bitter war and are now friends and allies.

Legal and Policy Issues

There are key legal and policy considerations when wrecks like these are discovered. The first consideration is the rights and interests of the identifiable owner. In many early treasure salvage cases applying the common law of finds ("finders keepers"), it was presumed the wrecks were abandoned by the mere passage of time and the fact that no potential owner had intervened to assert their rights of ownership. Under US maritime law of salvage, there is a presumption that there is an owner and a preference to respect the rights of the original owner through the application of the law of salvage over the common law of finds. Under this maritime law of salvage, the owner has the right to deny salvage. This right applies regardless, whether the owner is a private person or company or a government. Public vessels, those owned by a government, are also subject to the legal principle of sovereign immunity. Under this principal, the sovereign or government cannot be sued or subject to other legal action without the government agreeing to be sued. This immunity from arrest or a lawsuit extends to warships and other vessels on government (noncommercial) service. There are other considerations, such as the application of international and US historic preservation laws and whether or not the wreck may also be a grave site with human remains. If any salvage, recovery, or intrusive research is considered, there may also be laws protecting the marine environment that should be considered. However, in regard to the Pearl Harbor midget submarines, the interests of ownership, sovereign immunity, and war grave sites are at the heart of actions taken to protect them, consistent with international and US historic preservation law and policy.

While initially there was some question as to what exactly the three-piece midget submarine constituted—as of 1992, at least one dumped part, later determined to be three dumped parts of what together constituted one complete submarine—and whether it was a combat loss, discarded intelligence target, or war trophy. As it turned out, it was judged to be a combat loss that had been quietly removed from the original archaeological context of its loss inside or outside Pearl Harbor and taken to sea and dumped "out of sight and out of mind." A shift in its location did not change its legal ownership. As a Japanese "warship" not captured in battle but lost, and then subsequently raised from the seabed by the US Navy to be dumped in another location, it nonetheless would have remained a sovereign state craft belonging to a government—in this case not Japan but the United States by dint of Japan's surrender of all its vessels, afloat and sunken, at the end of the war. By the same token, the midget submarine sunk by USS *Ward*, lost during combat but not captured and not taken up or recovered, even in foreign waters and soil (the seabed), remained property of the Japanese government.

The path by which, 75 years after the battle, the current legal status of the two sunken submarines (the "three-piece midget" and the "*Ward* midget") was determined is a good case study of two former enemies cooperating in the protection of underwater cultural heritage and the use of maritime law in a US admiralty court for in situ preservation.

The Three-Piece Midget Submarine

The legal issues began with the July 27, 1992, discovery of the stern section of a Type A midget submarine several miles off Pearl Harbor by a team led by Terry Kerby of the University of Hawai'i's Undersea Research Laboratory (HURL) in the NOAA deep submersible vehicle Pisces V. It was a chance discovery as Kerby used annual test dives to also search areas where the submarine sunk by USS *Ward* could have been located. The target areas were developed in consultation with Dan Lenihan and Larry Murphy of the National Park Service (NPS). The Institute of Aeronautical Archaeological Research Inc. (IAAR) was in search of a 1930s aircraft and was allowed to come along on the 1992 Pisces V test dives. After Kerby's discovery of the sub on that dive, IAAR thought it was a piece of the "*Ward* midget" and subsequently took HURL's hard drive with the only video of the find. The institute engaged counsel and on August 11, 1992, used that footage as part of an in rem admiralty case against the wreck that their attorney filed on behalf of IAAR. The complaint asked the US District Court in the District of Hawai'i to award a "liberal salvage recovery with respect to the Defendant Wreck in the amount of $5,000,000" or whatever value the court set, with the institute entitled to "the sole and exclusive right to recover, control, deal with and transact with all such property without interference" (Civil No. 92-00522).

Upon learning of this action, Terry Kerby notified IAAR that HURL objected to the $5,000,000 finder's fee and notified the court of their objection. The US government was notified of the discovery of the submarine and the case against it. It was then the US government's determination that the three-piece midget submarine was government property and was possibly a war grave in addition to being a historical and archaeological site. This resulted in a two-pronged approach to protect the wreck from looting and unwanted salvage that was led by the Departments of State and Justice, respectively.

On September 19, the Department of State notified the government of Japan of the discovery. This set into motion the exchange of diplomatic notes agreeing that the wreck was the property of the US government. As it was thought to be the sub that was sunk on December 7, 1941, it was also recognized as being a war grave. The United States agreed that federal management would consider the interests of the government of Japan and the Japanese citizens presumed lost in its sinking. This was all done in coordination with NOAA, HURL, and the Department of Justice (DOJ). On January 12, 1993, in Washington, DC, the US government and the government of Japan exchanged diplomatic notes in which it was agreed that the wreck and its associated artifacts were the property of the United States and "that the wreck is a war grave, now owned by the U.S. and the desire of the Japanese Government that the United States protect the interests of the Government of Japan and its citizens therein" (US Department of State to Government of Japan, January 12, 1993).

The other prong for protection was led by maritime law experts Phil Berns and Mike Underhill in the DOJ, who filed a statement of interest on November 5 in the admiralty case filed on behalf of the institute. On November 12, the DOJ suggested at an appearance in court that in accordance with international law and United States salvage law, the owner of the wreck, the US government, did not wish it to be salvaged or disturbed, and the institute informally discussed a settlement. In a December 1, 1993, letter from Mathew Chung, IAAR's attorney, to the DOJ's attorney, Phil Berns, IAAR formally offered to settle the case, provided the government gave written assurances that the United States was the owner of the sub and accepted the responsibility for its protection and custodianship. Chung also asked for a finder's fee. In a December 4 e-mail, the government's response was to deny the request for a finder's fee and the request for reimbursement of expenses, and IAAR was provided with a copy of the diplomatic notes exchanged by the United States and Japan.

On July 1, 1993, a consent judgment and permanent injunction were entered in order to protect the Japanese craft that has subsequently become known as the "three-piece" midget submarine.[1] The US government appeared in this case as the owner of the wreck, pursuant to agreement with and the concurrence of the government of Japan. The institute agreed to this as well as the request for a permanent injunction (PI). Accordingly, Magistrate Judge Barry M. Kurren,

> ORDERED AND ADJUDGED that all persons and parties of any nature, unless they have obtained prior permission from the United States of America, are hereby enjoined and restrained from, directly or indirectly, taking any action of any nature in relation to defendant sunken vessel, including salvaging, attempting to salvage, moving, disturbing, removing, touching, making contact with the sunken vessel, its components, appurtenances, engines, boilers, appliances, furnishings, parts, etc., within the rectangular area encompassed by Latitudes 21°15′10″N. and 21°15′40″N. and Longitudes 1.S7°57′50″W. and 157°58′W.

The rectangular area for the PI was developed to address the need to provide reasonable notice to the public of the area subject to the permanent injunction so that it could be enforced while still withholding the precise location of the wreck from potential looters. The same cooperative protective approach was considered again when the wreck of the USS *Ward* midget submarine was discovered in 2002.

The *Ward* Midget Submarine's Legal Issues

On August 28, 2002, the "*Ward* midget" was discovered in another HURL expedition led by Terry Kerby in the NOAA deep submersible Pisces V within 3 miles of the coast. The legal and policy issues were raised again, and it was decided that the same path and process that ended up protecting the three-piece submarine applied, and the issue of ownership was not questioned. Accordingly, the United States and Japan, in a diplomatic note of February 12, 2004, agreed that the "the wreck and its associated property are now the property of the United States, that the wreck is a war grave, and . . . that the United State protect the interests of the Government of Japan and its citizens therein" (Embassy of Japan, February 12, 2004). "The United States desires to protect the wreck site and . . . does not wish it to salved or disturbed in any manner without its express authorization" (US Department of State, February 12, 2004). The United States promised that the utmost respect would be given to the vessel as a war grave and that the procedures the United States followed for this midget sub would be the same as those to be followed for the US treatment of its own sunken warships. It was also noted that the wreck site would be protected and managed consistent with international and US historic preservation laws and policies, including in situ preservation as the desired management option. A February 18, 2004, Department of State cable to Japan on the agreement states that the:

> discovery of the mini-sub and the exchange of notes are important for several reasons. The sub which was sunk on December 7, 1941, is evidence of the start of World War II in the Pacific (and together with one other mini-sub wreck), is the only known material evidence, of this particular part of the Japanese military operation at Pearl Harbor. It also verifies the account of the crew of the destroyer USS *Ward* who claimed that they fired a shot at a submarine in Pearl Harbor before the air attack on Dec. 7, 1941. As such, the submarine is a very significant historic resource and is likely to be eligible for National Register and perhaps even as a National Landmark. The treatment of the submarine, in situ, is in accordance with current U.S. archaeological standards and the respectful manner in which we would wish a U.S. war grave of this nature to be treated. (US Department of State cable to Japan, February 18, 2004)

It also stated that "wreck of the sub will be protected and preserved in situ (in place) by NOAA." Since then, the National Oceanic and Atmospheric Administration's National Marine Sanctuaries Program has been cooperating with the National Park Service and the Naval History and Heritage Command to manage and protect the *Ward* midget, including monitoring, education, scientific, and archaeological research.

All actions taken, therefore, by NOAA and the NPS follow the historic preservation principles, objectives, standards, and requirements of the 2001 UNESCO Convention on the Protection of Underwater Cultural Heritage, particularly the Annexed Rules. This means that the United States will seek the express authorization or consent of Japan before permitting any intrusive research, salvage, or recovery. Given this, in situ preservation is the primary management option, just as it is for sunken US warships like USS *Arizona*.

To date, NOAA, NPS, and HURL have conducted surveys of the wrecks, including a limited internal inspection by a camera carefully placed through an existing opening of the midget sub in a manner that minimized impact to the sub itself. However, since there was a possibility of observing and recording the existence of human remains, NOAA consulted with the government of Japan (through the embassy in Honolulu) in advance. The partial survey did not reveal any human remains in the command space of the midget sub, where remains would have likely been encountered.

Given the deterioration of the *Ward* midget, management decisions may have to be made within the next few years if, indeed, the craft continues to deteriorate and its status as a "sealed" site and war grave is further compromised. The three-piece midget is also deteriorating, and changes to the site, such as the collapse of the scuttling charge damaging portions of the hull, the disintegration of the conning tower, and the breaking off of the periscope and aft running light, beg the question of what to do beyond monitoring the deterioration. Is there a means by which the two craft can be better stabilized? Should a more aggressive program of monitoring and research take place? Should a more aggressive archaeological program, perhaps focused on the more accessible and more rapidly disintegrating three-piece midget, take place to learn more, perhaps through test excavation? If so, should some effort be made to recover key items? These are all key questions, all part of managing these two significant and ultimately fragile resources not only for the American public but also for the government and people of Japan. To that end, the Japanese government is kept informed of developments and research, most recently with a briefing held at the US State Department in September 2013.

Site Management Recommendations

Sufficient site investigations have been conducted at both the *Ward*'s midget site and the three-piece site to provide good data on deterioration and site formation processes. Changes to both sites have been observed over time. The following recommendations include critical steps for enhancing in situ preservation for both sites:

- Formal nomination of the midget sub sites to the National Register for Historic Places (NRHP)
- Secure collaborative joint-agency support for HURL maintaining the capacity for site engagement and intervention
- Selection and recording in situ of diagnostic artifacts currently threatened by site deterioration (three-piece sub site)
- Recovery and conservation of selected artifacts currently threatened by site deterioration (three-piece sub site)
- Sediment retention devices for halting (and potentially reversing) the scouring of supporting sediments beneath the forward and aft hull sections (*Ward*'s midget sub site)
- Quick response plan for handling any human remains that may be exposed by changes/deterioration to the site in the future (in coordination with the Japanese consulate)

Site identification, assessment, and monitoring and prevention of inadvertent (or intentional) human impacts to a site are all parts of in situ management. However, it is clear from the data gathered over the past two decades that the midget sub sites now exhibit the effects of advancing deterioration. Actions taken in response to this inevitable change over time for submerged archaeological sites range from "do nothing" to "full recovery and conservation." In this case, where archaeological sites are also war graves, where dangerous munitions are present, where depth and deterioration make recovery a less desirable option, the preferred alternative for the Japanese midget sub sites lies in between these extremes.

Vessels will deteriorate underwater, and there is little that can alter this fact. Nothing lasts forever. Protection of sites from undue damage, therefore, usually makes up the majority of management efforts in many places. But there are techniques that have emerged in the maritime archaeology field that provide cost-effective, low-impact measures for site stabilization. For instance, flat mesh mats with synthetic seagrass have been used on submerged archaeological sites in an attempt to reverse sediment scouring. Could scouring be reversed at the *Ward*'s midget sub site with such tools, increasing rather than decreasing the support for the forward and aft compartments? These measures need to be considered now.

It is the nature of submarines to hold their secrets securely within their hulls. Yet, as these hulls deteriorate, historically significant features and artifacts will be revealed. The capacity for site investigation needs to be maintained in order to take advantage of this "natural" excavation. Where possible, in situ measures should be implemented to protect these features and artifacts on site. If significant artifacts cannot be protected on site, consideration should be made for appropriate recovery and conservation. This plan is in compliance with an "in situ management as a first option" approach.

Key to all efforts in site stabilization, site recording, and artifact recovery is, of course, maintaining the capacity for deep ocean monitoring and management. Currently the only platforms with the proven track record of success in Hawai'i are the Pisces IV and Pisces V manned submersibles. Working dives to these sites by remotely operated vehicles (ROVs) have not yet been conducted. Whether by manned submersible or ROV, though, deep ocean archaeological investigation is costly. Today, by necessity (given the fiscal climate of tightening budgets), this means that joint-agency collaboration is a requirement for future research work.

As the management of the Japanese midget sub sites moves from baseline data collection and monitoring to more active in situ management, all activities directed at these significant locations must, of course, be conducted in a manner that is respectful of the agreed-upon preservation mandates for these historically significant archaeological sites and their special nature as war graves. At some stage, it may necessary to seek a protective order from federal court to help prevent looting and unwanted salvage.

Sharing with the Public

The investigation of these public properties by public resource management agencies is, by nature, "public" archaeology, which emphasizes interpretation. Archaeologists, historians, and resource managers, particularly those who work for public agencies, have an obligation to share their work and make resources accessible or available to the general public. Such access must be done in a responsible manner and format that takes into account the preservation and protection of the resource. The Japanese midget submarine wrecks from the Pearl Harbor attack have unique potential for public education and outreach and very specific obstacles to public access and availability. The midget sub is a deepwater site. Therefore, physical public access is not a practical matter. Publications, online access, and making the submarines accessible through media and film offer the only opportunities for the public to become familiar with these craft and why they "matter."

General information about Japan's midget submarines at Pearl Harbor is only available in the form of archival documents, many of them inaccessible except to researchers; history documentaries; published books; and visits to the partial craft at Etajima and the stripped hulk of Kazuo Sakamaki's submarine in Fredericksburg, Texas. Internet resources have shared a variety of documents and images, and these have grown exponentially since the 1990s. These include a "web presence" for the two sunken Pearl Harbor midget submarines by HURL, and a number of new sites that address the history and characteristics of the Type A and other midget submarines. Australia, notably, has done exceptional outreach with the story of the midget submarine attack on Sydney and in making the two craft more accessible, including complete, free online access to the documentation in the National Archives of Australia. Since the discovery of the "*Ward* midget" in 2002, HURL has placed a description of the site as well as a number of images on its web pages, and NOAA has also recognized the site online as a part of the Preserve America initiative.

A short article on the site's discovery was published by HURL in *Oceanography* magazine. All other research results to date until this book have remained internal to the management agencies. In part, this was due to the sensitive nature of the ongoing research. The midget sub is a war grave

Masao Yamamoto, a member of the Japanese Midget Submarine Association, holds up a sketch map of the islands where he and his fellow officers in the *kō-hyōteki* corps trained off Turtle Head (Kamegabuki) Cape near Kure. It was from here that the five midget submarines were loaded onto their I-boats for the voyage to Pearl Harbor. (David Jenkins)

Kazuo Sakamaki, the sole survivor of the Pearl Harbor midget submarine attack flotilla, pours water as an offering to the spirits of his fellow *kō-hyōteki* corps officers who died in the attack on Sydney during a 1988 visit to the site. (David Jenkins)

and due the appropriate protocols warranted by such status. (Potential human remains are neither displayed nor discussed in public.) The media has had a glimpse of the site; however, a general awareness of the ongoing research efforts and the full potential of the project to engage opportunities in education and outreach have not yet been realized. This book, as noted, is a key step in that direction. In addition, a more comprehensive website on the two craft has just been launched.

Kazuo Sakamaki and fellow classmate and *kō-hyōteki* corps survivor Teiji Yamaki at the central section of HA-21 in Sydney in 1988. Yamaki would have participated in the Sydney attack but was badly injured and his midget submarine damaged when batteries exploded while recharging the first day out from Truk. Yamaki's navigator, Petty Officer Shizuka Matsumoto, was killed in the accident. Their mother sub, I-24, returned to Truk and offloaded Yamaki and his submarine and loaded a replacement submarine and crew. The small number of veterans of the *kō-hyōteki* corps, like their few surviving craft, have passed into history. (David Jenkins)

As the seventy-fifth anniversary of the events of December 7, 1941, approaches, what we see in the passage of the decades is a complex mixture of history "as it was," recorded in the documents, language, and emotions of the time. We see the loss of the veterans of this battle and those that followed it, from both sides. We see the rediscovery of seemingly "lost" archival sources, and in particular, a wealth of sources now available from Japan tell us of the *kō-hyōteki* and those who designed, built, and crewed them. We also can see past the wartime propaganda from both sides that obscured the reality of these craft and those associated with them, especially the human side of the equation. In a telling and powerful discussion over dinner in Tokyo 10 years ago, one of the authors (Delgado) was alone with submarine veteran Takehashi Konada, an officer who ended the war as a "volunteer" in the *kaiten* corps. Konada told about how he did not "volunteer" but essentially joined in a nearly dazed state as just one man in a group of a few hundred. They stood at attention on a parade ground as a senior officer yelled that the war was being lost. They could turn the tide, however, with this new weapon. They needed volunteers. Looking side to side by shifting his eyes, he saw the men closest to him were doing the same.

This was *kichigai*, or crazy, he thought. And then he and every other man stepped forward, without having a conscious thought of doing so in his case. He simply joined the others as there was no other choice in the matter. "Have you ever been caught up in something bigger than yourself?" he then asked. Some of us have, especially in time of war, and when we were young. Some

MANAGING AUSTRALIA'S M24

A close parallel to the *Ward* midget rests in 54 meters (180 feet) of water off the northern beaches of Sydney. On November 12, 2006, divers discovered the final resting place of the last unaccounted for midget submarine from the attack of June 1942. Shrouded in fishing nets, the craft (designated M24 by the Australians, as it was the midget launched from I-24) was reported to the government. The significance of the site and its vulnerability caused immediate concern, and the government declared it a provisional historic shipwreck under the Commonwealth's Historic Shipwreck Act 1976 on November 24, 2006.

That action created a 500 meter radius exclusion zone and closed the site to diving. An in-water acoustic and camera surveillance system was installed and an immediate archaeological survey was planned as "observed cavities in the hull at the aft battery room and control room meant that the internal compartments and possible relic collections were at risk of disturbance" (Smith 2008:81).[2] A series of surveys took place between 2006 and 2008. There was also concern over human remains, as the sub is a war grave, as well as the unexploded scuttling charges inside the hull. Australia also notified the government of Japan, noting they did so to mirror the US consultation with Japan after the discovery of the *Ward* midget (Smith 2008:82). Japan has not issued any formal claim to ownership of the wreck. Australia is clear that the wreck is its responsibility to manage and formed an interdepartmental committee with representatives from the prime minister's office, the cabinet, the Departments of Foreign Affairs and Trade, the Department of Defence, federal and state heritage officials, and the Japanese Naval Attache, and tasked the Department of Sustainability, Environment, Water Population, and Communities to oversee the site with the New South Wales Heritage Branch.

The discovery sparked intense interest in both countries as well as international attention; among those who responded were the families of the two submariners interred inside the hull. The surviving brothers of Namori Ashibe and Katsuhisa Ban found the discovery aroused mixed emotions, with Mr. Itsuo Ashibe wanting to recover something to bury, while Kazutomo Ban felt his brother should be left to rest in peace (Sydney *Morning Herald*, December 12, 2006). Ultimately, what occurred was a ceremony in which nineteen relatives poured sake into the water over the wreck site. The Royal Australian Navy recovered clean sand from the wreck site, which they presented to the two brothers (Smith 2008:83–84).

go because they are willing, some go for love of country, or for ideology, or to protect that which we know—and it is all that we know. Rediscovery, archaeology, and integrating the human stories from both sides gives us more than a sense of these particular "midget submarines"; they provide insight and a reminder of more than battles or the waging of campaigns, but of the ingenuity, the heart, and the costs paid. Sitting inside the mud and sand of the *Ward* midget, and inside the muddy and rusty tomb that is USS *Arizona*, are men who will forever be young, and mourned, as they were on that fateful morning seventy-five years ago.

Buoy marking the wreck site of the wrecked midget submarine "M24" off Sydney Harbor, Australia. (Brad Duncan, Maritime Heritage Programs, Office of Environment and Heritage, Government of New South Wales)

Panorama of the damaged conning tower of M24, now open to the sea and a haven for marine life. (Brad Duncan, Maritime Heritage Programs, Office of Environment and Heritage, Government of New South Wales)

APPENDIX

Anatomy of the Type A *Kō-Hyōteki*

Much has been written about the construction, characteristics, and equipment of the Type A *kō-hyōteki*. The description that follows is based on Japanese sources, the archival records from the disassembly and analysis of HA-14 and HA-21 in Australia and HA-19 in the United States, and archaeological documentation of HA-8 in Groton, HA-36 at Kiska, the three-piece midget that is the likely I-16 *tou*, and the midget sunk by USS *Ward*.

General Arrangement

In describing the craft, all measurements for the submarine are reported with metric measurement

HA-19 at the Key West Naval Base in Florida in 1988, prior to being shipped to Fredericksburg, Texas, in 1990. (Dale M. McDonald, State Archives of Florida History, DM-0276)

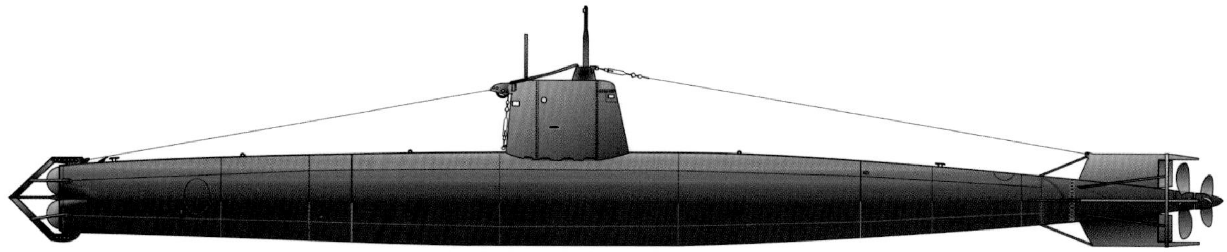

Plan view of a Type A submarine. (Burl Burlingame)

and in the English system, as many of the American and Australian analyses utilized that system.

The Type A *kō-hyōteki* is 23.90 meters (78 feet, 5 inches) in length, with a maximum beam (in the center section) of 1.850 meters (5 feet, 11 inches), and the maximum height, from the keel to the upper edge of the conning tower, is 3.100 meters (9 feet, 10 inches). The craft displaced 46 long tons submerged (Itani et al. 1993:121).[1] The basic form of the submarine is round except at the bow, where the sides taper to form an oval, and at the stern, where the diameter decreases to form a point at the propeller shaft gland. The hull "had the form of an enlarged torpedo with a conning tower" (Itani et al. 1993:121). The external fittings of the boat were few; in addition to the propeller and torpedo guards, a 9.5 meter long (50 mm × 12 mm) keel bar was welded to the bottom of the hull. The only projections aside from the conning tower were mooring cleats cut from 12 mm steel welded fore and aft (Itani et al. 1993:121). The basic design of the craft was simple enough to allow for modifications, as was the case with the post–Pearl Harbor changes and the subsequent Type B and Type C versions of the submarine.

The Royal Australian Navy analysis of the damaged HA-14 and HA-21 from the Sydney attack noted that the Type A submarine is "in general proportions . . . similar to a torpedo, i.e. overall length approximately twelve times the diameter; circular cross section for the greater part of its length; tail similar to British torpedo with vertical and horizontal fins and rudders, and right and left handed propellers" (RAN 1942:11).

The conning tower, as described for HA-19 in 1941, contains a "small tube leading to hatch which can be opened from inside only," a single periscope, a "vertical rubber covered radio antenna 32" high just forward of the conning tower hatch," two "white lights, one forward (screened), one aft," U-frame fairing periscope shears from "forward net cutting clearing line to top of sheers," and the battery ventilation exhaust (Description and Photographs of Japanese Midget Submarine No. 19, 1941:3).

As designed and built, the Type A boats are single-hull craft constructed in three sections, bolted together. Each section was joined by 2 3/8 inch (60 mm) flanges with threaded bolts 13/16 inches (20.6 mm) in diameter. A rubber gasket separated each section between the flanges.

The three parts to each of the submarines are the (1) forward section (17 feet / 5.18 meters long), (2) the center (control) section (34 feet, 11 inches / 10.64 meters long), and the (3) aft section (22 feet, 4 inches / 6.8 meters long). The bow section's primary function is to house the two torpedo tubes and the necessary equipment to fire the torpedoes. The center section contains the control compartment as well as two fore and aft battery compartments. The stern section contains the electric motor and gearing for the propeller and a free-flooding aft ballast tank.

An inventory and description of each compartment was laid out by the US Navy as part of

The disassembled bow of HA-19, 1941. (Naval History and Heritage Command)

The disassembled central section of HA-19, 1941. (Naval History and Heritage Command)

The disassembled tail section of HA-19, 1941. (Naval History and Heritage Command)

the examination of Sakamaki and Inagaki's HA-19. Here is their original description:

A. FORWARD BATTERY—contains:
   a. H.P. air and oxygen flasks on port side.
   b. One fourth of entire battery.
   c. 90.5 gallon trim tank under battery.
   d. Air purification.
   e. 284 lead pigs on port side forward weighing 3133 lbs.

B. CONTROL ROOM—contains:
   a. All depth and ship control instruments.
   b. Small crystal controlled radio.
   c. Periscope.
   d. Torpedo tube controls.
   e. Gyro compass.
   f. Electrically actuated directional gyro.
   g. Small electric trim pump.
   h. H.P. air manifold.
   i. Small regulator tank.

j. Hydrogen detector.

C. AFTER BATTERY—contains:

a. 3/4 of entire battery (36 cells).

b. Sound equipment.

c. Air conditioning apparatus.

d. Air purification.

e. 56.5 gallon trim tank under battery.

3. MOTOR ROOM—24'10-1/2" long to end of propeller hub,[2] bolted to center section—contains:

b. Motor control panels.

c. Motor.

d. Gear box.

e. Small free flooding tank.

f. Tail assembly.

2. CONNING TOWER—5'6" high to top of periscope shears, mounted directly over control room, contains:

1. Small tube leading to hatch which can be opened from inside only.
2. Periscope.
3. Vertical rubber covered radio antenna 32" high just forward of conning tower hatch.
4. Two white lights, one forward (screened), one aft.
5. Telephone jack connection for outside communication.
6. A U-Frame fairing periscope sheers from forward net cutting clearing line to top of shears.

The conning tower of HA-19, 1941. (Naval History and Heritage Command, NH 91335)

The top of the conning tower of HA-19, 1941. (Naval History and Heritage Command)

The hatch and periscope shears of HA 19, 1941. (Naval History and Heritage Command)

7. Battery ventilation exhaust.
8. No bridge. (Description and Photographs of Japanese Midget Submarine No. 19, 1941)

Construction

The Type A *kō-hyōteki* is made of butt-welded 8 mm (0.31 inch) cold-rolled, low-carbon, basic open-hearth steel plates (Itani et al. 1993:120) for the hull and 2.6 mm (0.1 inch) thick steel sheet for non-pressure-resistant parts of the craft (Description and Photographs of Japanese Midget Submarine No. 19, 1941:1; Itani et al. 1993:120). The hull is strengthened by 7.6 by 7.6 by .95 mm (3 by 3 by 3/8 inch) angle iron rings spaced 10 inches (25.4 cm) apart, intermittently tack welded to the shell. The hull also contains a 9.5 m long, 50 by 12 mm keel bar welded to the bottom of the hull. The selection of the steel and the use of all-welded hull construction minimize the submarine's weight. The crush depth of the craft was calculated to be approximately 200 meters, with a maximum operating depth set at 100 meters (Itani et al. 1993:121). The hull is divided by nonwatertight (but gas-tight) bulkheads with hatches.

Diving and Maneuvering

Ballasting for diving and trim was accomplished through free-flooded areas, ballast tanks, and lead pigs used as moveable ballast inside the pressure hull. The lead ballast in the bow consisted of lead pigs; the Australian analysis of 1942 noted each pig weighed approximately 10 lbs (4.53 kg) and was 6 by 2 by 2 inches (15.24 by 5.08 by 5.08 cm; RAN 1942:11). The lead pigs were sized to enable shifting by the crew "for any small adjustment in heel, trim and buoyancy" (RAN 1942:11). During the Pearl Harbor operation, Sakamaki and Inagaki laboriously shifted a number of weights inside HA-19 when they first ran aground.

The torpedo tubes pass through the forward ballast tanks, which lie beyond the forward end of the pressure hull, ending at a convex-shaped pressure bulkhead. The tanks are divided into the main ballast (diving) tank, which held 352.9 gallons (1336 liters) of water and the reserve ballast

Interior construction of HA-19, showing frames, 1990. (James P. Delgado)

Plywood bulkhead inside HA-19, 1941. (Naval History and Heritage Command)

tank (Itani 1993:121). The main tank was filled in advance of the mission by each "mother sub," as the diameter of the flood valve was too small and hence took more time than was at hand when the mission was under way (Itani 1993:121).

The reserve ballast tank forward is located "about 600 mm behind the forward pressure bulkhead" and was filled with water when the torpedoes were fired to compensate for the loss of weight; they proved inadequate as hard-learned experience demonstrated at Pearl Harbor and Sydney. "Even though this tank was filled through the sea valve comparatively quickly," it did not stop the bow and conning tower from bobbing above the surface, exposing the craft after even one torpedo was released (Itani et al. 1993:121).

The Royal Australian Navy estimated the diving rates for the submarines to be 3 feet per second down, 15 feet per second forward (Royal Australian Navy 1942). The Australian analysis noted "it appears the whole submarine has approximately neutral buoyancy. There is very little provision for alteration of buoyancy . . . The only provision for correction of heel appears to be by means of the port and starboard tanks in the control room—-these tanks are capable of being flooded independently:—Capacity, starboard 9 cu.ft., port 8 cu.ft." (RAN 1942:11).

The submarines were fitted with a depth-keeping mechanism, described as "a combination of pendulum and hydrostatic valve which operates, through a servomotor system, a hydraulic ram in the control room, this ram operating rods which move the horizontal rudders (an indicator in the control room shows a maximum of 26° up or down movement). The depth setting can be varied by altering the pressure of the spring on the hydrostatic valve" (RAN 1942:13).

Propulsion and Steering

The Type A *kō-hyōteki* was powered by batteries that drove a 600 hp motor. The Pearl Harbor submarines carried a main battery of 192 four-volt trays, arranged with 136 trays on racks in the aft battery compartment and 56 trays in the forward battery compartment. As built and used in all cases except at Pearl Harbor, the forward battery carried 88 trays, but 32 trays were removed to accommodate the additional air tanks for the

The forward battery compartment of HA-19, 1988. (Dale M. McDonald, State Archives of Florida History, DM-0281)

This view of a sailor disassembling the battery racks in HA-19 in 1941 offers a good view of the sub's interior construction. (Naval History and Heritage Command)

HA-19's batteries, 1941. (Naval History and Heritage Command)

The battery rack mounts inside HA-8, 1990. (James P. Delgado)

The surviving batteries inside HA-30 at Kiska, 1989. (National Park Service / Larry Murphy)

Pearl Harbor mission (Itani et al. 1993:121). The batteries powered the motor through settings at 52, 104, or 208 volts (RAN 1942:26).

The main motor has variously been described as 600 hp (Itani et al. 1993:121) and at 120 to 150 hp by the Royal Australian Navy (RAN 1942:26). It was a compound wound motor controlled by the central compartment, with the speed controlled by the field rheostat. "The scale of an indicator marked R.P.M. was marked from 0 to 2500, but it is considered that revs. would not exceed 2000, even for a short burst of speed" (RAN 1942:26).

The main motor was located in the tail section, with the resistance motor, the motor controller, the main contactors, the terminal board, relays, and the field and control rheostats just forward of the motor and just inside the bulkhead for the compartment. The rods for controlling the rudder and planes ran through the interior of this compartment.

The single propeller shaft was connected to the aft end of the main motor, passing through a welded pedestal, and then aft passed through the motor compartment, through the aft pressure bulkhead, and into the oil-filled compartment that housed a 5-1/2 to 1 double reduction gear (through twin trains of wheels), and then through another bulkhead to mount the twin counterrotating steel propellers, the sleeve shaft for the propellers, and at the stern, a ball-bearing, the stern gland, and the propeller boss. The gearing was supplied with forced lubrication through a pump that drew from "small tanks at the bottom of the Motor Room . . ." that also provided forced lubrication "to the pedestal bearing aft of the Main Motor" (RAN 1942:27). The Royal Australian Navy noted that "the workmanship of the main gearing is of the highest quality—all gear wheels, splines, etc. being ground all over—presumably to reduce gear noises to a minimum" (RAN 1942:27).

The engine mounts of HA-19 and HA-8, 1990. (James P. Delgado)

Shaft, propellers, and gears of HA-19, 1941. (Naval History and Heritage Command)

The twin cast-steel counterrotating four-bladed propellers were 55.25 inch (140.33 cm) outside diameter for the forward propeller and 49.25 inch (125.09 cm) diameter for the aft propeller. The forward propeller (as documented by the US Navy) had a 99.13 inch pitch, and the aft propeller had a 73.04 inch pitch (Description and Photographs of Japanese Midget Submarine No. 19, 1941). The Royal Australian Navy estimated through the efficiency coefficient of 0.8 and at a mean pitch of 100 inches at 1500 rpm equaled 18 knots and beyond with possible maximum speeds "greater than 20 knots" (RAN 1942:28).

Horizontally mounted hydroplanes were fitted to the stern, and two vertical rudders were mounted ahead of and above and below the propellers. Steering was accomplished using the vertical rudders, made of light steel tack welded to a framework, which were controlled by two steering wheels located in the control room that maneuvered a control rod that ran aft through the compartment and the tail section to the stern. The wheels (one power, one manual) are mounted on the port side of the compartment. In many ways, the design was a compromise between dynamic and hydrodynamic control. A lack of speed meant a loss in dynamic control, making

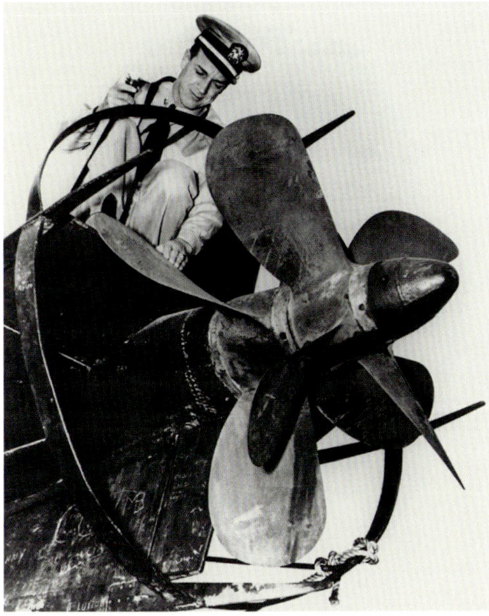

The "new" propellers placed on HA-19 after they were removed from the *kō-hyōteki* sunk by USS *Monaghan*. (Naval History and Heritage Command)

The original (damaged) propellers of HA-19, 1941. (Naval History and Heritage Command)

The propellers of Sakamaki's submarine were too badly damaged for wartime display and were replaced by those taken from the submarine sunk by USS *Monaghan*. Years later, the damaged propellers from HA-19 were discovered in downtown Honolulu. (Naval History and Heritage Command / Burl Burlingame)

the craft difficult to handle at low speeds. This was another example of how a craft designed for fast maneuvers in the open ocean was ill-suited for a stealth mission into an enemy harbor.

In addition to visual steering using the periscope, the submarine's commander could navigate with the Anschutz type gyrocompass inside the compartment and an emergency gyroscope. The gyrocompasses were powered by a motor alternator located on the port side of the forward (torpedo) compartment for the main gyro and from a motor alternator located at the after end on the port side of the forward battery compartment (RAN 1942:26).

Periscope

The US Navy described the periscope from HA-19 as 10 feet (3.04 meters) long, 3 5/8 inches (92 mm) in diameter, noting it was of "Japanese make but almost an exact copy of our Zeiss 30' periscope, two magnifications 1.5 and 6.0; raised and lowered by electric motor" (Description and Photographs of Japanese Midget Submarine No. 19, 1941:3). The HA-19 periscope's name plate indicated it had been manufactured by the Japan Optical Manufacturing Company in May 1941 as a "Type 92 No. 18" periscope (Description and Photographs of Japanese Midget Submarine No. 19, 1941:3). The periscope from HA-14, recovered at Sydney, had a name plate for a "Type 97 Telescope [*sic*] No. 18, Naval Technical Research Institute. Manufactured by the Japan Optical Industrial Co. Ltd., October 1939" (RAN 1942:32). It was otherwise identical to the periscope recovered from HA-19, with an upper tube of steel and a lower, inner tube of nickel-plated brass. The periscopes had a field of "40° at 1.5 magnification, and 10° at 6.0 magnification, and a line of

Interior of the central section and the steering gear and gyrocompass of HA-19, 1941. (Naval History and Heritage Command, NH 91337)

Interior of HA-8's control compartment, showing the access ladder from the conning tower, 1990. (James P. Delgado)

HA-19's gyrocompass, 1941. (Naval History and Heritage Command)

sight that could be moved from a 10° depression to 200 elevation only" (RAN 1942:33).

Air Replenishment

To maintain movement of air, and the purity of the air, a critical issue for any submersible, the submarine crews utilized two circulating fans. A fan mounted to starboard in the forward battery passed through an electric heater and was operated by a switch in the control compartment. "Air passes through [a] clack valve in Control Room to fan in Forward Battery Room; discharge is direct to Battery Room" (RAN 1942:29). The port fan was described as not only for circulation but primarily a discharge fan, "discharging through the pipe leading up the after valve of the conning tower to the atmosphere . . . This system can, of course, only be used when the conning tower is above water" (RAN 1952:29).

Portable canisters with CO_2 absorbent were also placed in the subs; the Royal Australian Navy noted that "about three dozen" of these "purifiers" were scattered about HA-14 and HA-21 (RAN 1942:29). Air bottles placed inside the subs also provided replenishment; for the Pearl Harbor attack, an additional bottle was placed inside each sub to deal with the expected lengthiness of the mission.

Motor meter board, HA-19, 1941. (Naval History and Heritage Command, NH 91336)

Oxygen bottles were also placed in the subs; the Royal Australian Navy found four 3.5 liter oxygen bottles; the US Navy found one 3.5 liter bottle in HA-19.

Armament

The bow carried two 5.4 m long, 45.7 cm diameter tubes, mounted vertically along the centerline of the bow, one over the other, in which two muzzle-loaded Type 97 oxygen torpedoes were carried. There was no breech. A "spherical casting riveted and welded to the tube . . . contained an adjustable tail stop with a thick rubber buffer and a housing for the air impulse air check valve" (Description and Photographs of Japanese Midget Submarine No. 19, 1941:1; Itani et al. 1993:121). The warheads of the torpedoes extended 300 mm outside of the tubes at the bow, with the tubes open to the sea and hence free-flooding and venting (Itani et al. 1993:121).

Itani et al. (1993) explain how the torpedoes were controlled and fired:

> The setting of the torpedo gyro and the depth-keeping gear was from the control room by means of mechanical linkages and shafts connected to the gyro and depth-setting spindles at the TT. The adjusted gyro angle and depth could be read on indicator dials in the control room. The torpedoes were fired by air pressure. Each tube had an impulse tank of 69.4 litres volume. Because the air was not lead to a tank a

The bow section of HA-19 in 1988, showing the torpedo tubes. (Dale M. McDonald, State Archives of Florida History, DM-0272).

Torpedo tubes, HA-8, 1990. (James P. Delgado)

The twisted figure-eight torpedo guard on Sakamaki's submarine. (Naval History and Heritage Command, NH 91334)

The bow of Sakamaki's HA-19 with the torpedo guard removed from the *kō-hyōteki* sunk by USS *Monaghan*. (Naval History and Heritage Command)

> stream of bubbles appeared on the surface after firing and there was much complaint about this from the crews. (121)

This in part draws from the US Navy's analysis in 1941, which has more detail, noting the impulse tanks and volume, though "impulse pressure was not indicated." It also indicates the following:

> Two and three sixteenth [inch diameter] copper impulse pipes lead from the tanks directly to the firing valve. On the valve housing is a small reducer with two copper service lines to the tube firing system . . . It appears there is a system of air piston interlocks operated by service air for each setting spindle and leading to the control room so that when tube is fired, service air goes to a "stop cylinder," lifting the stop bolt and releasing impulse air built up against the firing valve. Mechanical lugs and screws prevent operation of the stop cylinder unless the stop bolt and tripping latch are in the proper position. (Description and Photographs of Japanese Midget Submarine No. 19, 1941:2)

The report goes on to describe the action of the firing valve:

> The main valve of steel and cup shaped, is about two and three sixteenths in diameter and is held on its flat seat by impulse air, gravity and a large spring, This valve has a one inch hole in the center of its face and provides a flat seat for a brass, so called "auxiliary" piston valve. When air is released in the chamber of the piston valve, the valve lifts, thereby destroying the balance of forces holding the main valve on its seat and causing it to lift. A tapered lug integral to the lower face of the piston valve, controls the tube pressure and too rapid lifting of the main valve. A mechanically operated screw sleeve in the valve bonnet closes the line leading to the "stop" cylinder, when it is in the down position. An arrangement like this is necessary to charge the impulse line and in addition acts as a safety valve, no

> impulse stop being provided. (Description and Photographs of Japanese Midget Submarine No. 19, 1941:2)

Another problem inherent in firing the torpedoes as noted earlier was a loss of weight in the bow after firing even one torpedo, which caused the bow to rise dramatically and, at periscope depth, expose the bow and conning tower on the surface. After Pearl Harbor, a weighted counterbalance system was installed inside the submarines to deal with the problem.

Communications

The submarines each carried a wireless radio transmit-receive unit, located in the starboard forward corner of the control compartment. It was powered by a generator situated in the aft end of the torpedo compartment. The radio was connected to a rubber-sheathed metal aerial 2 feet, 3 inches (38.1 cm) long and 2 5/8 inches (6.6 cm) in diameter that was cranked from inside the sub to elevate it from a well at the top of the conning tower. The Royal Australian Navy examiners noted the radios were of "conventional design with curving showing extreme frequency limits of 7,900 to 10,100 kc/s. The model, manufactured by the Oki Electric Company,[3] was for telephony and telegraphy" (RAN 1942:6).

Conclusion

The Type A *kō-hyōteki* was and remains, even as a stripped hulk or as a wreck, an amazing technological and engineering achievement of the mid-twentieth century.

Notes

Introduction

1 Significant post-1989 battlefield archaeology of the next two decades included Fox and Scott (1991), Fox (1993), Foard (1995), Haucker and Mauck (1997), Curry (2000), Schoefield (2002), Newman and Roberts (2003), Sutherland (2003), Scott and Greene (2004), and Wilbers-Rost (2004). Since then, a wide range of projects have resulted in an extensive literature (e.g., Geier 2010; Pollard and Banks 2008; Schofield et al. 2002; Scott et al. 2007) as well as a dedicated peer-reviewed forum of the *Journal of Conflict Archaeology* (2005 to present).

2 As related to James Delgado by Burl Burlingame, who attended and reported on Sakamaki's reunion with other Pearl Harbor veterans and his submarine in Fredericksburg, Texas. See the Honolulu *Star-Bulletin* of May 11, 2002, available online at http://archives.starbulletin.com/2002/05/11/news/whatever.html. Accessed February 15, 2015.

Chapter 1

1 Great Britain, which "ruled the waves" with its vast navy, was particularly resistant to early experiments in undersea warfare. Clearly the submarine represented an immediate and unpredictable threat to the prevailing status quo of surface ships and established naval power. Despite resistance, the dream would nonetheless come to fruition. Truly some of the most interesting things about the development of submarines include the lack of any successful peacetime missions and the occasional reluctance of navies to fully adopt and support submarine programs while at the same time providing minimal funding in order to not be left behind.

2 At the same time, models of early, self-propelled torpedoes were developed and successfully tested, obviating the need for submarines to make as risky an approach as *Hunley*. See Epstein (2014).

3 Port Arthur is now known as Lüshunkuo and is part of Dalian in China's Liaoning Province.

4 Sold by Spain to Germany in 1899, the Caroline and Mariana Islands were occupied by Japan during World War I as an ally of the powers opposing Germany. Japan also occupied the Marshall Islands. In 1920, the Council of the League of Nations allowed Japan to control the islands under a mandate, which lasted until the end of World War II. Today these islands are part of the Federated States of Micronesia, the Republic of Palau, the Commonwealth of the Marianas, and the Republic of the Marshall Islands.

5 The Seto Inland Sea (*Seto Naikai*) is a long, relatively shallow body of water that separates Honshū, Kyūshū, and Shokokū, three of the four main islands of Japan. It has been used as an internal waterway as well as a route from the Pacific into the Sea of Japan for thousands of years.

6 The intelligence files of the Royal Australian Navy include a clipping noted as "Star 6/1934," which shows two men standing on the exposed floating topsides of the Nishimura sub, with others on a nearby boat, captioned "Japanese Army Officials watching the first tests of a midget submarine, which, it is believed, will be adopted for transporting

troops from the sea, up rivers, and into lakes, which have access to the oceans. Two men can man the craft, and it can cruise in waters too shallow to permit the passage of larger submersibles. This picture was banned by the Japanese Government, but was smuggled out to Europe" (Director of Naval Intelligence, Confidential No. 375-31).

7 Bywater was a spy for British naval intelligence in World War I and later was a naval correspondent for the *Daily Telegraph* and the *New York Herald*. Keenly interested in Japanese naval development, Bywater published a seminal work, *Sea-Power in the Pacific: A Study of the American-Japanese Naval Problem*, in 1921 and followed it four years later with a prescient volume, *The Great Pacific War*. As the book titles indicate, he was well aware of the likely coming conflict between the United States and Japan. Bywater's report on the Nishimura submarine trials is another indication of the man's genius. He died in London in August 1940, a year before the eruption of the Pacific War he had predicted.

8 The first two Nishimura boats remained with the Imperial Japanese Navy until 1945, when the original was destroyed by the US Navy. The second boat survived at Kure and in 1946 was shipped to the United States, where it survives in the collection of the Mariners' Museum in Newport News, Virginia.

9 A "submarine" is a craft that is built to spend most of its time underwater, while a "submersible" is a craft that operates on the surface but submerges to do its work (i.e., to wage war). World War I and World War II submarines were actually submersible craft, and it was not until the development of nuclear power that some historians consider the age of the "true" submarine to have begun.

10 In October 1992, James Delgado, working with then curator David Baumer, conducted a detailed survey and made measured drawings of the craft's exterior and interior; the team also took a series of black and white and color photographs documenting it.

11 The Imperial Japanese Navy never utilized this system for the midget submarines, but they were sequentially numbered.

12 *Ko-nekko*, for example, changes a cat, or *nekko*, into a kitten.

13 Tanaka's notebook was found inside a wrecked midget submarine, HA-8, at Guadalcanal and translated. The translation is now in the files of the Naval History and Heritage Command in Washington, DC.

Chapter 2

1 Gordon Prange interviewed Rear Admiral Sasaki on October 23, 1950 (Prange 1981:765).

2 When discovered in 2002, the submarine was found to lie some 640 yards (587 m) east of and just outside the defensive zone boundary. It drifted out of the zone when sunk.

3 The gun was conserved by the Minnesota Historical Society in 2006. See http://www.mnhs.org/preserve/conservation/reports/ward_gun.pdf. Accessed February 17, 2015.

4 This will be discussed in greater detail in chapter 6.

5 Analysis of Sakamaki's HA-19 by the US Navy after its capture showed that a mechanically operated "screw sleeve" in the valve bonnet that allowed air from the impulse tanks to fire the torpedoes was "found in the closed position, preventing firing of the tube" (Description of Japanese Submarine No. 19 1941:2). The torpedo guard at the bow was also mangled, blocking the torpedoes, but unless Sakamaki had figured out the screw sleeve problem, even without mangled guards, HA-19 would have been unable to fire. Either the equipment was faulty or Sakamaki was not fully prepared for the mission. Given the haste of training and preparations after the late-hour shift to the harbor-penetration attack plan, and the fact that Sakamaki also could not make his gyrocompass work (but the US Navy examiners could), this suggests perhaps some young submariners were being pushed beyond their limits.

6 It was not a deliberately misleading measurement. A US Navy intelligence report shared with the Royal Australian Navy, dated December 15, 1941, noted the captured sub was 41-feet long with a 4.5-foot-high conning tower; notations in pencil indicate a corrected length of 80 feet (Chief of Naval Operations 1941).

7 The scuttling charge was intended, where possible, to be a "third torpedo" when there was no other option, necessitating maneuvering next to or below an enemy warship.

8 HA-19's periscope was removed by CMM Michael "Mike" Cuello and F1C James E. "Jim" Green in January 1942 and replaced with a wooden replica for its war bond tour. The navy saved the periscope, which is currently on loan to and displayed at the USS *Arizona* visitor center and museum in Honolulu, Pearl Harbor, Hawai'i.

9 See the Vallejo Naval and Historical Museum's page on the visit at http://vallejomuseum.blogspot.com/2008/09/fdr-at-mare-island.html and http://vallejomuseum.blogspot.com/2008/10/fdr-at-mare-island-part-two.html. There is online footage of the visit showing the submarine on its trailer as the president inspects it from his car at https://www.youtube.com/watch?v=NX2Kb2R3IXo. Accessed February 17, 2015.

Chapter 3

1 https://www.youtube.com/watch?v=NL8qp20FqAM. Accessed February 7, 2015.

2 The British discovered the remains of I-20 *tou*, above water but breaking apart, on a reef at Nosy Antali Keli. The wreck, now submerged, remains there in an active surf zone, but the propellers have reportedly been salvaged and mark the grave of its crew ashore (Boogaerde 2009:285). Starting in the 1970s, members of the Japanese Midget Submarine Association began visiting the site of Akieda and Takemoto's final stand, and a memorial was erected in 1976 (Association of Midget Submariners 1984:48; Warner and Seno 1986:183).

3 The wreck of I-24 *tou* was discovered by recreational divers from the private club No Frills Divers in November 2006 in 178 feet of water approximately 3 miles off Bungan Head near Sydney's Northern Beaches. The submarine is intact, with its hatches sealed. An archaeological assessment and management plan has been completed for this site. See Tim Smith, "Wreck of the Japanese Type 'A' Midget Submarine M24," Australian Heritage Office, 2007.

4 The Australians shared their intelligence gathered from the submarines with the United States, and US naval intelligence shared what they had discerned. In July 1942, Vice Admiral Robert L. Ghormley and Lieutenant Commander J. W. Wintle were allowed to inspect the remains of the Sydney midget submarines (Commander South Pacific Area and South Pacific Force 1942:11).

5 Delgado attended the exhibition in November 1992.

6 The Australia-Japan Research Project, a joint initiative between the two nations centered at the Australian War Memorial, commenced in 1996 to initially promote research and dialogue on the World War II interactions of the two nations. The project has ended, but the website created for it is still online. The page on the midget attack is at http://ajrp.awm.gov.au/ajrp/ajrp2.nsf/26de8347ac6e7658ca256da3002479e5/bd273c64c0d01ad7ca2576120023607e?OpenDocument. Accessed February 19, 2015.

Chapter 4

1 The remains of the base and the last remaining midget submarine at Kiska were archaeologically documented by the National Park Service's Submerged Resources Center in the 1980s.

2 Both men were shipped north to the Aleutians to join the midget submarine base at Kiska.

3 Their sub, numbered HA-8, was raised by USS *Ortolan* (ASR-5). There is an excellent website discussing the maritime and underwater battlefield archaeology of the Guadalcanal campaign by Archaehistoria.org at http://www.archaehistoria.org/solomon-islands-archaeology/27-wwii-archaeological-sites-of-savo/176-site-savo13-japanese-midget-submarine-ko-hyoteki-30–11-november-1942.

4 Frank (1990), in his landmark study of the Guadalcanal campaign, discusses the limited successes of the midget submarines, noting the three torpedo hits, the loss of the boats and crews, and no lasting impact (501).

5 The details of the deployment and losses of these midget submarines comes from Japanese sources, as noted in http://www.combinedfleet.com/Bismarcks.htm. The primary source is a postwar recap of submarine operations prepared by the Defence Training Unit of the Japan Defence Agency. A copy of the report is in the National Library of Australia as MS 3108.

6 See http://www.archaehistoria.org/index.php/solomon-islands-archaeology/27-wwii-archaeological-sites-of-savo/176-site-savo13-japanese-midget-submarine-ko-hyoteki-30-11-november-1942. Accessed March 4, 2016.

7 See http://www.combinedfleet.com/Philippines.htm. Accessed February 13, 2015. US landings at Dumaguete on April 26 encountered weak resistance from a small group of defenders who then fled to the interior.

8 Five men were listed as killed in the ship's log with another twelve noted as missing. It was soon confirmed all were dead. Two other men died of their wounds in the next two days. The lost men are listed and commemorated at http://www.maritimequest.com/daily_event_archive/2014/02_feb/21_uss_renshaw_dd499.htm. Accessed February 13, 2015.

9 See http://www.ussrenshaw.org/Logs/log45.pdf. Accessed February 13, 2015.

10 Willoughby and Prange (1994) is available online at http://www.history.army.mil/books/wwii/MacArthur%20Reports/MacArthur%20V2%20P2/. Accessed February 13, 2015.

11 Following the capture of Cebu, USS *Snatch* (ARS-27) engaged in harbor clearance from May 26 through December 30, 1945, during which time a series of photographs taken by crew member Lieutenant Louie C. Weed, USNR, document the raising of a scuttled *kō-hyōteki* by *Snatch*. We are indebted to Lieutenant Weed's son, Robert "Bob" Weed of Abbeville, Alabama, for sharing the images and information.

12 In 1998, historian and naval officer E. Andrew Wilde privately published a detailed account of *Halligan*'s career and loss, which contains many original documents. It can be found online at http://destroyerhistory.org/assets/pdf/wilde/584halligan_wilde.pdf.

13 As reported on http://www.combinedfleet.com/Okinawa.htm.

14 Working from Japanese records, Hackett and Kingsepp reported on their Combined Fleet Sensuikan website that on May 19, 1944, a detachment of two Type C *hei-gata* under the overall command of Lieutenant (j.g.) Fukasa Yasuzo departed Yokohama for Saipan under tow by *Horaisan* and *Shoken Maru* in a convoy. The convoy was spotted by the submarine USS *Silversides* (SS-236) on May 29, 1944, which fired a spread of three torpedoes, sinking the two transports and presumably their midget submarines. Given the timing and location, Hackett and Kingsepp suggest that the Guam submarine(s) may be the same craft that drifted ashore after the attack.

15 ID no. 66-02-1125. The submarine was visible at low tide with a hole aft of the conning tower, which was the result of *Halford*'s shelling on July 10, 1944. In May 1986, a local resident sawed off the conning tower hatch and recovered it, much to the dismay of preservation officials (*Pacific Daily News*, May 17, 1986). As of 2002, the wreck was reportedly no longer visible (Thompson 2002:185). It likely was buried in bottom sediments with the upper hull collapsed or broken off and hence obscured by seasonal coastal change in 2002. A more recent image shows what appears to be part of the submarine off the end of the sandbar.

16 The hull number does not make sense as HA-51, under tow, was sunk in deep water hundreds of miles away from Guam en route to Rabaul with *Tarushima Maru* by USS *Whale* on January 17, 1944 (Cressman 2000:205). The confusion may result from the report of the number "651" on the boat shelled by USS *Halford* at Umatac Bay on July 10, 1944. That craft was not recovered and remains in situ as an archaeological resource. It is possible that the hull number of the Umatac Bay craft was HA-65.

17 After the fall of Okinawa, the minecraft vessels USS *Capstan* (AN-60) and *Baretta* (AN-41) raised the scuttled midget during harbor clearance operations.

18 However, they would have made no difference in a battle decided by carrier-based aircraft.

Chapter 5

1 Historians and aficionados have made observations based on the latest discoveries on the Internet; two of the most prominent are Bob Hackett and Sander Kingsepp's Sensuikan! website on Pearl Harbor at http://www.combinedfleet.com/Pearl.htm and Parks Stephenson's website at http://www.i-16tou.com, which is in large measure based on the work done by Steve Price and Terry Kerby of HURL. (See Hackett and Kingsepp's discussion before the link to the I-16 *tou* website.)

2 *Ward* crew member Will Lehner noted the following in a November 2002 radio interview: "There was a lot of doubt. People said, 'Oh, you didn't find it, so you didn't sink it.' I said, 'Yes we did. I know we sunk it. I know we sunk it.' Different ones I'd tell the story to, they'd say, 'Oh, you just think you sunk it. There's no evidence that you sunk it.'" See http://wpt2.org/wisconsinStories/worldwar2/moreStories.cfm?action=Lehner. Accessed January 18, 2015.

3 The online discussion about *Ward*'s attack on the midget on PearlHarborAttacked.com demonstrates the sensitivities of the veterans and their families about any suggestion the midget sinking was a "myth." See http://www.pearlharborattacked.com/cgi-bin/IKONBOARDNEW312a/ikonboard.cgi?act=Print;f=1;t=12. Accessed January 18, 2015.

4 One of the authors (Delgado) was part of the 1990 mission, which was in part sponsored by National Geographic. A 13-minute documentary, "Secret Subs of Pearl Harbor" (1991), told the story of the midgets and the ultimately unsuccessful 1990 search.

5 The dispatches from the mission are found on National Geographic's website for the expedition. See http://www.nationalgeographic.com/pearlharbor/dispatches/dispatch_01.html. Accessed January 19, 2015.

6 NURP's funding declined, as did NOAA's budget in recent years. In October 2012, NURP and NOAA's Office of Ocean Exploration were merged, and funding for HURL was reduced. At the same time NOAA transferred its assets to HURL—notably the Pisces submersibles in the NURP inventory, which HURL had been already expertly maintaining and operating. The budget cut has created a budget crisis for HURL, which announced that unless it can find a quick replacement for the nearly $3 million cut, it anticipates serious reductions and possible closure. See http://news.sciencemag.org/2012/04/no-love-nurp. Accessed March 7, 2016.

7 See http://www.soest.hawaii.edu/HURL/. Accessed January 19, 2015.

8 See http://www.soest.Hawaii.edu/HURL/subops/, http://www.soest.Hawaii.edu/HURL/subops/piscesIV.html and http://www.soest.Hawaii.edu/HURL/subops/piscesV.html. Accessed February 20, 2015.

9 See http://www.soest.Hawaii.edu/HURL/. Accessed January 19, 2015.

10 See http://www.soest.Hawaii.edu/UMC/cms/kaimikai-o-kanaloa/. Accessed February 20, 2015.

11 See http://www.soest.Hawaii.edu/HURL/science/accomplishments.html. Accessed January 19, 2015.

12 See http://www.soest.Hawaii.edu/HURL/gallery/archaeology/. Accessed January 19, 2015.

13 The wreck was discovered just outside of the defensive zone.

14 The NPS assumed management of the USS *Arizona* in 1980 and began managing the USS *Oklahoma* and then the USS *Utah* Memorials at Ford Island in 2007 and 2008, when World War II Valor in the Pacific National Monument was created by integrating the three memorials with six mooring quays on Battleship Row; six historic CPO bungalows on Ford Island; the Pearl Harbor Visitor Center; World War II elements on the Aleutian islands of Kiska, Atka, and Attu; and the former Japanese-American internment camp at Tule Lake, California. See http://www.nps.gov/valr/parkmgmt/index.htm. Accessed January 19, 2015.

15 Now the Naval History and Heritage Command (NHHC).

16 See http://www.routledge.com/archaeology/articles/author_innes_mccartney_on_how_shipwrecks_reveal_history/?utm_source=shared_link&utm_medium=post&utm_campaign=SBU3_SCS_3RF_6sl_3ARC_AMC15_X_X_McCartneyInterview. Accessed March 7, 2016.

17 See http://www.ibiblio.org/hyperwar/USN/ships/logs/DD/dd139-DL.1241.html. Accessed March 7, 2016.

18 See http://www.ibiblio.org/hyperwar/USN/ships/logs/DD/dd139-Pearl.html. Accessed March 7, 2016.

Chapter 6

1 Mr. Northrup (1906–91) was a critical figure in postwar nuclear weapons assessment. Graduating from MIT, Northrup, a physicist, joined the Naval Ordnance Laboratory in 1940 and was sent to Pearl Harbor. There he worked on two projects—demagnetizing ships to thwart undersea mines and a system to detect submarines trying to enter the harbor. In 1948, he transferred to the US Air Force and served as technical director of the Air Force Office of Atomic Energy (AFOAT) and the USAF Special Weapons Squadron. This work included top-secret aerial reconnaissance to detect radioactivity from air samples and seismographic monitoring to detect Soviet nuclear weapons tests. In 1949, the system detected the first atomic blast by the USSR, code named "Joe 1." This led to a presidential commendation. When his role in the discovery was released, *Time* magazine described him as a "cloak and Geiger man." Mr. Northrup later served as scientific advisor to the US delegation at Geneva during the atomic test ban negotiations.

2 It has been on display there since 1972. See http://www.combinedfleet.com/Pearl.htm. Accessed January 25, 2015. One of the authors (Delgado) has viewed it at Yasukuni's museum, the Yūshūkan.

3 An important observation is necessary here. It has been suggested that the "three-piece midget submarine" is in fact the disinterred *Monaghan*-sunk submarine. The condition of the submarine raised in 1941 and then buried as described by contemporary observers is not the same as the "three-piece" craft. Notable differences include no shell hole through the conning tower, no depth-charge induced "washboarding" of the hull, and the survival of the bow and torpedo tubes on the "three-piece" craft.

4 See article in the *Baltimore Sun* available at http://articles.baltimoresun.com/1992-08-03/news/1992216090_1_attack-on-pearl-pearl-harbor-midget-submarine. Accessed March 7, 2016. They initially indicated that they were representing Erickson Air-Crane Company. See also discussion of case and other legal action below.

5 The Sacramento *Bee* of August 3, 1992, identified Mr. Larkins and Mr. Carter as "Sacramento area men" and Mr. Larkins as "director of Aeronautical Archaeological Research." See also the *Baltimore Sun* at http://articles.baltimoresun.com/1992–08–03/news/1992216090_1_attack-on-pearl-pearl-harbor-midget-submarine. Accessed March 7, 2016.

6 Including one of the authors (Delgado).

7 Alexandria, Virginia.

8 For example, some, notably Burl Burlingame, author of *Advance Force: Pearl Harbor*, believe that a severed mine-sweeping paravane floating near the harbor entrance was mistakenly identified as a submarine and fired on by USS *St. Louis* (Burlingame 1992:226–27).

9 In the aftermath of the NOVA show, the host published a detailed website, I-16tou.com, which offers the view that the craft is I-16 *tou*. The site, like the documentary film, presents the conclusions of the HURL team and an archaeological research design prepared by NOAA and the NPS and tested by the NOVA team as part of their show.

10 In 2013, this disarticulated light was shifted away from its precarious position beneath the deteriorating conning tower and placed in a labeled, yellow plastic bucket, which was filled with sand to protect the artifact.

11 The African American Diversity Cultural Center Hawai'i (AADCCH.org) is currently engaged in research into the West Loch disaster and honors the African American soldiers who lost their lives in the explosions, now buried at the National Memorial Cemetery of the Pacific, in an annual remembrance event.

12 Captain Pineau (1916–93) was a graduate of the US Navy's Japanese Language School and worked as a code breaker in the Office of Naval Intelligence in Washington, DC, from 1943 to 1945. He then traveled to Japan

as an interpreter and analyst for the Strategic Bombing Survey and then the Washington Document Center. In 1947, the navy transferred him to the Office of Naval History. He worked at Naval History for Admiral Morison for 10 years. He then worked in the state department as chief for far eastern intelligence, the Institute for Defense Analyses, and as social science officer for Cultural and Educational Affairs. After 1965 he worked at the Smithsonian until 1972, when he was recalled to active duty and served as director of the Navy Memorial Museum in Washington, DC, until his retirement in 1978. Captain Pineau died in Bethesda, Maryland, in 1993. Fluent in Japanese and extremely knowledgeable, Pineau was a trusted and reliable source. It is highly unlikely his letter reflected anything but the truth.

13 Osborne was doing research to assist Walter Lord during the completion of Lord's *Day of Infamy* (1957), which was originally serialized in *Life* magazine in 1956.

14 Vanderbilt (1914–61) was a member of the prominent Vanderbilt family of New York, an avid yachtsman with a strong interest in marine biology and ocean exploration. Vanderbilt sponsored and participated in a number of expeditions around the world. Vanderbilt served in the navy during World War II. After the war, he founded the George Vanderbilt Foundation at Stanford University and accompanied some of the expeditions the foundation sponsored. The foundation sponsored a number of expeditions in the Pacific from 1951 to 1961. Vanderbilt's 175 foot yacht *Pioneer* was the platform for research, and hence Vanderbilt would join the trips. There was no 1950 expedition, but in 1951, Vanderbilt departed on the Pacific Equatorial Expedition in conjunction with the Philadelphia Academy of Natural Sciences and the California Academy of Sciences. It started in California, headed to Hawai'i, and from there went to Midway, the Marquesas, and Society and Tuamoto Islands. *Pioneer* was equipped with nets, dredges, and diving equipment for the expedition.

15 This refers to the entrance buoy, which was a second-class hand channel buoy.

16 We know of no instances where an aviator from the Pearl Harbor attack carried a sword, but Sakamaki carried one, as did his compatriots in the attack on Sydney, and Ikieda, when killed after the Diego Suarez attack, was carrying his. This suggests the midget submarine officers did bring their swords into battle.

Chapter 7

1 See Institute of Aeronautical Archaeological Research, Inc. v. Wreck of Type A "Midget" Japanese Submarine, Civ. No. 92-0052-BMK, reported in *Digest of United States Practice in International Law*: 2004, 1991–99: 1619–20.

2 The need for protection was underscored in September 2012, when an archaeological monitoring dive discovered that despite the legal protection and surveillance, unknown parties had entered the exclusion zone and anchored to the wreck, breaking off two propeller blades (Sydney *Morning Herald*, March 14, 2013). The surveillance system was not active at the time, as it was being repaired. The culprits have not been located to date.

Appendix

1 Both the United States and Australian analyses of 1941 and 1942 list the length at 80 feet, with a 6 foot beam and a conning tower height of 11.5 feet from the keel.

2 The Australians used the interior measurement.

3 The company, a pioneer in Japanese telephones established in the late nineteenth century, did extensive work for the Japanese Army and Navy during World War II. Surviving the war and an attempt to break up the company during the occupation of Japan, Oki is today one of Japan's "big six" electronics firms. See http://www.fundinguniverse.com/company-histories/oki-electric-industry-company-limited-history/. Accessed March 10, 2015.

References

Books

Agawa, H.

1979 *The Reluctant Admiral: Yamamoto and the Imperial Navy*. Kodansha International, Tokyo, New York, and San Francisco.

Appleman, R. E., J. M. Burns, R. A. Gugeler, and J. Stevens

1948 *The United States Army in World War II, War in the Pacific: Okinawa, The Last Battle*. Center for Military History, United States Army, Washington, DC.

Association of Midget Submariners, eds.

1984 *Ah Tokushu Senkotei*. Tokusen Kai, Tokyo.

Bailey, Major Alfred Dunlop USMC (Ret.)

1986 *Alligators, Buffaloes, and Bushmasters: The History of the Development of the LVT through World War II*. USMC HQ History and Museums Division, Washington, DC.

Beck, C. M., W. G. Johnson, and J. Schofield

2002 *Matériel Culture: The Archaeology of Twentieth-Century Conflict*. Routledge, New York.

Boyd, C., and A. Yoshida

1995 *The Japanese Submarine Force and World War II*. Naval Institute Press, Annapolis, Maryland.

Burlingame, B.

1992 *Advance Force Pearl Harbor*. Pacific Monograph, Kailua, Hawai'i.

Burt, R. A.

1986 *British Battleships of World War One*. Naval Institute Press, Annapolis, Maryland.

Campbell, J.

1985 *Naval Weapons of World War Two*. Naval Institute Press, Annapolis, Maryland.

Carpenter, D., and N. Polmar

1986 *Submarines of the Imperial Japanese Navy*. Naval Institute Press, Annapolis, Maryland.

Carruthers, S. L.

1982 *Australia under Siege: Japanese Submarine Raiders, 1942*. Solus Books, Sydney.

Chandonnet, F., ed.

2008 *Alaska at War: The Forgotten War Remembered*. University of Alaska Press, Fairbanks.

Chihaya, M., trans., D. M. Goldstein, and K. V. Dillon, eds.

1991 *Fading Victory: The Diary of Admiral Matome Ugaki, 1941–1945*. University of Pittsburgh Press, Pittsburgh, Pennsylvania.

Cohn, A. B., A. Kane, C. R. Sabick, and E. R. Scollon

2003 Valcour Bay Research Project, 1999–2002: *Results from the Archaeological Investigation of a Revolutionary War Battlefield in Lake Champlain, Clinton County, New York.* Lake Champlain Maritime Museum, Vergennes, Vermont.

Compton-Hall, R.

1983 *Submarine Boats: The Beginnings of Underwater Warfare.* Conway Maritime Press, London.

Compton-Hall, R.

1985 *Submarine Warfare: Monsters and Midgets.* Blandford Press, Poole, Dorset.

Cook, H. T., and T. F. Cook, eds.

1992 *Japan at War: An Oral History.* New Press, New York.

Coyle, B.

2014 *Kiska: The Japanese Occupation of an Alaska Island.* University of Alaska Press, Anchorage.

Craddock, J.

2006 *First Shot: The Untold Story of the Japanese Minisubs That Attacked Pearl Harbor.* McGraw-Hill, Camden, New Jersey.

Cressman, R.

2000 *The Official Chronology of the U.S. Navy in World War II.* Naval Institute Press, Annapolis, Maryland.

Cruse, J. B.

2008 *Battles of the Red River War: Archaeological Perspectives on the Indian Campaign of 1874.* Texas A&M University Press, College Station.

Curry, A.

2000 *The Battle of Agincourt: Sources and Interpretations.* Boydell, Woodbridge.

Cybriwski, R. A.

2011 *Historical Dictionary of Tokyo.* Scarecrow Press, Lanham, Maryland.

Delgado, J. P.

2006 *Khubilai Khan's Lost Fleet: In Search of a Legendary Armada.* University of California Press, Berkeley, Los Angeles, and London.

Delgado, J. P.

2011 *Silent Killers: Submarines and Underwater Warfare.* Osprey Publishing, Botley, Oxford.

Dorsey, J., and D. Slaymaker

2010 *Literary Mischief: Sakaguchi Ango, Culture and the War.* Lexington Books, Lanham, Maryland.

Dower, J. W.

1986 *War without Mercy: Race and Power in the Pacific War.* Pantheon Books, New York.

Doyle, R. C.

2010 *The Enemy in Our Hands: American Treatment of Enemy Prisoners of War from the Revolution to the War on Terror.* University Press of Kentucky, Lexington.

Dull, P.

1978 *A Battle History of the Imperial Japanese Navy, 1941–1945.* Naval Institute Press, Annapolis, Maryland.

Dyer, G. C.

1972 *The Amphibians Came to Conquer: The Story of Admiral Richmond Kelly Turner.* US Government Printing Office, Washington, DC.

Earhart, D. C.

2008 *Certain Victory: Images of World War II in the Japanese Media.* M. E. Sharpe, Armonk, New York.

Epstein, K. C.

2014 *Torpedo: Inventing the Military-Industrial Complex in the United States and Great Britain.* Harvard University Press, Cambridge, Massachusetts, and London.

Evans, D. C., ed.

1986 *The Japanese Navy in World War II: In the Words of Former Japanese Naval Officers, Second Edition.* Naval Institute Press, Annapolis, Maryland.

Evans, D. C., and M. R. Peattie

1997 *Kaigun: Strategy, Tactics and Technology in the Imperial Japanese Navy, 1887–1941.* Naval Institute Press, Annapolis, Maryland.

Foard, G.

1995 *Naseby: The Decisive Campaign.* Pryor Publications, Whitstable.

Foster, M., and P. Stone

1994 *Rabaul's Forgotten Fleet.* Oceans Enterprises, Yarram, Victoria.

Fox, R. A.

1993 *Archaeology, History and Custer's Last Battle: The Little Bighorn Reexamined.* University of Oklahoma Press, Norman.

Frank, R. B.

1990 *Guadalcanal.* Random House, New York.

Freeman, T. W., and J. P. Delgado

1991 *Pearl Harbor Recalled: New Images from the Day of Infamy.* Naval Institute Press, Annapolis, Maryland.

Friedman, N.

1982 *U.S. Destroyers: An Illustrated Design History.* Naval Institute Press, Annapolis, Maryland.

Fukui, S.

1961 *Japanese Naval Vessels Survived: Their Post-War Activities and Final Disposition.* Shuppan Kyodo Publishers, Tokyo.

Fukui, S.

1980 *Kaigun Kantei Shi.* KK Bestsellers, Tokyo.

Fukui, S.

1991 *Japanese Naval Vessels at the End of World War II.* Naval Institute Press, Annapolis, Maryland.

Garfield, B.

1995 *Thousand-Mile War: World War II in Alaska and the Aleutians.* University of Alaska Press, Fairbanks.

Geier, C. R., L. E. Babits, D. D. Scott, and D. G. Orr, eds.

2011 *The Historical Archaeology of Military Sites: Method and Topic.* Texas A&M University Press, College Station.

Geier, C. R., and S. R. Potter, eds.

2000 *Archeological Perspectives on the American Civil War.* University Press of Florida, Gainesville.

Gill, G. H.

1968 *Australia in the War of 1939–1945: Series Two, Navy, Volume II, Royal Australian Navy, 1942–1945.* Australian War Memorial, Canberra.

Goldstein, D. I., and K. V. Dillon, eds.

1993 *The Pearl Harbor Papers: Inside the Japanese Plans.* Brassey's, Washington, DC.

Gray, R., ed.

1985 *Conway's All the World's Fighting Ships, 1906–1921.* Conway Maritime Press, London.

Greene, J. A., and D. D. Scott

2006 *Finding Sand Creek: History, Archaeology, and the 1864 Massacre Site.* University of Oklahoma Press, Norman.

Grose, P.

2007 *A Very Rude Awakening.* Allen & Unwin, Crows Nest, NSW.

Grose, P.

2009 *An Awkward Truth: The Bombing of Darwin, February 1942.* Allen & Unwin, St. Leonards, NSW.

Haecker, C. M., and J. G. Mauck

1997 *On the Prairie of Palo Alto: Historical Archaeology of the U.S.–Mexican War Battlefield.* Texas A&M University Press, College Station.

Hashimoto, M.

1955 *Sunk: The Story of the Japanese Submarine Fleet, 1942–1945.* Cassell, London.

High, P. B.

2003 *The Imperial Screen: Japanese Film Culture in the Fifteen Years' War, 1931–1945.* University of Wisconsin Press, Madison.

Holmes, W. J.

1966 *Undersea Victory: The Influence of the Submarine Operations in the War in the Pacific.* Doubleday, Garden City.

Howarth, S.

1983 *The Fighting Ships of the Rising Sun: The Drama of the Imperial Japanese Navy, 1895–1945.* Atheneum, New York.

Ito, M., and R. Pineau

1986 *The End of the Imperial Japanese Navy.* Jove Books, New York.

Jackson, C. L.

1982 *On to Pearl Harbor and Beyond.* Pacific Ship and Shore, Dixon, California.

Japanese Defense Agency, Defense Research Institute

1971 *Senshi Sosho: Nanto Homen Kaigun Sakusen, Volume 83.* Defense Research Institute, Office of War History, Tokyo.

Japan Times

1942 *Special Attack Flotilla: Bushido in the War of Greater East Asia.* Japan Times, Tokyo.

Jenkins, D.

1992a *Battle Surface! Japan's Submarine War against Australia, 1942–1944.* Random House Australia, Sydney and Melbourne.

Jenkins, D.

1992b *Hitting Home: The Japanese Attack on Sydney, 1942.* Random House Australia, Sydney and Melbourne.

Jentschura, H., D. Jung, and P. Mickel

1986 *Warships of the Imperial Japanese Navy, 1869–1945.* Naval Institute Press, Annapolis, Maryland.

Johnson, W.

1986 *The West Loch Story: Hawai'i's Second Greatest Disaster in Terms of Casualties.* Westloch Publications, Seattle.

Johnston, I., and M. French, eds.

2014 *Battleship Ramillies: The Final Salvo.* Seaforth Publishers, Barnsley, U.K.

Kemp, P.

1999 *Midget Submarines of the Second World War.* Chatham, London.

Kinderman, B., ed.

1983 *USS* Ward *Fires First Shot WWII.* Impressions, St. Paul, Minnesota.

Klobuchar, R. P.

2006 *USS* Ward*: An Operational History of the Ship That Fired the First American Shot of World War II.* McFarland, Jefferson, North Carolina, and London.

Kurihara, R.

1974 *Ko Hyoteki*, Nami Shobo, Tokyo.

Lacroix, E.

1997 *Japanese Cruisers of the Pacific War.* Naval Institute Press, Annapolis, Maryland.

Lane, F. C.

2001 *Ships for Victory: A History of Shipbuilding under the U.S. Maritime Commission in World War II.* Johns Hopkins University Press, Baltimore.

Lenihan, D. J., ed.

1990 *Submerged Cultural Resources Study: U.S.S. Arizona Memorial and Pearl Harbor National Historic Landmark.* National Park Service, Submerged Cultural Resources Unit, Santa Fe, New Mexico.

Lord, W.

1957 *Day of Infamy.* Henry Holt, New York.

Mair, M., and J. Waldron

2014 *Kaiten: Japan's Secret Manned Suicide Submarine and the First American Ship It Sank in WWII.* Berkley Caliber, New York.

Manvell, R.

1974 *Films and the Second World War.* A. S. Barnes, South Brunswick and New York.

Martin, C.

1975 *Full Fathom Five: Wrecks of the Spanish Armada.* Viking, New York.

Martin, C., and G. Parker

1988 (rev. ed. 1999) *The Spanish Armada.* Manchester University Press, Manchester.

Maru Magazine

1995 *Maru Magazine Special No. 12, Imperial Japanese Navy Submarines, I-GO, RO-GO, HA-Go, Midget Submarines.* Maru Special, Tokyo.

McCartney, I.

2015 *The Maritime Archaeology of a Modern Conflict: Comparing the Archaeology of German Submarine Wrecks to the Historical Text.* Routledge, New York.

Mesko, Jim.

1993 *AMTRACS in Action.* Squadron Signals Publication, Carrollton, Texas.

Meyer, R., J. Köhler, and A. Lomburg

2002 *Explosives, Fifth Edition.* Wiley—VCH Verlag GmbH, Weinheim.

Morison, S. E.

1963 *History of United States Naval Operations in World War II: Volume XIII, The Liberation of the Philippines: Luzon, Mindanao, the Visayas, 1944–1945.* Little, Brown, Boston.

Newman, P. R., and P. R. Roberts

2003 *Marston Moor 1644: The Battle of the Five Armies.* Blackthorn, Pickering.

Ohnuki-Tierney, E.

2002 *Kamikaze, Cherry Blossoms and Nationalisms.* University of Chicago Press, Chicago.

O'Neill, R.

1988 *Suicide Squads of World War II.* Military Heritage Press, New York.

Orita, Z., and J. D. Harrington

1976 *I-Boat Captain.* Major Books, Canoga Park, California.

Parshall, J. B., and A. B. Tully

2007 *Shattered Sword: The Untold Story of the Battle of Midway.* Potomac Books, Washington, DC.

Pollard, T., and I. Banks

2008 *Scorched Earth: Studies in the Archaeology of Conflict.* Brill eBook Titles.

Prange, G. W.

1981 *At Dawn We Slept: The Untold Story of Pearl Harbor.* McGraw-Hill, New York.

Prenatt, J., M. Stille, and P. Wright

2014 *Axis Midget Submarines*. Osprey Publishing, Botley, Oxford.

Reilly, R. L.

2010 *Kamikaze Attacks of World War II: A Complete History of Japanese Suicide Strikes on American Ships, by Aircraft and Other Means*. McFarland, Jefferson, North Carolina.

Rohwer, J.

1983 *Axis Submarine Successes of World War II: German, Italian and Japanese Submarine Successes, 1939–1945*. Naval Institute Press, Annapolis, Maryland.

Sakamaki, K.

1949 *I Attacked Pearl Harbor*. Association Press, New York.

Salecker, G. E.

2014 *The Second Pearl Harbor: The West Loch Disaster, May 21, 1944*. University of Oklahoma Press, Norman.

Sano, H.

1975 *Tokushu Senkotei*. Tosho Shuppan Sha, Tokyo.

Schofield, A. J., W. G. Johnson, and C. M. Beck, eds.

2002 *Matériel Culture: The Archaeology of 20th Century Conflict*. Routledge, London and New York.

Scott, D. D., L. Babits, and C. Haecker

2007 *Fields of Conflict: Battlefield Archaeology from the Roman Empire to the Korean War*. Praeger, Westport, Connecticut.

Scott, D. D., R. A. Fox, M. A. Connor, and D. Harmon

1989 *Archaeological Perspectives on the Battle of the Little Bighorn*. University of Oklahoma Press, Norman.

Shibuya, T.

1952a *Submarine Operations, December 1941–April 1942, Japanese Monograph No. 102*. Office of the Chief of Military History, Department of the Army, Washington, DC.

Shibuya, T.

1952b *Submarine Operations in Second Phase Operations, Part I, April–August 1942, Japanese Monograph No. 110*. Office of the Chief of Military History, Department of the Army, Washington, DC.

Shores, C., B. Cull, and Y. Izawa

1993 *Bloody Shambles: The Defence of Sumatra to the Fall of Burma*. Grub Street Publishers, London.

Shores, C., B. Cull, and Y. Izawa

2002 *Bloody Shambles: The Drift of War to the Fall of Singapore*. Grub Street Publishers, London.

Smith, R. R.

1991 *United States Army in World War II: The War in the Pacific, Triumph in the Philippines*. Center for Military History, United States Army, Washington, DC.

Spennemann, D. H. R.

2011 *The Cultural Landscape of the World War II Battlefield of Kiska, Aleutian Islands. Findings of a Cultural Heritage Survey, Carried Out in June 2009*. Institute for Land, Water and Society, Charles Sturt University, Albury, NSW.

Stille, M.

2014 *Axis Midget Submarines, 1939–45*. Osprey Publishing, Botley, Oxford.

Stille, M., and T. Bryan

2007 *Imperial Japanese Navy Submarines 1941–45*. Osprey Publishing, Botley, Oxford.

Stillwell, P., ed.

1981 *Air Raid: Pearl Harbor: Recollections of a Day of Infamy*. Naval Institute Press, Annapolis, Maryland.

Sutherland, T.

2005 *Battlefield Archaeology—A Guide to the Archaeology of Conflict*. British Archaeological Jobs Resource, England.

Thompson, C.
2002 *The 25 Best World War II Sites: Pacific Theater*. Greenline, San Francisco.
Tomlinson, M.
1976 *The Most Dangerous Moment: The Japanese Assault on Ceylon 1942*. William Kimber, London.
US Naval Technical Mission to Japan
1946a *Characteristics of Japanese Naval Vessels, Article 1—Submarines, S-01-1*. United States Navy, Washington, DC.
US Naval Technical Mission to Japan
1946b *Characteristics of Japanese Naval Vessels, Article 6—Submarines, Supplement I, S-01-6*. United States Navy, Washington, DC.
US Naval Technical Mission to Japan
1946c *Characteristics of Japanese Naval Vessels, Article 7—Submarines, Supplement II, S-01-7*. United States Navy, Washington, DC.
US Naval Technical Mission to Japan
1946d *Japanese Suicide Craft, S-02*. United States Navy, Washington, DC.
US Naval Technical Mission to Japan
1946e *Ordnance Target: Japanese Torpedoes and Tubes, Article 1, Ship and Kaiten Torpedoes, O-01-1*. United States Navy, Washington, DC.
Van Den Boogaerde, P.
2009 *Shipwrecks of Madagascar*. Eloquent Books, New York.
Vego, M. N.
2006 *The Battle for Leyte, 1944: Allied and Japanese Plans, Preparations and Execution*. Naval Institute Press, Annapolis, Maryland.
Warner, P., and S. Seno
1986 *Coffin Boats: Japanese Midget Submarine Operations in the Second World War*. Leo Cooper, London.
Watts, A. J.
1966 *Japanese Warships of World War II*. Doubleday, New York.
Watts, A. J., and B. G. Gordon
1971 *The Imperial Japanese Navy*. Macdonald, London.
Willoughby, C. A., and G. W. Prange
1994 *The Reports of General MacArthur: Volume II, Part II, Japanese Operations in the Southwest Pacific Area*. Department of the Army, Center for Military History, Washington, DC.
Wise, J. E., Jr.
2005 *U-505: The Final Journey*. Naval Institute Press, Annapolis, Maryland.
Yokota, Y., and J. D. Harrington
1962 *Suicide Submarine! The Story of Japan's Submarine "Kamikaze" of Manned Torpedoes!* Ballantine Books, New York.
Zimm, A. D.
2013 *Attack on Pearl Harbor: Strategy, Combat, Myths, Deceptions*. Casemate, Philadelphia and Newbury.

Articles and Contributions

Anonymous
1945 Untitled article on USS *Ward*. *All Hands Magazine* (335) February: 24–26.

Carman, J.

2005 "Battlefields as Cultural Resources." *Post-Medieval Archaeology*, 39: 215–23.

Conlin, D. L., and M. A. Russell

2010 "Maritime Archaeology of Naval Battlefields," in C. R. Geier, L. E. Babits, D. D. Scott, and D. G. Orr, eds., *The Historical Archaeology of Military Sites: Method and Topic*, 39–56.

Daniels, G.

1982 "Japanese Domestic Radio and Cinema Propaganda, 1937–1945: An Overview." *Historical Journal of Film, Radio and Television*, 2 (2): 115–32.

Date, J. C.

1998 "Japanese 'A' Class Midget Submarines." Naval Historical Society of Australia, Sydney. Monograph No. 65.

Delgado, J. P.

1991 "The Japanese Midget Submarine HA-19: A Unique Artifact That Helps Us 'Remember Pearl Harbor.'" *CRM Bulletin*, 14 (8).

Fox, R. A., and D. D. Scott

1991 "The Post–Civil War Battlefield Pattern." *Historical Archaeology*, 25 (2): 92–103.

Friedman, N.

1980 "United States of America," in R. Gray, ed., *Conway's All the Worlds Fighting Ships, 1906–1921*, 105–33.

Fukaya, H.

1952 "Three Japanese Submarine Developments." *Proceedings of the United States Naval Institute*, 78 (8) August: 863–64.

Gould, R. A.

1983 "The Archaeology of War: Wrecks of the Spanish Armada of 1588 and the Battle of Britain, 1940," in R. A. Gould, ed., *Shipwreck Archaeology*, School of American Research, Albuquerque, 105–42.

Henry, T., and K. Dinsley

1998 "Pisces Ascending: The Little Sub That Could," in H. White, ed., *Raincoast Chronicles 18*. Harbour Publishing, Madeira Park, British Columbia, 7–18.

Hohjo, S.

1942 "The Nine Heroes of Pearl Harbour Attack." *Contemporary Japan: A Review of Far Eastern Affairs*, 11 (4) April: 564–84.

Itani, J., H. Langerer, and T. Rehm-Takahara

1993 "Japanese Midget Submarines: Kō-hyōteki Types A to C," in J. Gardiner, ed. *Warship 1993*, Conway Maritime Press, London, 113–29.

Jameson, J. H., Jr., and D. Scott-Ireton, eds.

2007 *Out of the Blue: Public Interpretation of Maritime Cultural Resources*, Springer US, New York.

Kimura, J., M. Staniforth, and L. Thi

2014 "Naval Battlefield Archaeology of the Kublai Khan Fleets." *International Journal of Nautical Archaeology*, 43 (1): 76–86.

Knauss, J. A.

2000 "The Emergence of the National Science Foundation as a Supporter of Ocean Science in the United States," in Ocean Studies Board, National Research Council, eds., *50 Years of Ocean Discovery: National Science Foundation 1950–2000*, National Academy Press, Washington, DC, 3–10.

Lacroix, E.

1960 "The Japanese Imperial Navy: Submarines ('Sensuikan')." *The Belgian Shiplover*, 76 (205) Part III: 255–78.

McCandless, B.

1962 "Comments and Discussion." *US Naval Institute Proceedings* (88) July: 120.

McCarthy, M.

1998 "The Submarine as a Class of Archaeological Site." *Bulletin of the Australian Institute for Maritime Archaeology* (22): 61–70.

Merriman, A., and C. Olson

2010 "Minnesota's Naval and Maritime Memorials." *The Minnesota Preservationist*, May/June: 7–8. Available online at http://maritimeheritagemn.org/MNPreservationist.pdf

Moonesum, M., and P. Charmdooz

2012 "General Arrangement and Naval Architectural Aspects in Midget Submarines." Paper presented at the Fourth International Conference on Underwater System Technology: Theory and Applications 2012 (USYS'12), December 5–6, Shah Alam, Malaysia. Available online at http://dl.kashti.ir/ARTICLES/USYS-2012.pdf

Murphy, L. E., and D. J. Lenihan

1995 "Recent Archaeological Investigations of World War II Material in Kiska Harbor, Aleutian Islands," in F. Chandonnet, ed., *Alaska at War, 1941–1945: The Forgotten War Remembered: Papers from the Alaska at War Symposium, Anchorage, Alaska, November 11–13, 1993*, Alaska at War Committee, Anchorage, 353–57.

Potter, S. R., R. C. Sonderman, M. C. Creveling, and S. L. Dean

2000 "No Maneuvering and Very Little Tactics: Archaeology and the Battle of Brawner Farm," in C. R. Geier and S. R. Potter, eds., *Archeological Perspectives on the American Civil War*, 3–28.

Riley, J. E., and B. L. Delanoy

1961 "The Last of the Midgets." *US Naval Institute Proceedings* 87 (December): 127–28.

Silcock, D.

2015 "Ghosts of the Machines: Kavieng's World War II Wrecks." *X-Ray Magazine* 66 (May): 8–15.

Smith, Col. C. C., Jr.

1981 "A Hell of a Christmas," in P. Stillwell, ed., *Air Raid Pearl Harbor*, 223–25.

Smith, T.

2007 "Wreck of the Japanese Type 'A' Midget Submarine *M24*." Heritage Office, NSW Department of Planning, Australia.

Smith, T.

2008 "Managing an Australian Midget: The Imperial Japanese Navy Type A Submarine *M24* at Sydney." *Bulletin of the Australasian Institute for Maritime Archaeology*, 32: 79–89.

Snow, D. R.

1981 "Battlefield Archaeology." *Early Man* 3 (1): 18–21.

Spennemann, D. H. R.

2013 "Hindcasting the Japanese Military Base on Midway Atoll (Central Pacific)." *Journal of Conflict Archaeology*, 8 (2): 136–59.

Stewart, A. J.

1974 "Those Mysterious Midgets." *US Naval Institute Proceedings*, December: 55–63.

Sutherland, T. L.

2003 "The Towton Battlefield Archaeological Survey Project: An Integrated Approach to Battlefield Archaeology." *Landscapes* 4 (2): 15–25.

Tibbets, R. H.

1996 "Only Her Crew Kept Her Afloat." *Naval History*, 10 (3): 46–50.

Tusa, S., and J. G. Royal

2012 "The Landscape of the Naval Battle at the Egadi Islands (241 B.C.)." *Journal of Roman Archaeology*, 25: 8–48.

Van Tilburg, H.K.

2002 "Underwater Archaeology, Hawaiian Style," in C. V. Ruppé and J. Barstad, eds., *International Handbook of Underwater Archaeology*, Kluwer Academic/Plenum Publishers, New York, 247–66.

Van Tilburg, H.K.

2003 "US Navy Shipwrecks in Hawaiian Waters: An Inventory of Submerged Naval Properties." Legacy report submitted to Naval Historical Center, Washington, DC.

Van Tilburg, H.K.

2006 "Japanese Midget Sub at Pearl Harbor: Collaborative Maritime Heritage Preservation." *Underwater Cultural Heritage at Risk: Managing Natural and Human Impacts*, 67–69.

Van Tilburg, H.K.

2007 "Unseen Battlefields: The Japanese Midget Sub at Pearl Harbor," in J. H. Jameson Jr. and D. Scott-Ireton, eds., *Out of the Blue: Public Interpretation of Maritime Cultural Resources*, 182–95.

Van Tilburg, H.K., and D. Conlin

2007 "Pearl Harbor: West Loch Site Reconnaissance, August 2007." NOAA: National Marine Sanctuary Special Report; Submerged Resources Center: Technical Report Number 25. Maritime Heritage Program, NOAA ONMS and National Park Service, Submerged Resources Center, Silver Spring, Maryland, and Santa Fe, New Mexico.

Westerdahl, C.

1992 "The Maritime Cultural Landscape." *International Journal of Nautical Archaeology*, 21 (1): 5–14.

Wilbers-Rost, S.

2004 "The Battle of Varus (9 A.D.)—Archaeological Remains, Museum and Park Kalkriese." Paper presented at the Fields of Conflict Battlefield Archaeology Conference, Nashville.

Wilson, B., D. L. Johnson, H. Van Tilburg, M. A. Russell, L. E. Murphy, J. D. Carr, R. J. De Angelis, and D. L. Conlin

2007 "Corrosion Studies on the USS *Arizona* with Application to a Japanese Midget Submarine." *Journal of Minerals, Metals and Materials Society*, 59 (10): 14–18.

Wiltshire, J., T. Kerby, and A. Kalvaitis

2002 "The Search, Discovery, and Survey of a World War II Japanese Type 'A' Midget Submarine." *Oceanography*, 15 (4): 35–40.

Yamamoto, M.

2005 "The Sinking of Submarine No. 6 and Response of the Imperial Japanese Navy." *NIDS Security Reports* (6), September: 93–119.

Manuscripts

US National Archives, Washington, DC, and College Park, Maryland

RG 38, Records of the Office of the Chief of Naval Operations (1875–1993), 38.2.4, Records Relating to US Navy Operations Received from the Operational Archives Branch, Naval Historical Center

Commander-in-Chief, Pacific Fleet

1942 "Action Report," February 15, Serial No. 0479. RG 38.2.4.

Commander Destroyer Division Eighty

1941 "Attacks by Japanese of December 7; Report on Participation by Destroyer Division EIGHTY," Memorandum to Commandant Fourteenth Naval District, December 12, A16-3 (W). RG 38.2.4.

Commander Escort Division Thirty-Two

1944 "War Diary, 1 December," CED32/A16/A4-3. RG 38.2.4.

Commander Fifth Fleet

1946 "War Diary, ComFIFTHFleet, January 1946," A12-1(1). RG 38.2.4.

Commander Forward Area, Central Pacific

1945 "Japanese Midget Submarines," Memorandum to Commander Marianas Patrol and Escort Group, Commander Western Carolines Patrol and Escort Group, January 22, A16-3 (10). RG 38.2.4.

Commander Mine Squadron Four

1945 "War Diary for the Month of July, 1945," August 9. A12/1. RG 38.2.4.

Commander Service Squadron Twelve

1944 "War Diary, 1 August," A9-4(3). RG 38.2.4.

Commander South Pacific Area and South Pacific Force

1942 "War Diary . . . From 1 July 1942 to 31 July 1942," No serial. RG 38.2.4.

Commanding Officer, USS *Alchiba*

1942 "U.S.S. *Alchiba*, Torpedoing Of," Memorandum to Commander-in-Chief, Pacific Fleet, December 15, A16-4 (0015). RG 38.2.4.

Commanding Officer, USS *Antares*

1941 "Air Raid on O'ahu December 7, 1941; Report On," Memorandum to Commander-in-Chief, Pacific Fleet, December 10, A16-3 (0661). RG 38.2.4.

Commanding Officer, USS *Bennett*

1944 "War Diary, July," A12 (039). RG 38.2.4.

Commanding Officer, USS *Blue*

1941 "U.S.S. *Blue*—Action during December 7 Air Raid, Report Of," Memorandum to Commander-in-Chief, Pacific Fleet, December 11, A16-3. RG 38.2.4.

Commanding Officer, USS *Bobolink*

1941 "Offensive Measure Taken by the USS *Bobolink* against Japanese Air Attack of December 7, 1941," Memorandum to Commander-in-Chief, Pacific Fleet, December 10, A16-3 (0221). RG 38.2.4.

Commanding Officer, USS *Boise*

1945 "Report of Operations Incident to Amphibious Assault and Landings on Luzon Island, Philippine Islands, 1 January 1945 to 31 January, 1945, Inclusive," February 5, A16-3/A9-8 (08) RG 38.2.4.

Commanding Officer, USS *Breese*

1941 "Action, Pearl Harbor Air Raid, Report Of," Memorandum to Commander-in-Chief, Pacific Fleet, December 9, A16-3. RG 38.2.4.

Commanding Officer, USS *Callaghan*

1945 "Action Report," June 22, A16-3 (0053). RG 38.2.4.

Commanding Officer, USS *Case*

1944 "Action Report," November 22, A16-3 (0179). RG 38.2.4.

Commanding Officer, USS *Catclaw*

1945 "History of the Ship," October 21, AN60/A12-1. RG 38.2.4.

Commanding Officer, USS *Curtiss*

1941 "Raid on December 7, 1941, Report Of," Memorandum to Commander-in-Chief, Pacific Fleet, December 16, A16-3 (071). RG 38.2.4.

Commanding Officer, USS *Dale*

1941 "Detailed Report of Offensive Measures Taken during Air Raid, December 7, 1941," Memorandum to Commander-in-Chief, Pacific Fleet, December 28, A4-3 (667). RG 38.2.4.

Commanding Officer, USS *Helena*

1941 "Brief Report of the Japanese Attack of December 7, 1941," Memorandum to Commander-in-Chief, Pacific Fleet, December 14, A16-3 (0149). RG 38.2.4.

Commanding Officer, USS *Helm*

1941 "Action during Air Raid on December 7—Report On," Memorandum to Commander-in-Chief, Pacific Fleet, December 11, A16-3 (483). RG 38.2.4.

Commanding Officer, USS *Industry*

1946 "War History, 3 May," RG 38.2.4.

Commanding Officer, USCG *Ironwood*

1945 "Salvage of Japanese Midget Submarine, January 4–30, 1945," Memorandum to Commander-in-Chief, Pacific Fleet, April 8, A16-3 (005800). RG 38.2.4.

Commanding Officer, USS *Johnnie Hutchins*

1945 "Anti-Submarine Action, Report of, Memorandum to Commander-in-Chief," Pacific Fleet, August 11, A16-3 (21). RG 38.2.4.

Commanding Officer, USS *Lansdowne*

1942 "Additional Data on Anti-Submarine Action," Memorandum to Commander-in-Chief, Pacific Fleet, November 16, A16-3 (051). RG 38.2.4.

Commanding Officer, USS LST-225

1945 "Report of Action, 12 January, 1945, Kossol Roads." January 13, A16-k (002-045), RG 38.2.4.

Commanding Officer, USS *Medusa*

1941 "Report of Action of 7 December, 1941," Memorandum to Commander-in-Chief, Pacific Fleet, December 16, A16 (0593). RG 38.2.4.

Commanding Officer, USS *Molala*

1946 "War History, 9 May," RG 38.

Commanding Officer, USS *Monaghan*

1941 "Engagement with Enemy on December 7, 1941, Report Of." Memorandum to Commander-in-Chief, Pacific Fleet, December 30, A16-3 (0655). RG 38.2.4.

Commanding Officer, USS *Perry*

1941 "Japanese Air Raid on Pearl Harbor, December 7 1941," Memorandum to Commander-in-Chief, Pacific Fleet, December 22, A16-3 (0234). RG 38.2.4.

Commanding Officer, USS *Rall*

1944 "Action Report," Memorandum to Commander-in-Chief, Pacific Fleet, November 20, A16-3. No serial. RG 38.2.4.

Commanding Officer, USS *Ringness*

1945 "Anti-Submarine Action of 27 April 1945, Report Of," Memorandum to Commander-in-Chief, Pacific Fleet, April 28, A16-3 (450). RG 38.2.4.

Commanding Officer, USS *St. Louis*

1941 "Offensive Measures Taken During Air Raid, December 7, 1941—Report Of," Memorandum to Commander-in-Chief, Pacific Fleet, December 25, A16-3. RG 38.2.4.

Commanding Officer, USS *Tangier*

1942 "Raid, Air, December 7, 1941, USS *Tangier* (AV-8)—Report On," Memorandum to Commander-in-Chief, Pacific Fleet, January 2, A16-3. RG 38.2.4.000.

Commanding Officer, USS *Ward*

1941 "Sinking of a Japanese Submarine by U.S.S. *Ward*," Memorandum to Commander-in-Chief, Pacific Fleet, December 13, A16-3 (759). RG 38.2.4.

Commanding Officer, USS *Zane*

1941 "Air Raid on Pearl Harbor, Report Of," Memorandum to Commander-in-Chief, Pacific Fleet, December 10, A16-3 (0366). RG 38.2.4.

Headquarters XIV Corps, Office of the AC of 3, G-2

1943 Letter of Instructions from CO *Chiyoda* to Ensign Tanaka, Chiaki, Document Translation, May 9, Serial No. 17. RG 38.2.4.

Headquarters XIV Corps, Office of the AC of 3, G-2

1945 Lakin, Lieutenant Commander R., RN, "Material Report on Japanese Submarines" by British Submarine Liaison Officer, US Pacific Fleet, November 1. No serial. RG 38.2.4.

Sommer, Lieutenant F. X., USNR

1943 "Salvage and Flotation of Japanese Two-Man Submarine #8," Memorandum to the Commanding Officer, June 7. No serial. RG 38.2.4.

Vice Chief of Naval Operations

1942 "Enemy Submarines—Recovery of Information From," May 11, Confidential Serial #01225416. RG 38.2.4.

US Air Force Historical Research Agency, Maxwell AFB, Alabama

Northrup, Doyle L.

1973 Oral history, file K239.0512-685. Interviewed July 19, 1973, declassified December 31, 1981.

National Archives of Australia

Commanding Officer, HMAS *Yandra*

1942 "Attack on Japanese Midget Submarines—31st May 1942," Memorandum to NCC Sydney, Ref. No. N.O./5/4/42, NAA SP338/1 201/37.

Department of the Navy

1942 "Technical Report on Japanese Midget Submarines," July. NAA MP 1049/5 2026/21/36.

Department of the Navy

1942a "Salvage of Midget Submarine," August 31. NAA MP 1049/5 2026/21/33.

Department of the Navy

1942b "Midget Submarine Attack on Sydney Harbour, May 31–June 1," July 16. MP 1049/5 2026/21/22.

Eastern Fleet Intelligence Survey

1942 "Midget Submarines, Midget Submarines: Addendum 1, Addendum 2," NAA B6121, 174S.

Naval Intelligence Division

1942 "Japanese Submarine General Arrangement Plan," NAA B6121, 174S.

Naval Intelligence Division

1942a "Japanese Development of Midget Submarines in Attack on Sydney Harbour," Description of the Midgets Used and Suggested Methods of Countering This Form of Attack, August. NAA B6121, 174S.

New Zealand Naval Intelligence

1942 "Japanese Midget Submarine Tactics," Memorandum, Serial No. 20, November 29. NAA B6121, 174S.

US Navy, Chief of Naval Operations, Intelligence Division

1941 "Japanese Midget Submarines," Intelligence Report, Serial No. 81–41, December 15. NAA B6121, 174S.

Public Records Office, Kew, United Kingdom

Flag Officer Commanding Force F

1942 "Attack on Diego Suarez Bay by Japanese Midget Submarines," Enclosure No. 7, Ironclad Diaries, No. 60/48, June 16. ADM 199/937.

Wastell, Captain R.

1942 "British Loyalty." Report of an interview with the master, Captain R. Wastrell, M.V., Shipping Casualties Section, Trade Division. TD/139/1457, September 15. ADM 100/2140.

Miscellaneous Archives and Collections

David Aiken Collection, Honolulu, Hawai'i

Baham, P.

1986 Letter to David Aiken on salvage from the *Monaghan* Midget Submarine, June 9.

Hawai'i Undersea Research Laboratory, University of Hawai'i, Manoa

Kerby, T.

2002 "Discovery and Survey of WWII Japanese Type 'A' Midget Submarine," August 28.

Kerby, T.

2008 Survey Plan: Japanese 3-Piece Sub Site, February 2009 Expedition.

Pacific Fleet Submarine Memorial and Museum, Pearl Harbor

Eigell, R. W.

n.d. "To Clean Up a Day of Infamy." Unpublished manuscript.

Naval War College, Newport, Rhode Island

Riffer, Cdr. W. J., USN

1989 "A Study in Operational Failure: Japanese Submarine Operations in World War II." Unpublished paper submitted to the Faculty of the Naval War College in satisfaction of the requirement for a research paper for the Operations curricula.

The Mariners' Museum, Newport News, Virginia

Nihon Kaiyo Sangyo Kenkyusho Gmbh.

1976 Letter to William D. Wilkenson, Director, The Mariners' Museum, Newport News, Virginia, January 30.

Index

Italic page numbers indicate illustrations.